3 6854 00018743 3

S0-BIN-428

Energy Conservation

Energy Conservation

Successes and Failures

JOHN C. SAWHILL *and* RICHARD COTTON
Editors

THE BROOKINGS INSTITUTION
Washington, D.C.

Library of Congress Cataloging in Publication data:

Main entry under title:

Energy conservation.

Includes bibliographical references and index.
1. Energy conservation—United States. 2. Energy policy—United States. 3. Public utilities—United States—Energy conservation. 4. Petroleum industry and trade—Government policy—United States. I. Sawhill, John C., 1936– . II. Cotton, Richard, 1944– .
HD9502.U62E478 1986 333.79′16′0973 85-26894
ISBN 0-8157-7716-7
ISBN 0-8157-7715-9 (pbk.)

9 8 7 6 5 4 3 2 1

THE BROOKINGS INSTITUTION is an independent organization devoted to nonpartisan research, education, and publication in economics, government, foreign policy, and the social sciences generally. Its principal purposes are to aid in the development of sound public policies and to promote public understanding of issues of national importance.

The Institution was founded on December 8, 1927, to merge the activities of the Institute for Government Research, founded in 1916, the Institute of Economics, founded in 1922, and the Robert Brookings Graduate School of Economics and Government, founded in 1924.

The Board of Trustees is responsible for the general administration of the Institution, while the immediate direction of the policies, program, and staff is vested in the President, assisted by an advisory committee of the officers and staff. The by-laws of the Institution state: "It is the function of the Trustees to make possible the conduct of scientific research, and publication, under the most favorable conditions, and to safeguard the independence of the research staff in the pursuit of their studies and in the publication of the results of such studies. It is not a part of their function to determine, control, or influence the conduct of particular investigations or the conclusions reached."

The President bears final responsibility for the decision to publish a manuscript as a Brookings book. In reaching his judgment on the competence, accuracy, and objectivity of each study, the President is advised by the director of the appropriate research program and weighs the views of a panel of expert outside readers who report to him in confidence on the quality of the work. Publication of a work signifies that it is deemed a competent treatment worthy of public consideration but does not imply endorsement of conclusions or recommendations.

The Institution maintains its position of neutrality on issues of public policy in order to safeguard the intellectual freedom of the staff. Hence interpretations or conclusions in Brookings publications should be understood to be solely those of the authors and should not be attributed to the Institution, to its trustees, officers, or other staff members, or to the organizations that support its research.

Foreword

THE extraordinary increases in the price of oil that occurred in the wake of the 1973 Arab oil embargo, together with the possibility of future embargoes, forced the United States to seek effective measures to reduce its dependency on imported oil. In the ensuing policy debate, strong disagreement developed over the extent to which more efficient use of energy resources could contribute to solving the energy crisis. A number of studies argued that theoretically the United States could maintain its standard of living and produce a growing gross national product through the end of the century with minimal, if any, increases in the use of fuel resources by using these resources more efficiently.

The worldwide recession of the late 1970s and early 1980s clouded analytic conclusions about whether the reductions in oil use experienced in those years resulted from the general economic slowdown or from real increases in the efficient use of energy resources. Moreover, there has been little analysis of the effectiveness of various governmental measures intended to promote energy efficiency.

This book presents seven essays that seek to answer these questions. The results indicate that significant increases in energy efficiency have occurred and that further increases (still attributable to the price increases of the 1970s) can be expected as capital stock with a long lead time, such as factories, buildings, and durable goods, is replaced. The effectiveness of government policy in accelerating the market's response to higher prices has been mixed. But the authors suggest that the experiences of the past decade offer important lessons to future government leaders about which policies will work and which will not.

At a time when the oil glut dominates news in the energy field, it may be tempting to believe energy problems are a thing of the past. But the continuing tensions in the Middle East caution against such a view. Moreover, even without an abrupt supply disruption, most forecasts predict that the 1990s will once again see a tightening of supplies. This volume should assist policymakers in drawing upon the lessons of the past to formulate energy policy for the end of the century.

These essays are based on papers that were initially presented at a conference held at the Brookings Institution in October 1982 attended by economists, oil and gas industry representatives, utility officials, energy policy experts, congressional staff, and local, state, and federal government officials.

John C. Sawhill is a director of McKinsey and Company and has served as chairman of the U.S. Synthetic Fuels Corporation, deputy secretary of the Department of Energy, and administrator of the Federal Energy Administration. Richard Cotton is a partner in the law firm of Dewey, Ballantine, Bushby, Palmer and Wood, and has served as special counsel to the deputy secretary of the Department of Energy and in advisory positions to the California Energy Commission.

Nancy Davidson edited the manuscript; Carolyn Rutsch verified its factual content; Michael J. Coda provided research assistance; and Florence Robinson prepared the index. Dawn Swindells, Ann Fouke, and Catherine DuBose shepherded the essay manuscripts through their many production phases.

The project was supported with funds provided by the Andrew W. Mellon Foundation, for which we are most grateful.

The views expressed in this book are those of the authors and the conference participants and should not be ascribed to the Andrew W. Mellon Foundation or the trustees, officers, or staff members of the Brookings Institution.

BRUCE K. MACLAURY
President

November 1985
Washington, D.C.

Contents

Tables

Figures

Energy Conservation

JOHN C. SAWHILL *and* RICHARD COTTON

Introduction

THE 1973 Arab oil embargo stimulated a wide-ranging response on the part of public officials. Policies were developed to curb the growth of energy demand, increase the domestic oil supply, and substitute alternative domestic fuels for imported oil. Now—more than a decade later—it is apparent that some of these policies were very effective, while others were either counterproductive or had minimal effects. Yet the current oil glut suggests that on balance the country achieved its objectives of reducing oil imports, strengthening national security, and mitigating the effects of rising oil prices on the economy. Indeed, energy demand growth has slowed and energy consumption is now a significantly lower portion of GNP than it was in the early 1970s; the decline in oil production has been halted; the United States has diversified its sources of foreign oil supplies; and alternative fuels—primarily natural gas and coal—have been substituted for oil in a variety of boiler fuel uses.

We embarked on this project to gain a better understanding of the effectiveness of energy policy and to draw from this experience lessons for the future. We looked at the policies that had been aimed at curbing demand and asked what happened, what worked, what failed, and why? We were particularly interested in understanding the role that institutions such as public utilities, large energy-consuming corporations, governments, and financial intermediaries played in the adjustment process. To what extent did they impede or accelerate the efficient use of energy? What actions could policymakers have taken to help these institutions function more effectively?

Specifically, our objectives were to: (1) analyze and assess trends in energy use in the United States (and to a lesser extent abroad) over the decade from 1973 to 1983; (2) identify institutional barriers that impeded basic market forces from working to stimulate the more efficient use of energy; (3) identify steps that might be taken to remove these barriers; and (4) determine whether there are additional practical and realistic steps that specific institutions could take to accelerate and enhance the more efficient use of energy beyond the efficiencies likely to be attained in the marketplace.

When we began our study in 1982, there was still strong sentiment that energy conservation was important.[1] Oil imports in 1981 were still a relatively large portion of U.S. oil consumption (37 percent); tensions in the Middle East remained high; and most forecasters predicted that further oil price increases or supply shortages would occur throughout the remainder of the decade. By 1985, however, this situation had changed dramatically. Oil prices had already fallen 33 percent in real terms from their 1980 peak and were predicted to decline still further for the balance of the 1980s.[2] Overcapacity existed in all sectors of the energy industry: drilling rigs, tankers, oil refineries, and retail outlets. OPEC production, which had been as high as 31.3 million barrels per day in 1977, had fallen to 17.6 million by 1984, or about 62 percent of current OPEC capacity.[3]

In view of this sharp turn of events, it seems appropriate to ask whether a study focused on energy conservation remains relevant. Are the lessons learned from an assessment of institutional performance during the 1970s and early 1980s useful for policymakers in a world characterized by energy surpluses rather than shortages?

We believe the answer is yes. There are a number of reasons to think that continued efforts should be made to improve the effectiveness of institutions in stimulating reductions in energy demand growth. First, the probability of another oil supply disruption in the Middle East (the source of 63 percent of the free world's oil reserves) is difficult to assess but remains large enough to merit taking actions in advance to protect energy security.[4] Second, the current oil glut is unlikely to be permanent. Even without a supply disruption, longer-term forecasts of oil supply and demand point to rising U.S. imports and general market tightness in the 1990s. Third, investments in improving energy efficiency remain

1. The research and writing of most of the essays in this book were carried out in mid-1982 and presented at a conference held at the Brookings Institution in October 1983.

2. U.S. Department of Energy, Energy Information Administration, *Monthly Energy Review* (March 1985), pp. 41, 95, 113.

3. OPEC, *Annual Statistical Bulletin, 1982,* p. 13; and *Petroleum Intelligence Weekly,* March 18, 1985, p. 11.

4. DeGolyer and MacNaughton, *Twentieth Century Petroleum Statistics, 1984* (Dallas: DeGolyer and MacNaughton, 1984), p. 1.

Figure 1. *Relationship between World Oil Price and Capacity Utilization, 1973–84*

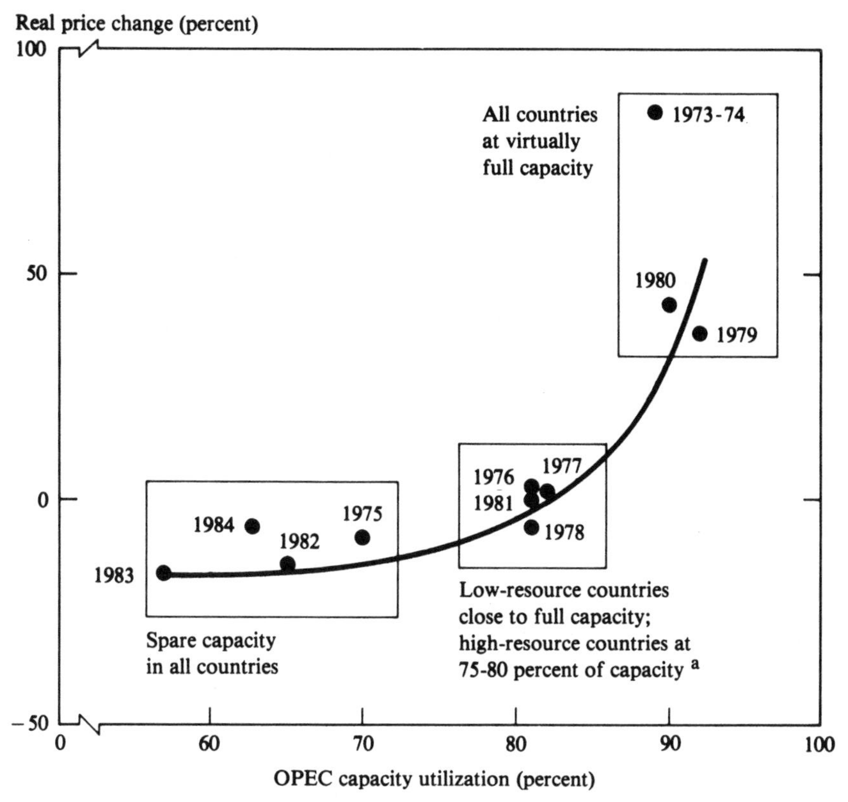

Source: U.S. Department of Energy, Energy Information Administration, *1984 Annual Energy Review*, p. 131; and *Petroleum Intelligence Weekly*.

a. Low-resource countries include all of OPEC except Saudi Arabia, Kuwait, and United Arab Emirates; high-resource countries include Saudi Arabia, Kuwait, and United Arab Emirates.

attractive even at today's oil prices, and—if undertaken—can dampen inflation and improve the overall competitiveness of the U.S. economy in world markets. Finally, conservation investments have a number of advantages over alternative ways of reducing import dependency. For example, compared with most supply increase options, they are more environmentally benign and can usually be achieved more rapidly.

Figure 1 shows the behavior of oil prices in relation to the demand and supply of OPEC oil. In those years in which the high-resource countries (Saudi Arabia, Kuwait, and United Arab Emirates) were operating at 75 to 80 percent of capacity and the lower-resource countries

Figure 2. *Potential for Oil Price Increases, 1985–2000*[a]

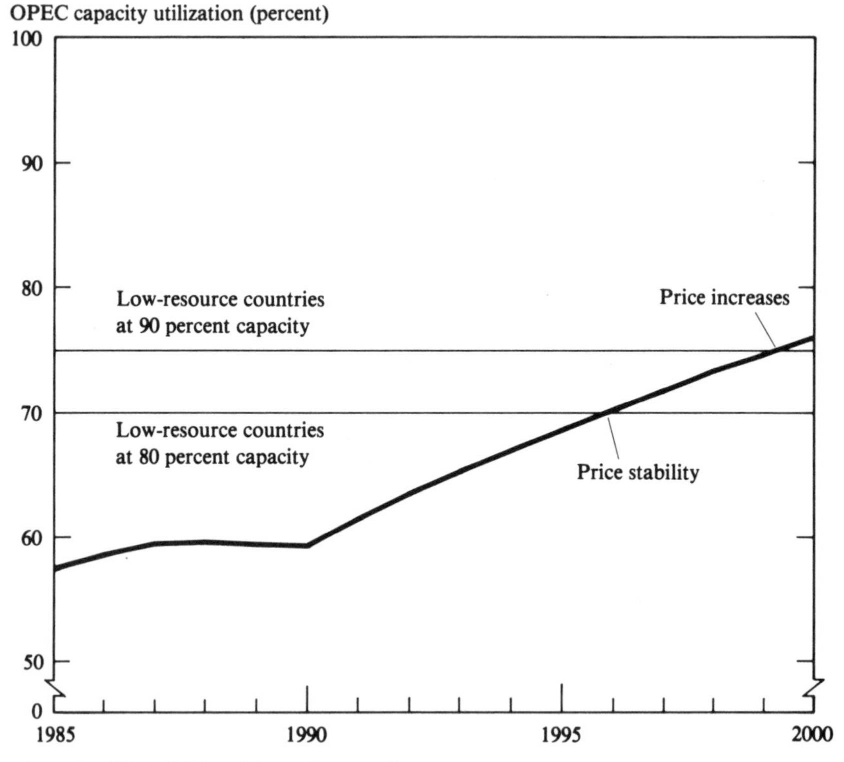

Source: DOE, EIA, *1984 Annual Energy Review,* p. 131.

a. Assumes no additions to capacity except by Iran and Iraq (reaching a total production by those two countries of 7.5 million barrels a day by 1995), and assumes that high-resource countries' production is held fixed at the level agreed to at the October 1984 OPEC meeting.

(Indonesia, Ecuador, Venezuela, Nigeria, Libya, and Algeria) were operating at 90 percent of capacity, real oil prices remained stable. In those years when all countries operated close to full capacity, real oil prices rose; and when all countries had significant excess capacity, real oil prices fell. Most forecasters project that the present situation of falling real prices is likely to persist for the next few years and could last longer depending on the outcome of the Iran-Iraq war and how this affects OPEC production.

Figure 2 illustrates that the potential for sharp price increases will remain minimal until the late 1990s because OPEC capacity utilization will not increase dramatically. Given reasonable assumptions about world demand growth of 1.7 percent a year and a gradual increase in Iran-Iraq production, it is likely that there will be a return to conditions consistent with real price stability toward the end of the 1980s and that rising real oil prices could occur somewhere in the mid-1990s.

No one knows for sure how future market conditions will evolve. There are too many imponderables, including political developments in the volatile Middle East. But it does seem reasonable to expect that the oil glut—like the oil shortage—will not persist indefinitely. By the mid-1990s, U.S. oil imports will probably rise to between 50 and 60 percent of consumption, given expectations of gradually declining domestic production and the possibility of expanded product imports.[5] Thus any tightening in oil market conditions could pose a threat to the economy (as a result of rising prices) as well as to national security. For this reason, we believe that actions taken in the interim to remove institutional barriers to energy conservation would be highly desirable.

We feel, however, that there is an equally compelling reason to improve U.S. institutions' energy efficiency apart from national security considerations. In many cases it simply makes good economic sense. Energy efficiency and energy production should be viewed as alternative investment opportunities. Investments—in either energy efficiency improvement or expanding domestic supplies—should be judged on the basis of the same economic criteria. Society should optimize (in an economic sense) its use of scarce resources so that those investments that promise the highest rate of return are the ones that get funded—assuming, of course, that all costs are accounted for and subsidies are equalized or eliminated. From the policymakers' point of view, the return on investment in retrofitting homes to make them more energy efficient should be compared with such supply-enhancing investments as off-shore drilling rigs and nuclear plants. Viewed in this framework, investments to improve energy efficiency are no different from coal mines or geothermal wells. They are merely alternative investments that ultimately will contribute to the health of the economy and to reduction of oil imports. The one promising the highest payoff should have first call on society's resources.

For example, the Department of Energy has estimated that fairly simple steps such as insulation, storm windows, and weatherizing could reduce energy use for heating by up to 40 percent in existing homes.[6] These improvements are cost effective if the savings on the price per

5. DOE, EIA, *Annual Energy Outlook 1984 with Projections to 1995,* DOE/EIA-0383(84) (DOE, 1985), p. 203.

6. Department of Energy, *Reducing U.S. Oil Vulnerability: Energy Policy for the 1980s,* DOE/PE-0021 (GPO, 1980), p. V-F-1.

barrel of oil provides ample incentive. Investments in "producing" this saved energy would obviously compare favorably with the costs of importing oil at the current world price and also with the per barrel costs of exploring for oil in many parts of the United States. Unfortunately, there is a long list of institutional barriers to residential conservation investments, such as lack of information and the short-term orientation of many homeowners and renters who plan to leave the home before a conservation investment can pay off. Furthermore, as Robert Hemphill and Edward Myers describe, most utilities still have not developed the expertise required to market residential conservation programs effectively. And, as Henry Lee points out, the experience of local governments with mandatory retrofit programs, point-of-sale ordinances, and the like has not been very successful.

Similarly, even though industry has dramatically reduced the amount of energy it uses, there are still substantial opportunities to increase the efficiency of energy use. The Alliance to Save Energy recently published a study that looked at energy use by major companies in several different industries and found that energy conservation could be quite profitable. They found, for example, that one company studied could reduce its energy use by 20 percent through a series of projects, all of them with a highly favorable internal rate of return of more than 40 percent. A shortage of capital and poor profit performance had postponed these investments.[7]

Merton Peck and John Beggs point out that in some industries such as steel, energy conservation is inextricably linked to general economic conditions because project economics often dictate that the introduction of energy-saving techniques be delayed until major renovations are made or new plant and equipment are built.

Yet numerous studies, such as those cited above, have identified energy efficiency projects with returns that exceed returns to investment elsewhere in the economy. Where there are institutional barriers to making investments, it makes sense to remove them. Furthermore, to the extent that there are externalities associated with conservation investments—such as favorable environmental impacts or improvements in national security—then it may be desirable to take steps to accelerate energy efficiency investments beyond the market's natural

7. Alliance to Save Energy, *Industrial Investment in Energy Efficiency: Opportunities, Management Practices, and Tax Incentives* (Washington, D.C.: Alliance to Save Energy, 1983), pp. 193–94.

response to higher energy prices. We have not attempted to measure these externalities, but we do feel that their existence strengthens the case for institutional change.

Changes in Energy Demand

In 1972, the last year before the Arab oil embargo, total primary consumption of energy in the United States was 71.6 quadrillion British thermal units (quads) and had grown for more than a decade at a compound rate of 4 percent a year. For electric utilities, consumption stood at 18.5 quads and had been growing at a rate of nearly 7 percent a year. Adjusted for economic activity, the level of primary energy consumption reached a new peak in 1972 at 34,000 Btus per 1980 dollar of GNP.[8] Most energy economists accepted the fact that increasing energy consumption was necessary to fuel the engine of economic growth and that the energy-GNP ratio was stable.

In the following decade, primary energy consumption rose and then fell, leaving total energy usage in 1982 just below what it had been in 1972. Electricity consumption continued to grow, but the annual growth rate slowed from 7 percent to 2.8 percent, and the primary energy-GNP ratio fell by 24 percent.[9] This sharp drop shattered the myth of an immutable energy-GNP ratio.

As William Hogan points out, the improvements in energy efficiency were shared across major sectors of the economy, with the industrial sector showing the greatest decline in the growth rate, 4.8 percentage points. As a result, industrial primary energy consumption actually decreased over the decade.

Hogan segmented the aggregate data into electric and nonelectric energy consumption and found that over the twenty years between 1960 and 1980 the share of electricity in delivered energy almost doubled in industry and more than doubled in the residential and commercial sectors. This result is consistent with predictions that would flow from a simple price response. Thus in the first half of the period—1960–72—when the real price of electricity fell, one would expect to see a shift toward electricity consumption. But even after 1972, when the price of

8. DOE, EIA, *1984 Annual Energy Review,* pp. 5, 11.
9. Ibid.

electricity increased, the price of competing nonelectric fuels grew even faster, which explains the continued growth in the share of electricity.

Using this electric-nonelectric split, he developed a model that explains electric and nonelectric consumption over the 1960–82 period with surprising accuracy. Using his model, he concludes that there has been a significant improvement in energy efficiency since 1972 that can be attributed to "a cost-effective response to higher energy prices." Furthermore, his model provides a useful perspective on the rate of the economy's adjustment to higher energy prices. The essay by Peck and Beggs describes how the process worked in three large energy-consuming industries—steel, aluminum, and cement. As they point out, opportunities and constraints exist within a single industry. In the cement industry, for example, a new technology (dry process with preheater system) has permitted savings of up to 30 percent in energy used in individual plants. The analyses by Peck and Beggs and by Hogan both suggest that the rate at which the stock of energy-using equipment is replaced is relatively slow, which constrains the rate at which technologically possible energy savings are achieved. Moreover, further efficiency gains that are theoretically possible cannot be made quickly because of high transportation costs and the location of appropriate raw materials distant from the growth markets for cement.

Hogan concludes that there is still substantial conservation to be achieved as a result of the price increases that occurred in 1973 and 1979. He points out that most energy usage is linked to durable capital-intensive machines, equipment, and buildings. Since there are limits to how rapidly major new capital investments can be made, Hogan's analysis recognizes that conversion to more energy-efficient durable goods and equipment will be "a slow process stretched out over many years." For example, new houses are almost twice as energy efficient as older ones, but only 1 or 2 percent of the housing stock is replaced each year. Using these lagged relationships, Hogan forecasts that with stable real energy prices and a 2 percent annual growth in GNP, nonelectric energy demand will not reach its historical peak until the end of this century and electricity consumption will enjoy only modest growth, compared with historical levels. Given the economic and non-economic benefits associated with a slowdown in energy consumption, it would seem important that institutions take steps to facilitate rather than impede this long-term adjustment process.

Barriers to Improving Energy Efficiency

Our framework for analyzing barriers has been an economic one. We began with the proposition, as set out above, that the rapid increase in energy prices in the late 1970s would lead over time to adjustments through normal market forces. Specifically, since fuel had become more expensive, simple economics would dictate substitution of other factors for fuel. For example, where it once paid to buy cheap electric motors that consumed large amounts of inexpensive electricity, it was now better economics to buy more expensive motors that would reduce consumption of increasingly expensive electricity. Where it once paid to burn lots of cheap oil and not insulate a building, more expensive oil now made it more economic to buy insulation and weatherproofing to reduce the amount of oil consumed. In these ways, normal market forces responding to higher fuel prices would stimulate what we have called greater energy efficiency—that is, achieving the same level of service or production with less fuel.

We have assumed that over a substantial period of time these market forces will ultimately lead to a new equilibrium in which the U.S. economy will use fuel far more efficiently than it did before the 1970s. We have further assumed that these market forces are by far the most powerful forces driving the economy toward greater fuel efficiency. But our effort in this study has been to identify the counterweights—the forces that slow down these market-driven adjustments to higher energy prices.

There is a strong temptation to label as a "barrier" anything that slows down achievement of greater fuel efficiency through market adjustments to higher energy prices. But it is important to recognize that, as an analytic matter, giving in to such a temptation leads to confusion. Our study has, in fact, identified a number of "barriers" that have their roots in what economists call market imperfections. Lack of information, or misunderstanding about energy efficiency, for example, on the part of individual consumers or the owners of small businesses may delay or prevent cost-effective investments in energy efficiency that market economics would justify. Similarly, the refusal of utility managers in the early 1970s to consider the economic attractiveness of load management and efficiency programs out of a tradition-bound commitment to production may have foreclosed economically justified efforts to increase efficiency.

There are, however, many economic factors at work to slow down investment in increased energy efficiency that flow from a rational assessment of the economics of particular investment decisions. These factors cover a wide gamut. For example, energy economics alone will rarely justify immediate replacement of multimillion-dollar plant and equipment. In this sense, the slow turnover time of the capital stock discussed earlier constrains more rapid improvement in the efficiency with which the economy uses energy.

Similarly, other rational economic considerations may have negative effects on decisions about whether to invest in energy efficiency. For example, to the extent that high interest rates discourage investment, that energy conservation technology is untried and properly regarded as more risky than other technology, and that a company concludes that other investments are more important to its economic success, all these factors may work against rapid increases in investment in energy conservation.

The challenge for policymakers is to understand the forces they confront. They must recognize whether the constraints they seek to remove rest on market imperfections and irrational decisionmaking or on real economic forces. The essays in this book provide vivid examples of the importance of understanding the reasons behind an apparent lack of action on energy efficiency investments. Consider, for example, what the authors found in investigating the actions of industrial concerns, financial institutions, and utilities.

Peck and Beggs concluded that most industrial concerns have made the easy housekeeping changes that lead to more efficient use of fuel. Real improvements in energy efficiency will now have to come from substantial investments in changing industrial processes and in more fundamental changes in the way industries do business (such as relocations to reduce transportation needs). In particular, increases in energy efficiency will flow from investment in new plants. New machinery, new processes, and new facilities will incorporate state-of-the-art knowledge on a variety of fronts, including use of energy.

But major investments in new plant and equipment obviously constitute fundamental capital decisions for an industrial concern. These decisions are often driven by factors other than energy efficiency. Peck and Beggs found that one of the most important reasons energy efficiency does not rank high as a driving force in the investment decisions of most firms is that energy costs are generally a relatively small percentage of the firms' total costs. In particular, plant investment decisions tend to turn on general economic conditions, the specific competitive situation in a particular industry, the economic health of the particular firm involved, and government policies affecting investment decisions generally. And more generally, their investment strategies often focus on enhancing products and market share before allocating capital to cost-cutting investments.

Arnold Sametz found that investments to promote energy efficiency face tough sledding in obtaining financing. The reasons for these high hurdles included (1) high real interest rates; (2) the riskiness of expected return flows over time; (3) the greater uncertainty associated with longer-term investments and with investment in more innovative projects; (4) the high information and transaction costs that often discourage the small businessman and consumer; and (5) lenders' lack of experience with energy efficiency investments. But Sametz concludes that the hurdles energy efficiency investments face are almost always rational and reasonable, rooted in an accurate assessment of their economic riskiness.

Hemphill and Myers looked hard at the experience utilities have accumulated over the past five to ten years in energy conservation programs. They found that most utilities have made a bow in the direction of conservation. But the authors found it more difficult to ascertain how many utilities treat conservation as a serious dimension of their strategic planning for meeting future commitments. Moreover, they found that those utilities that have made serious decisions to rely on conservation programs to control the growth of demand face enormously complicated planning challenges and that the difficulties of the obstacles have not been widely acknowledged by conservation advocates.

In assessing utility performance, the authors point out that it is critical to recognize that utilities will differ in how they view conservation, depending on each utility's characteristics, including the size of its reserve margin and the type of service area it serves. For example, utilities in low-growth areas with excess capacity will view conservation activities very differently than utilities facing a high-growth service area with low reserve margins. Hemphill and Myers found that these internal motivations are by far the most powerful determinants in whether utilities develop effective programs.

The authors found that federal conservation programs had minimal effects. State-inspired stimuli were effective only where state public utility commissions had strong commitments and carried through on those commitments with a substantial degree of competence and tenacity. It is also true that most of the state public utility commission programs that were effective occurred in high-growth, low-margin areas where the conservation programs were in fact congruent with the economic self-interest of the regulated utilities.

In sum, these authors found that in many circumstances careful analysis could identify important countervailing considerations that tended to block more rapid investment in energy efficiency.

Lessons for the Future

We believe that energy policymakers must never lose sight of the fundamental proposition in this area: price signals and market forces remain by far the most powerful engines driving more efficient use of energy. On that score, our study has left us optimistic. The many studies emphasizing the great potential for more efficient use of energy have, in our judgment, been substantially validated by the analysis set out by Hogan.

From the point of view of promoting greater energy efficiency, the most effective tools in the policymakers' arsenal are plain: elimination of regulatory constraints on accurate price signals and constraints that interfere with the working of market forces in responding to those price signals.

At a minimum, this means that utilities and utility commissions should continue to work toward rate structures that give consumers strong and accurate price signals reflecting changes in operating and capital costs. It means that policymakers should resist any move back toward increased regulation of energy prices and should seek to continue the move toward deregulation of natural gas prices. Finally, it means that if increased taxes are needed to reduce the current federal deficit, policymakers should recognize that one benefit of energy taxes is that increased prices will continue to stimulate more efficient use of fuel.

Beyond those most important steps, the message of our study for the policymaker is twofold. First, it is critical to distinguish barriers based on market imperfections from countervailing economic forces that work to slow down the adjustment to higher fuel prices. Policies designed to remove market imperfections will differ significantly from those intended to address underlying economic factors. If government seeks to increase investment in energy efficiency that is being slowed by real economic forces, it will be necessary to change the economics of the situation in order to achieve change—and it is often very expensive to do that.

Second, while government has only a limited ability to affect barriers that operate fundamentally in the private sector, it can have an important influence if it focuses its effort sharply, does not seek to carry out activities that are beyond its ken, and seeks to mesh its actions with the economic and political self-interests of those whose actions it seeks to influence.

To be effective, policymakers will have to work through particular institutions. Our examination of the institutions with the largest potential effect on energy efficiency leads to quite specific conclusions. Industrial concerns clearly play a major role in energy use in the United States. Their record demonstrates that they respond to energy price increases by moving strongly toward increased energy efficiency. Faster gains in energy efficiency would probably flow most effectively from general economic policies that produced more investment and faster turnover in the capital stock, rather than from any narrowly focused energy policies.

The type of more narrowly focused initiatives worth considering appears limited. The most important role for government in this area is probably in long-term research and development. Many industries may not have the profit margins or capacity to do such research. The aluminum industry demonstrates that without feasible energy-efficient technology an industry has few options available to reduce its fuel use significantly. In particular, the government can provide economic incentives to the industries involved to encourage them to carry out the research and development or it can provide direct grants to research institutions. Government has experience in both of these approaches to funding research and development and has successfully carried out effective programs in the past.

Somewhat less important but still potentially valuable are initiatives seeking to promote specific energy-efficient technologies. Such technologies include cogeneration and the use of waste products. Such efforts might be particularly effective if they were directed to the types of industries Peck and Beggs suggest would be receptive—competitive industries where energy costs are a high percentage of total costs. We regard it as an open question whether tax credits or subsidies could be structured to influence industrial investment decisions. The big-payoff investments from an energy efficiency perspective are new plant and equipment. Energy-oriented tax credits seem unlikely to affect these big decisions significantly. Whether energy savings from less significant investment decisions would be worth the cost to the public treasury seems questionable.

Like industry, utilities have proved themselves major actors in affecting energy efficiency investment decisions. Any effort to stimulate utilities to promote energy efficiency must begin from three propositions. First, only utilities where demand management is congruent with the utilities' economic self-interest are likely targets. Second, the focal point for influencing the utility should be, if at all possible, the agency that regulates the utility. Third, programs to stimulate energy efficiency need to be consistent with the utility's rate structure and with its overall approach to serving its customers.

State and federal programs designed to support utility efforts to solve admittedly difficult problems of planning, management, and integration of energy efficiency programs appear worthwhile. Overregulation appears counterproductive in light of the experience of the late 1970s. In situations where a state believes more efficient use of existing production capacity makes better economic sense than adding more capacity, state public utility commission constraints on investment in new capacity or incentive rates of return appear to have been productive methods to convince utilities that demand management is in their own economic self-interest. That goal should be the policymakers' target. Overly prescriptive efforts to tell the utility how to achieve demand management do not have a good track record and seem unlikely candidates for success in the future.

Finally, the lesson of the past decade on the capacity of state and local governments seems quite clear. Their ability to affect private decisions about energy efficiency is limited.

First, both Karen Griffin's essay on state governments and Henry Lee's essay on local governments suggest that governments must have strong motivation, produced by local circumstances. Thus states with strong energy programs tended to be both net importers of energy and heavily dependent on oil. Hence they were most affected by the 1970s price increases. Municipalities that ventured effectively into the business of energy conservation in general acted because local political developments generated strong community support for such activity. Where these motivations did not exist, municipal efforts consistently foundered.

Second, both state and municipal governments failed badly when called on to perform functions outside their traditional functions and types of activities. State government success stories were limited to programs in which states made fairly traditional construction grants to schools and hospitals for energy conservation or set statewide standards for buildings and appliances. Similarly, municipal success stories appear to be limited to three areas: municipal building codes, efforts directed at improved management of municipal buildings and vehicles, and cooperative ventures with utilities.

Thus the empirical record of state and local government efforts to promote energy conservation emphasizes that a limited number of states and municipalities are strong candidates for such activities—namely, those that strongly view energy conservation in their self-interest. Those that have the requisite motivation will probably succeed only in projects that call upon the skills and capacities traditionally exercised by these governments.

But they can do well if their assignments are directed at particular barriers and draw on their natural skills and capacities. Our study has clearly suggested that energy efficiency investments will frequently face high costs in securing financing. Grant or subsidy programs aimed narrowly at particular target groups or institutions have a good chance of succeeding. Standard-setting actions such as building codes, zoning, or other legislated guidelines can prove effective at the state and local level. Both state and local government actions to achieve greater efficiencies in the management of government buildings and operations can be important and effective.

The federal government can play a constructive role by accepting the lessons described above and focusing its support on approaches that are likely to succeed. Providing incentives to industry and to state and local governments to act in the areas set out above seems likely to be productive. But the most important role for the federal government—at least in the absence of a new crisis—appears to be to provide leadership and to demonstrate new technologies and new approaches. But, as John Gibbons, Holly Gwin, and Richard Pool point out, the federal government's record has been spotty at best.

The federal government is the nation's largest energy consumer, using

2.5 percent of the fuel consumed nationally. Yet the federal government's record of efficient use of energy shows only minimal and inconsistent progress. The government's mediocre performance in achieving gains in energy efficiency came in the face of many congressional mandates and executive orders directing government agencies to reduce their use of fuel. The authors report that, with a few exceptions, these directives have been ignored, and high government officials have not been interested in the goal of greater energy efficiency. The authors contrast the government's performance with that of the Bell System, which used 12 percent less energy during the first two-thirds of 1982 than it did in the same period of 1973, even though the volume of its business had grown 97 percent during that period.

Plainly government agencies respond only sluggishly to price signals. They are not guided by profit imperatives, but only by the more abstract need to cut costs to keep within budgetary restraints. Cost-cutting investments often fare poorly against an opportunity for an agency to seek program expansion, new space, or other more visible bureaucratic symbols of the agency's success.

Strong, effective federal government leadership in energy efficiency, by way of example and demonstration, has the potential for significant success. The United States fares poorly in international comparisons of energy efficiency. Both France and Japan, in particular, have launched aggressive programs that have begun to yield impressive results. There is no reason the U.S. government could not achieve similar results if the necessary commitment could be developed at the agency level.

Conclusions

The importance of energy efficiency has been established by now. It is now accepted wisdom that greater energy efficiency played an important role in creating the current oil glut and in reducing U.S. dependency on imported oil. The United States will continue to benefit from gains in energy efficiency as new plants and equipment are acquired during the next decade. Moreover, significant but gradual change may be under way in which efficiency becomes the central focus of the provision of energy services. But the challenge to policymakers of how to promote more rapid movement toward more efficient use of fuel will become increasingly subtle and difficult as time goes on. The "easy" gains will have been made. The gains that have not yet been realized will be those where there are strong counterweights. As we have emphasized, these counterweights may be imperfections such as lack of information, but they may also be situations where real economic considerations weigh against the energy efficiency investment.

The task ahead is to analyze constraints carefully and not to make quick assumptions about the cause of particular constraints. The only way to remove a barrier is to have an accurate understanding of its nature and its cause and to devise policies that focus on the real problem. In the increasingly sophisticated world of energy policy, that will be no easy task. But in the event of another supply disruption, it could easily become one of the most important facing the nation.

WILLIAM W. HOGAN

Patterns of Energy Use

ENERGY conservation dominated the adjustments of the energy decade from 1973 to 1983. Before the oil shocks of 1973, the potential for improved energy efficiency enjoyed little credibility in the energy industry. But by the end of a decade of higher energy prices, the irrefutable evidence of decreased energy use confirmed the power of energy conservation. A new belief in energy efficiency as a permanent structural change replaced the earlier assumption of ever-increasing energy consumption.

Reductions in energy use, surprising even to conservation enthusiasts, have had a profound effect on the world economy. This was most notable in the collapse of the demand for OPEC oil, which declined from 31 million barrels per day (bpd) in 1979 to 19 million bpd in 1982.[1] Improvements in energy efficiency left surplus power plants scattered about the electric utility industry, spawned a metamorphosis in the design and production of automobiles, contributed to the stillbirth of the heralded synthetic fuels business, and visibly altered architectural design.

The new puzzles, and the new dangers of orthodoxy, appear in the definition of what is permanent and what is transitory among the changes in energy utilization. In the long run how much reduced energy use can be attributed to new technical opportunities and how much to substitution of capital and labor in response to altered relative prices? The answer to this question should affect imminent decisions in industries that have

Colin Blaydon, Dale Jorgenson, Joseph Kalt, William Hieronymus, and James Sweeney provided helpful criticisms of the dynamic adjustment model applied here. Thomas Birdsall and William Klitgaard helped organize the data and formulate the long-run analysis. Thomas Graham suggested the concentration on the disequilibrium evidence of the long-run transition. Henry Lee, Henry Linden, Alan Manne, John Meyer, Michael O'Hare, Stephen Peck, Marc Ross, Robert Stobaugh, Philip Verleger, and Daniel Yergin criticized a draft of the paper.

1. U.S. Department of Energy, Energy Information Administration, *Monthly Energy Review* (May 1983), p. 97.

long lead times, such as electric power production. In the short run how much reduction in energy use has followed from conservation and substitution and how much from reduced economic growth? The answer should affect near-term plans, such as continued national investment in a strategic petroleum reserve.

A complete analysis of the changes in energy use will require many investigations with attention to the details of institutions and technologies. The costs of a thorough study would be large, as would the potential for concentrating on a biased sample of extreme cases of success or failure. In contrast, an examination of the aggregate data can provide a good deal of insight, and the focus on the whole establishes a background for the study of the parts. The purpose of this essay is to offer an interpretation of the aggregate evidence on the use of energy in the United States. It concentrates on separating the major effects of economic activity, the role of energy use, the effects of interfuel substitution, and the dynamics of adaptation of these factors during a period of substantial market turmoil.

The results confirm the new conventional wisdom of the high potential for energy conservation. There will continue to be significant improvements in energy efficiency. But the same results refute the claims of permanent structural change. Soft energy markets or shifts in relative prices could produce additional surprising changes in the level and mix of energy demand.

Energy Consumption

In 1972, the last year before the market convulsions wrought by the oil embargo, total primary consumption of energy in the United States was 71.6 quadrillion British thermal units (quads), and had grown for more than a decade at the compound rate of 4 percent a year. For electric utilities, the growth leader, consumption stood at 18.5 quads and had been growing at a rate of nearly 7 percent a year. Adjusted for economic activity, the level of primary energy consumption reached a new peak in 1972 at 34,000 Btus per 1980 dollar of gross national product.[2] The prospect of ever-increasing energy consumption was accepted as inevitable, even necessary to fuel the engine of economic growth.

2. DOE, EIA, *1982 Annual Energy Review*, pp. 7, 13.

Figure 1. *Primary Energy Annual Growth Rates, by Sector, 1960–72 and 1972–82*

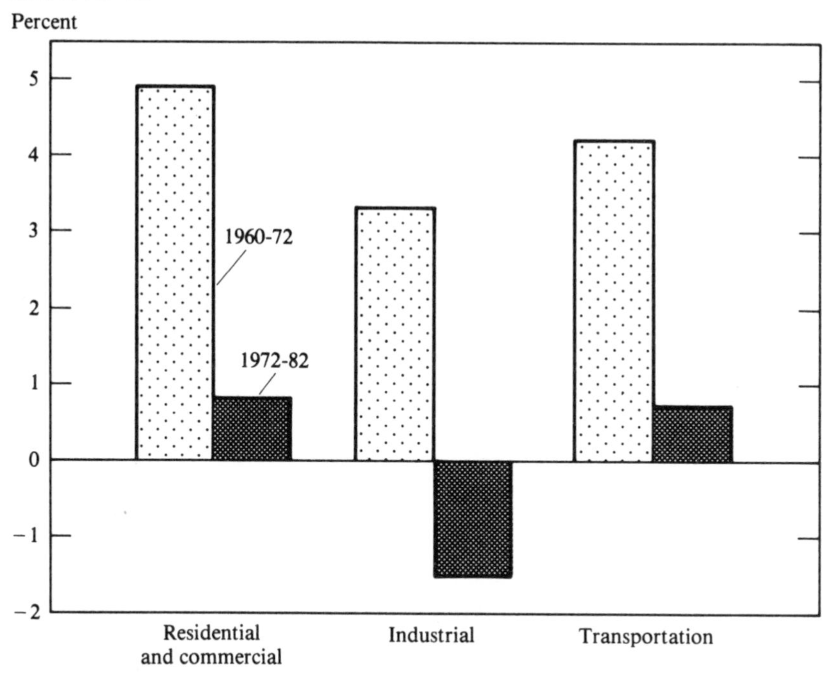

Source: U.S. Department of Energy, Energy Information Administration, *1982 Annual Energy Review*, p. 9.

In the decade following, primary energy consumption rose and then fell, leaving total energy use in 1982 just below the 1972 level. Electricity consumption continued to grow, but at only 2.8 percent a year. With intermittent growth in the economy, the calculus of energy efficiency revealed a 24 percent reduction in the ratio between primary energy and GNP.[3] The impact of energy conservation was indisputable. Faced with this evidence, even skeptics recognized energy conservation as an essential technology for efficient operation of the economic engine.

The improvements in energy efficiency were shared across the major sectors of the economy. As shown in figure 1, the rapid pre-1972 growth in total primary energy use dropped dramatically in the residential-commercial, industrial, and transportation sectors. The growth rate declined the most in the industrial sector, a total of 4.8 percentage points, and industrial primary energy consumption actually decreased over the

3. Ibid.

decade. Under the pressure of congressionally mandated automobile efficiency standards, average fuel economy bottomed out at 13.1 miles per gallon (mpg) in 1973 and began the long climb toward the 27.5 mpg target for new automobiles. Even U.S. government energy use in 1982 was less than in 1975, despite a growth in federal expenditures.[4]

Although further disaggregation might reveal exceptions to these trends, tighter houses, lighter cars, shifts to less energy-intensive industries, and growth in the use of cogeneration contributed to the impressive triumph of the predictions of the energy conservationists. S. David Freeman and his colleagues were widely criticized in 1974 when they offered their unprecedented scenario for moving to zero energy growth. Yet Freeman actually overestimated 1980 energy consumption by 15 percent.[5]

Inspection of one natural segmentation of the aggregate data, into electric and nonelectric energy, reveals a steady trend with important implications for the aggregate analysis of energy statistics. Figure 2 provides a summary of data describing the gradual electrification of energy demand. Between 1960 and 1980 the share of electricity in delivered energy demand almost doubled in industry and more than doubled in the residential and commercial sectors. During this same period, despite the high cost of electricity, the percentage of homes using electric heat rose from under 2 percent to over 17 percent, with distillate oil heat absorbing the loss in market share.[6] The move to greater use of electricity is part of the story of energy conservation.

Both the improvements in energy efficiency and the shift toward electricity are consistent with the predictions that would flow from a simple economic characterization of energy utilization. The higher energy prices that followed the oil embargo of 1973 and the Iranian revolution of 1979 could be expected to have profound effects on energy choices. At the new level of relatively high energy costs, it should be

4. Ibid., pp. 191, 209.

5. Ford Foundation, Energy Policy Project, *Exploring Energy Choices: A Preliminary Report* (Washington, D.C.: Ford Foundation, 1974). Figures interpolated from the graph on page 41 imply an estimate by Freeman of 87 quads for 1980 in the zero energy growth case. According to the *Monthly Energy Review,* actual gross consumption was 75.9 quads. Hence Freeman overestimated demand by 15 percent. For a description of the surrounding controversy, see Martin Greenberger, *Caught Unawares: The Energy Decade in Retrospect* (Ballinger, 1983). Freeman offered his own thoughts in "Still Time to Choose . . . Ten Years Later," *Energy Journal,* vol. 4 (April 1983), pp. 9–14.

6. DOE, EIA, *1982 Annual Energy Review,* p. 195.

Figure 2. *Electric and Nonelectric Energy Shares, by Sector, 1960–80*

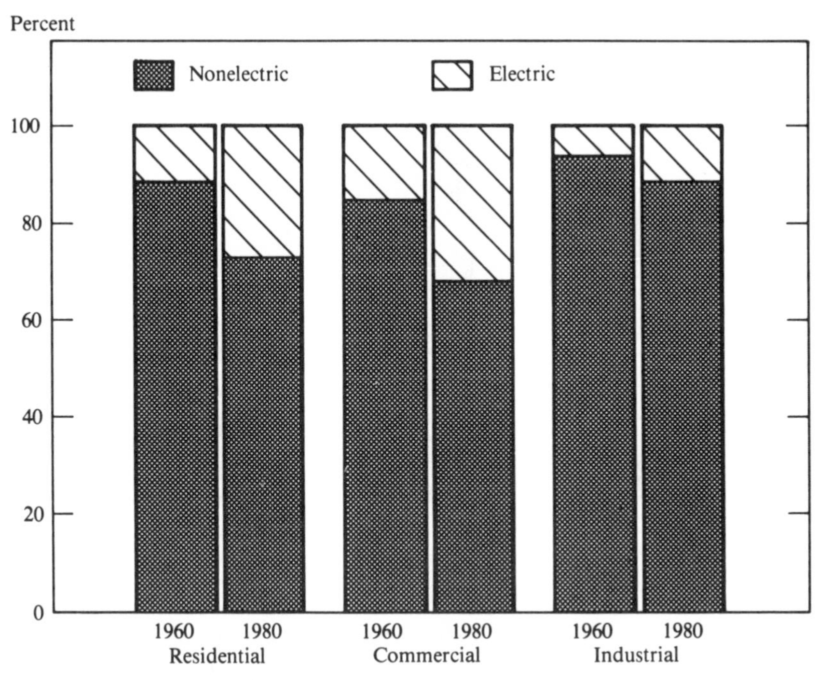

Source: Data derived from U.S. Department of Energy, State Energy Consumption Data Base, 1960–80.

economic to substitute away from energy through energy conservation and the greater use of capital and labor. At the same time, the relative prices of nonelectric energy and electricity were changing significantly, as shown in figure 3. From 1960 to 1972 the real price of electricity was falling, and one would expect a move toward electricity then. But even after 1972, when the price of electricity increased, the price of competing nonelectric fuels grew faster, and just as consistently the share of electricity continued to grow.[7]

Energy conservation can be viewed as part of the process of improving the overall efficiency of the economy. Overall improvements in energy efficiency suggest a substitution of other factors of production—capital and labor—to achieve an increased level of economic output with a constant level of energy use. However, it is important to point out here

7. This refers to the aggregate prices estimated with a Tornquist index, as discussed in the Appendix.

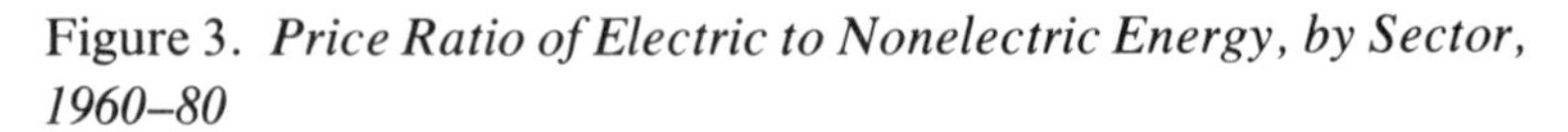

Figure 3. *Price Ratio of Electric to Nonelectric Energy, by Sector, 1960–80*

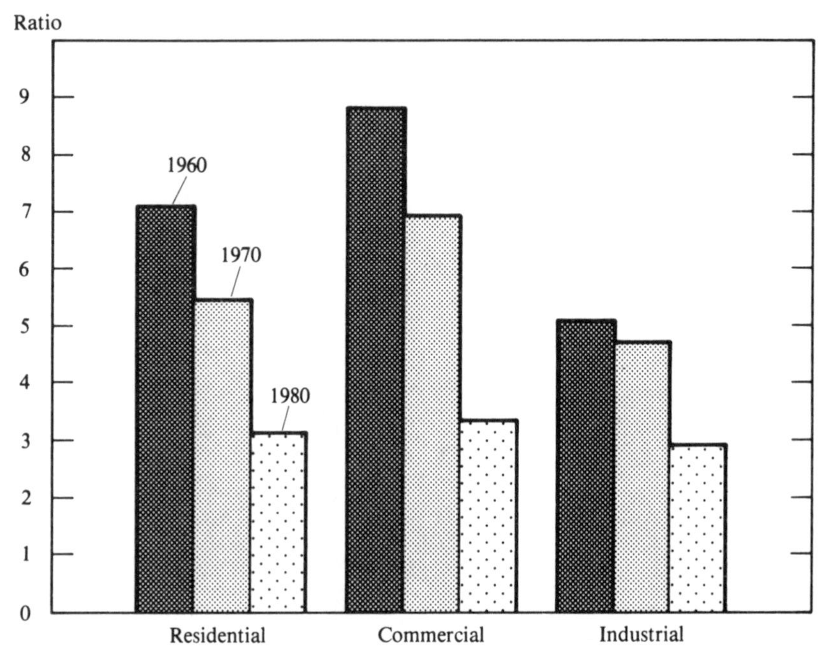

Source: Data derived from DOE, State Energy Consumption Data Base.

that reductions in energy demand that follow from changes in total output—"doing without"—are not the same as cost-effective energy conservation. For example, changing the energy used in making steel is conservation within an industry, and reducing the steel needed to make automobiles is an indirect way to conserve energy. This adaptation in the mix of products in the economy may be among the most important sources of energy conservation. Mandating car pools, however, might reduce the number of cars sold and reduce energy use, but it would not meet the test of cost effectiveness.

Slow but Sure

Although the importance of energy conservation appears in even a few selected statistics, the limited sample of years with higher energy prices obscures the story of the long-run adjustments that are yet to come. Furthermore, the examination of the aggregate data soon presents familiar dilemmas concerning the proper definition and measurement of energy efficiency. Both these issues need at least partial resolution before proceeding with an examination of the trends in energy consumption.

Flexibility in Energy Use

In the long run, there is an impressive potential for achieving an improved level of energy efficiency—at a price. In an earlier discussion of the same theme,[8] I summarized a diverse array of arguments and indirect evidence pointing to a high degree of flexibility in energy use. Later studies, such as the work of Eric Hirst and others, further extend and elaborate the collection of detailed statistical and anecdotal evidence of the potential for energy conservation.[9]

International comparisons, for instance, provide many examples of countries with high consumer costs for energy and low aggregate energy demand when figured on a per capita basis or adjusted for economic activity. And Canada, the one instance of a developed country with lower energy prices, conveniently displays a greater use of energy than the United States.[10] These international comparisons are not without their criticisms and pitfalls. Each country has its unique patterns of weather, economic activity, and behavior that could confound the aggregate statistical comparison. But the example of Sweden, with its low energy use, persuades many that energy conservation represents a huge resource only partly tapped in the United States.

At another level of sophistication, and less subject to the criticisms of international comparisons, careful examination of energy use across the fifty states provides alternative evidence of the potential for energy

8. See William W. Hogan, "Dimensions of Energy Demand," in Hans H. Landsberg, ed., *Selected Studies on Energy: Background Papers for Energy: The Next Twenty Years* (Ballinger, 1980), pp. 1–92. The summary results without all the supporting data appear in Hans H. Landsberg and others, *Energy: The Next Twenty Years* (Ballinger, 1979), chap. 2.

9. Eric Hirst and others, "Recent Changes in U.S. Energy Consumption: What Happened and Why," *Annual Review of Energy*, vol. 8 (1983), pp. 193–245.

10. In addition to the summary in Hogan, "Dimensions of Energy Demand," a detailed comparison of more recent OECD data appears in Kazuya Fujime, *Structural Changes in Energy Demand in the OECD Nations, with Emphasis on the United States and Japan, and on Cyclical Behavior in Oil Markets*, MIT-EL 83-015WP (MIT Energy Laboratory, March 1983).

conservation. Although the variations in prices across states are not as great as those across nations, the states are far from being homogeneous in their energy costs or patterns of energy use. For instance, electricity in the Northwest, provided by abundant hydropower, has long been less expensive than elsewhere in the country; natural gas has traditionally been more expensive at the end of the long pipelines than close to the source of production. These variations in conditions provide one test of flexibility in energy use. And the cross-state studies confirm the results found in the comparisons across nations. There is a large potential for energy conservation, and to a first approximation the interstate and international comparisons yield the same degree of aggregate flexibility in energy use.[11]

Interstate comparisons gain further credibility when tested in aggregate studies of the United States with pre-1972 data, which can be viewed as close enough to equilibrium to allow econometric estimation of long-run parameters. Fortunately, such studies estimate parameters consistent with the international and interstate comparisons. In the most complete and careful attempt to compare and analyze representative models from each of these classes, the Energy Modeling Forum found that for all empirically based models considered, the long-run flexibility in energy use exceeds all but the most optimistic estimates of the energy conservationists.[12]

No amount of care in the analysis could fully eliminate all the objections to top-down estimation of the net effect of millions of individual energy choices. But engineers have generated an alternative data base describing the conservation potential inherent in a variety of technologies. In every case, from automobiles to freezer-refrigerators, from building design to industrial process control, the individual analyses demonstrate that over a wide enough range of prices, many energy utilization patterns would be feasible and sensible. Overall, the conservation potential estimated in the engineering studies is at least as large as that obtained from straightforward international comparisons and indirect econometric estimates.[13]

11. For an example of an extensive investigation using a data base of state statistics, see Martin L. Baughman, Paul L. Joskow, and Dilip P. Kamat, *Electric Power in the United States: Models and Policy Analysis* (MIT Press, 1979).

12. Energy Modeling Forum 4 Working Group, "Aggregate Elasticity of Energy Demand," *Energy Journal,* vol. 2 (January 1981), pp. 33–75.

13. See Hogan, "Dimensions of Energy Demand" or Hirst and others, "Recent Changes in U.S. Energy Consumption."

The collective message of these alternative studies is impressive in its consistency. Casual observation and the weight of evidence across many periods, regions, and types of analysis combine to provide firm underpinnings for the conclusion that energy consumption is a variable of choice, not a rigid requirement for economic growth. To a first approximation at 1980 prices, the combined estimates fall in a range just below a level that would dictate constant long-run expenditure shares for delivered energy. In other words, a doubling of delivered energy prices would result in almost a halving of energy consumption.[14] This suggests a good deal of energy conservation yet to come in response to the price changes already experienced in the energy decade.

Speed of Adjustment

This conservation estimate will be defined more precisely below, but it raises a second issue of the speed at which the long-run target can be approached. When higher prices did not lead to immediate conservation results on the scale suggested by the international comparisons, critics questioned the validity of the long-run estimates. When the conservation adjustments did appear, others attributed all the force of the adjustments to contemporaneous changes in the marketplace and ignored the cumulative impacts of earlier shocks. However, both views neglect the implications of an alternative hypothesis of a slow process of adjustment to new incentives and opportunities.

It is inherent in the nature of energy utilization that the bulk of energy use is tied to durable capital-intensive devices. When purchasing a new car, one may devote a good deal of attention to an evaluation of gasoline mileage, but once the car is purchased it will usually be driven for many years, even with a wide range of gasoline prices. When the car model is replaced in the fleet there will be a major change in fuel efficiency. So too with appliances, although the life of an appliance may be a few years for an air conditioner, rather than the decade for the car. Given a large jump in energy prices, homeowners might add new insulation, but this has a limited effect compared with building a new house many years later, and even the retrofit may await an external event such as sale to a new owner. Utilities and large industrial users may shift away from oil

14. A unitary elasticity is on the high end of the range of estimates. However, given the high price increases of the energy decade, the qualitative impact of differences in elasticities diminishes rapidly for values above 0.5.

and toward coal, but there are limits as to how much switching is possible before requiring the expensive and slow construction of new boilers.[15] It follows that for most energy-using activities the conversion to more energy-efficient configurations is a slow process stretched out over many years.

When prices first rose in 1973–74, there was much discussion but relatively little tangible evidence in average energy consumption patterns to support the most ambitious conservation estimates. But as the years passed, adjustments accumulated, and conservation incentives were reinforced through further increases in prices in 1979. By 1980 the aggregate record included a complicated overlay of adjustments driven by a series of energy shocks. It is fair to conclude that the entire decade after 1972 was one of disequilibrium in which average aggregate statistics disguised the long-run choices being made at the margin. Therefore, in examining the aggregate data it is essential to adopt a framework that approximates the slow adaptation to the long-run target.

In previous discussions of this adjustment process, I applied a simple adaptive adjustment mechanism.[16] In effect, I estimated for each year the long-run target energy utilization, based on current conditions, and compared this target with the existing configuration. I assumed that a percentage of the gap was removed each year in the gradual march toward equilibrium. Hence, if the target is stable, equilibrium is approached. And if the target moves because of a sequence of shocks to the system, the annual adjustments rise or fall in proportion to the distance from equilibrium. This would be the minimal characterization needed to capture the dynamics of the energy decade. In more complicated descriptions, the speed and type of adjustment might depend on other factors, such as the cost of new equipment or the state of the economy.[17]

15. For an investigation of the causes of the lengthy delay between changes in energy prices and installation of new industrial boilers, see Alvin L. Alm with Joan P. Curhan, *Coal Myths and Environmental Realities: Industrial Fuel Use Decisions in a Time of Change* (Boulder, Colo.: Westview Press, 1984).

16. See Hogan, "Dimensions of Energy Demand."

17. Reister examined a similar ad hoc model of energy adjustment in David B. Reister, "Energy Conservation: The Post-Embargo Record," *Energy*, vol. 7 (May 1982), pp. 403–11. For a further discussion of alternative approaches to the characterization of dynamics, an excellent overview can be found in Ernst R. Berndt and Barry C. Field, eds., *Modelling and Measuring Natural Resource Substitution* (MIT Press, 1981). See also G. C. Watkins and E. R. Berndt, "Energy-Output Coefficients: Complex Realities

If energy-using equipment has a fixed efficiency, then only the entry of new equipment alters the average energy intensity of the economy. If one further assumes that equipment utilization is independent of energy efficiency, then the average efficiency will follow the average configuration of equipment. Finally, for a large economy composed of many energy-using devices, an exponential decay and replacement of old equipment can be assumed. With these assumptions, my dynamic approximation will apply, and the rate of annual adjustment toward the long-run target will equal the percentage of new equipment. Hence if the average stock of energy-using equipment is replaced at a rate of 10 percent a year, each year the economy will move 10 percent closer to the long-run equilibrium of average energy efficiency. The speed of adjustment, therefore, will depend upon the depreciation and growth rates in the economy, because these two figures will identify the percentage of new equipment each year.

The average life of energy-using equipment is the reciprocal of the depreciation rate. For instance, an average life of ten years implies a depreciation rate of 10 percent, an average life of eight years implies a rate of 12.5 percent, and so on. Recognizing that an attempt to average the expected life of everything from electric toasters to high-rise apartments does not justify a great deal of precision, I think it is reasonable to adopt an average life of somewhere between six to twelve years. Adding on a few percentage points for growth should produce total adjustment rates of from 10 percent to 20 percent a year, with the midpoint of 15 percent used as the focus of discussion.

These calculations provide the background for examining the consistency of the aggregate data with the hypothesis that energy conservation adjustments are slow but sure. Over the long run, the incentive of high energy prices creates an enormous potential for adjustment in the patterns of energy utilization. But because of the need to replace the stock of energy-using equipment, the lags in adjustment extend over many years. However, there is an additional pitfall in interpreting the aggregate energy data that can be avoided. This requires a description of the proper measurement of energy prices and quantities.

---

behind Simple Ratios," *Energy Journal,* vol. 4 (April 1983), pp. 105–22. An interesting application of a dynamic model with specific costs of adjustment appears in Robert S. Pindyck and Julio J. Rotemberg, "Dynamic Factor Demands, Energy Use, and the Effects of Energy Price Shocks," MIT-EL 82-024WP (MIT Energy Laboratory, April 1982).

Energy or Btus?

Not all Btus are alike. The natural gas burned at home is much cleaner than the coal firing a utility's boiler. The Btus captured in gasoline are more useful than the Btus of residual oil in bunker fuels. And the price of Btus of electricity is much higher than the price of Btus of heating oil. Unfortunately, the productivity and value of energy products are not fully summarized by the Btu measure of the equivalent heat content.

In preparing and using energy statistics, rough attempts are made to deal with the most egregious disparities. Hence the energy content of electricity is often represented in terms of the heat content of the fuels needed to generate the electricity. In the case of hydropower, this often means the equivalent heat content if the hydropower had been coal instead. This has led to speaking loosely about energy products as though they could be substituted on an equivalent Btu basis, an important simplification that serves to remind that energy products are substitutes. Without protection from outside the market, the price of one product cannot move out of line for long without precipitating a competitive response and shift in market share. But the extent of the shift depends on many factors. The electricity customer buys electricity, not the heat content of the coal needed to generate the equivalent hydropower, or any of the other approximations in the standard convention. And the conventional Btu measure does not capture all the information needed to evaluate a changing mix of energy use patterns. The standard energy Btu in the energy statistics is in part a fiction, which in some applications serves well. But for the purposes of this discussion, more attention must be given to measuring the differences in the energy forms.

Fortunately, E. R. Berndt has dealt at length with the history of energy accounting conventions, the deficiencies of the standard Btu measure, and the natural alternative approach from the perspective of the energy model.[18] The alternative to adding up the Btus is to treat energy as an economic good and follow the procedure applied in aggregating economic goods in other sectors of the economy. In essence,

18. Ernst R. Berndt, "Aggregate Energy, Efficiency, and Productivity Measurement," *Annual Review of Energy*, vol. 3 (1978), pp. 225–73. Peck and Beggs speak from a similar economic perspective and urge the use of costs, not Btu per unit of output, as the measure of economic efficiency. See Merton J. Peck and John J. Beggs, "Energy Conservation in American Industry,"this volume.

the recommended procedure is to use the price of the product as the best measure of its overall value and to aggregate across products, weighting the quantities by the prices. Any of several index formulas might be applied. If prices are used as the best available measure of value, the index formulas preserve a consistent evaluation.

The Energy Modeling Forum examined a number of index formulas in the context of energy statistics.[19] I believe the Tornquist index provides the best mix of flexibility and consistency across a range of underlying economic assumptions.[20] For convenience I benchmark the parameters of the index to 1972 to reproduce the total number of quads obtained by straight addition of the Btus consumed in that year. But for other years, when relative prices change, the index estimate of total energy (interpreted as the homogeneous good of the type delivered in 1972) diverges from the unweighted sum of Btus found in conventional statistics. To illustrate, figure 4 displays the index-based estimate of total consumption per 1980 dollar of GNP and the traditional unweighted sum of the Btus. In 1980, for instance, the difference between the two measures was about 10 percent. Given that the improvement in energy efficiency is of the same order of magnitude, the choice of the index can have a significant impact on the estimate of the short- and long-run impact of energy conservation.

The measurement problems compound during a period of extended disequilibrium in energy markets. When relative prices are changing, the average energy mix will differ from the long-run target. Yet the underlying theory of index measurement is based on long-run equilibrium conditions. To illustrate the difficulty, consider oil and gas used for heating; they are nearly perfect substitutes, but a switch from one to the other occurs with the replacement of the furnace. Assume a start at equilibrium with equal prices and equal market shares. Suddenly the price of oil rises, but regulation prevents any change in the price of natural gas. The aggregate energy statistics will show an increase in the average price of energy. But for purchasers of new furnaces, gas will be the choice and the price of "energy" will not have changed. And for the

19. See Energy Modeling Forum 4 Working Group, "Aggregate Elasticity of Energy Demand."

20. The Tornquist (or "Divisia" or "translog") index calculates the aggregate price index between two sets of input price observations as a linear logarithmic approximation using the average of the value shares between observations as the weights in the average. See the Appendix for details.

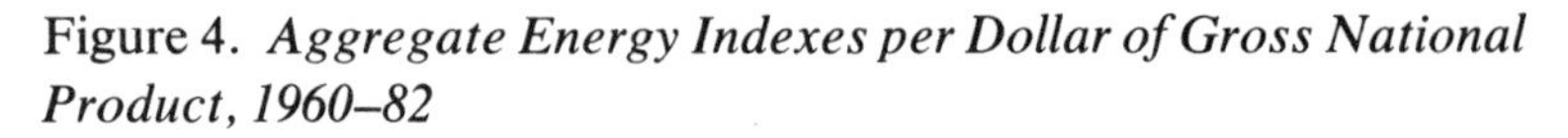

Figure 4. *Aggregate Energy Indexes per Dollar of Gross National Product, 1960–82*

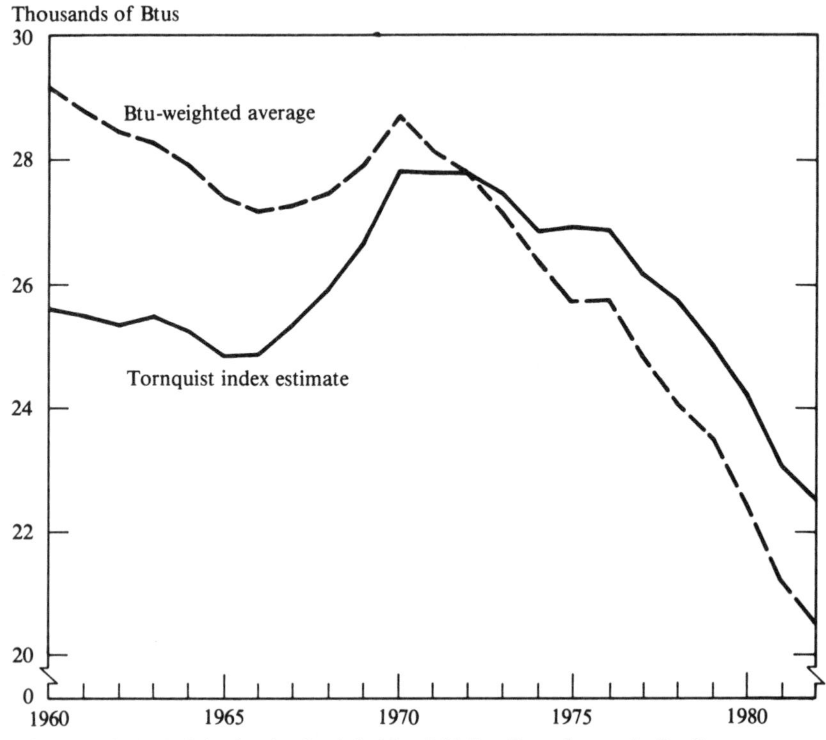

Source: Author's calculations based on data derived from DOE, State Energy Consumption Data Base.

owners of old furnaces, energy efficiency cannot change. Hence the aggregate data will reveal no energy conservation in response to an increase in average energy price. Eventually, as the old oil furnaces are replaced by new natural gas furnaces, reported average prices will drop to the original level and consistency will be restored. But in the interim an incorrect picture is being presented of the response of energy conservation.

Several solutions are available to deal with this disequilibrium problem. My previous investigation applied the Pindyck estimates of long-run substitution in order to calculate the relevant aggregate energy price for new consumption decisions,[21] and thereby avoided the use of Btu

21. See Hogan, "Dimensions of Energy Demand." The long-run price equations were drawn from Robert S. Pindyck, *The Structure of World Energy Demand* (MIT Press, 1979).

average prices. The chief deficiency in this method was the lack of a corresponding estimate of the quantity of energy use on a consistent basis. With the shorter period of disequilibrium in the earlier data base, the Btu approximation appeared adequate, but as I argued above, this assumption is less applicable as the number and duration of the shocks increase. Another method would call for a carefully disaggregated data base that distinguished the vintages of energy equipment, but this would go beyond the realm of an examination of the aggregate data.

The approach adopted here is to disaggregate the energy products to separate the data with the greatest differences and changes in relative prices. To the extent that heterogeneous products are accounted for separately, the disequilibrium problem does not arise. Or for aggregates of products, the problem does not arise if there are no relative price changes among the products in the subset being aggregated. As discussed, the most significant difference in relative prices and aggregate shares is between electric and nonelectric energy products. For example, more than half the discrepancy between the index estimates and Btu-weighted averages of all energy prices can be attributed to the change in the mix between electric and nonelectric shares. Therefore, as the minimal step away from the complete aggregation of all energy into a single commodity, I disaggregate to the changes in efficiency for electric and nonelectric energy as measured with a Tornquist index of prices and quantities.

The resulting national data for delivered energy prices and quantities appear in figures 5 and 6. For reference the Tornquist indexes for total petroleum and total energy consumption are also shown. Delivered energy consumption, not primary energy production, is emphasized, because it is the final product that consumers purchase and this is where they make their conservation decisions.

These delivered price data do not conform to the usual shorthand summary of the movements of energy prices over the energy decade. For example, it is commonplace to note that after the first oil shock the real price of crude oil declined until 1978. But the delivered price of petroleum products did not decline during this period, and the delivered price of all energy moved up steadily (see figure 5). In part this was caused by the effects of the gradual elimination of price controls on petroleum products and natural gas and by the increasing price and greater weight of electricity in the total energy index.

The second price shock, in 1979, was more significant than the first,

Figure 5. *Delivered Energy Prices, by Type of Source, 1960–82*

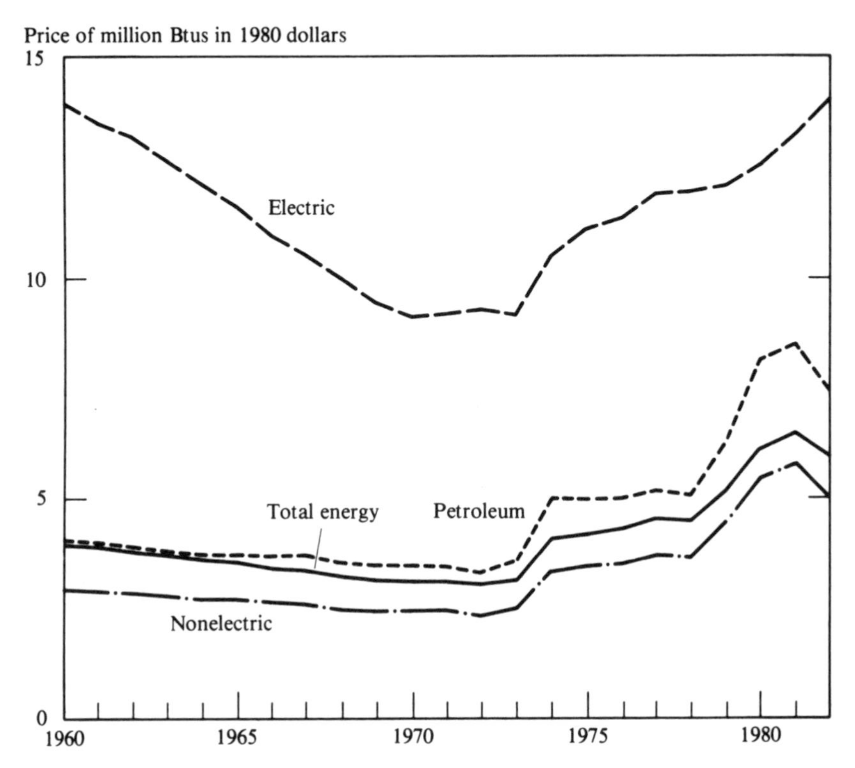

Sources: Data for 1960–80 derived in disaggregate form from DOE, State Energy Consumption Data Base. Aggregate data for 1981–82 from DOE, EIA, *1982 Annual Energy Review*, pp. 44, 116, 142, 164.

although more so for nonelectric than electric energy. And the price drops that occurred in the early 1980s were small compared with the earlier price increases. It is not surprising, therefore, that the move toward energy conservation, as shown in figure 6, appeared to accelerate after 1979. Of course, the simple graphs tell only part of the story. An accounting for the shift in energy mix and the long-run implications in the short-run data depend on the analysis of the dynamics of this adjustment.

Accounting for Adjustment

My framework for the energy-economy interactions includes three sectors: electric energy, nonelectric energy, and other inputs to the

Figure 6. *Energy Quantities per Dollar of Gross National Product, by Type of Source, 1960–82*

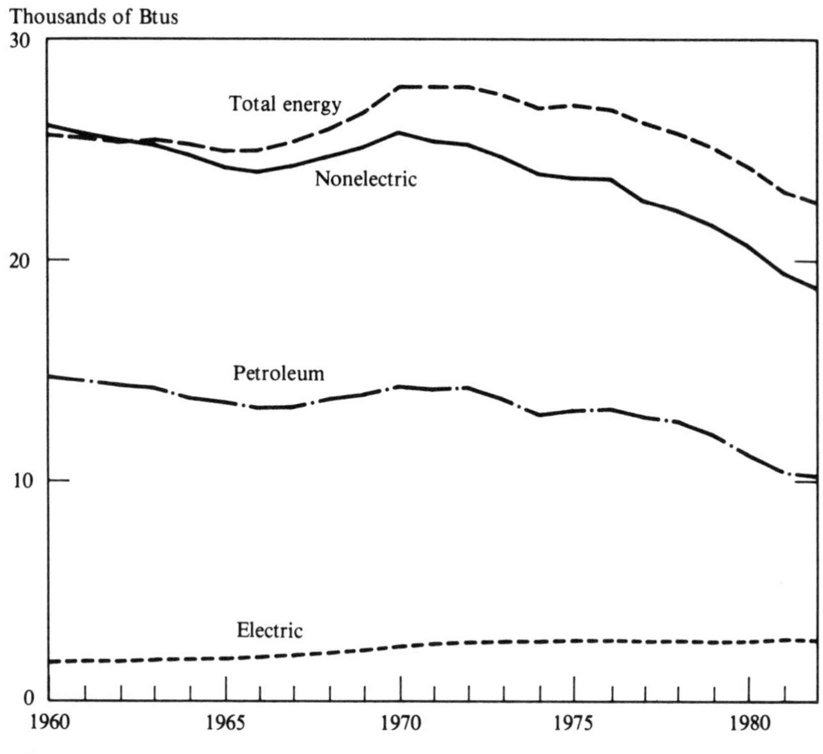

Sources: Same as figure 5.

economy. It is assumed that without relative price changes the level of energy demand is proportional to the level of economic activity. But changes in relative prices can affect the long-run mix of energy and other factors. (I considered interactions between the level of activity and prices in determining the value shares, but found that the prices alone provided the better description.) Although somewhat arbitrary, this accounting scheme is familiar in aggregate models of energy and the economy.[22] Of course other factors could influence energy demand, but to the extent that this simple model provides an adequate explanation of the data, it will be applied to separate the effects of economic activity,

22. See Energy Modeling Forum 4 Working Group, "Aggregate Elasticity of Energy Demand."

Figure 7. *Actual and Estimated Demand for Electric and Nonelectric Energy, 1961–82*

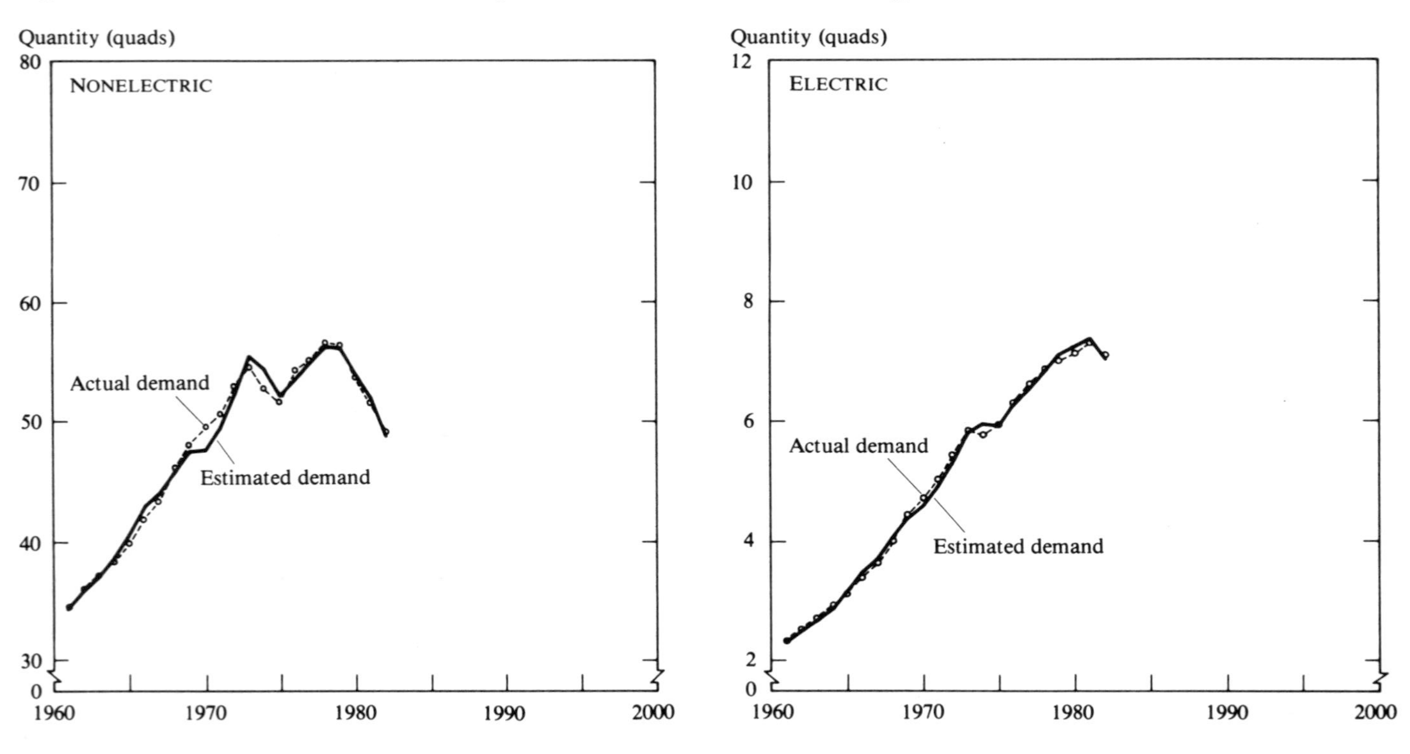

Sources: Same as figure 5.

price changes, and gradual adjustments to the elusive long-run equilibrium.

Estimation

Within this accounting framework I used a flexible translog approximation to estimate the long-run substitution relationships. This translog model is embedded in the adjustment process and estimated over a range of assumptions for the speed of adaptation. The details of the model design and estimation appear in the Appendix.

The results of the estimation are shown in figure 7, which compares the actual and estimated demands for electric and nonelectric energy. The fit of this simple model is impressive, especially considering the turmoil of the period after 1972. The model does *not* use the actual data in the lagged values of the adjustment equations, which otherwise would hide the accumulation of errors. The somewhat ad hoc estimation procedure is equivalent to preparing a forecast beginning in 1959 and then using the estimated quantities as the lagged values in the prediction of the next-period estimates. Nor is there a technical problem with an inadequate number of degrees of freedom: the combined model includes eight parameters. The twenty-three-year sample contains forty-six independent observations on the value shares of electric and nonelectric energy.

Given the importance of the two energy price shocks, the total degrees of freedom might not be as impressive if the eight parameters were tracking only four real changes in price (electric and nonelectric for 1973 and 1979). Hence it would be useful to examine the structural estimates in the model and compare the substitution parameters with those obtained from the long-run models and international studies mentioned above. For these purposes I focus on the aggregate elasticity of energy demand. For equal percentage changes in electric and nonelectric energy prices, an aggregate elasticity can be defined as the ratio between the percentage change in energy quantity and the percentage change in price. My model yields an elasticity estimate for each assumption on the speed of adjustment, relying on a priori arguments in preference to the usual statistical estimates, which provide little discrimination. For a given level of total adjustment in energy demand, a faster assumed rate of adjustment must result in a lower estimate of the elasticity of demand.

As an internal check on these estimates, I can compare the stability

Table 1. *Comparative Estimates of Elasticity of Energy Demand, by Speed of Adjustment and Period*

Source of estimate	*Estimate*
Hogan	
1960–78	
10 percent per year adjustment rate	0.92
15 percent per year adjustment rate	0.57
20 percent per year adjustment rate	0.39
1960–82	
10 percent per year adjustment rate	1.00
15 percent per year adjustment rate	0.63
20 percent per year adjustment rate	0.45
Energy Modeling Forum	
Pindyck	1.00
Baughman-Joskow	0.86
Griffin OECD	0.71
BESOM/H-J	0.57
MEFS	0.42

Source: Author's estimates based on the long-run empirical models reported in Energy Modeling Forum 4 Working Group, "Aggregate Elasticity of Energy Demand," *Energy Journal*, vol. 2 (January 1981), pp. 37–75. The high and low estimates apply to Pindyck and the MEFS model, from table 6 in the EMF report. The conversion to delivered or retailed elasticities was made using the ratio of 0.7 between secondary and retail elasticities in 1980 as shown in figure 6 of the EMF report.

of the estimates for the period through 1978, which includes one price shock, and the period through 1982, which includes the larger second price shock. For comparison, I use the estimates from the long-run empirical models as reported by the Energy Modeling Forum, adjusted to the equivalent measures for delivered energy prices. To establish the scale for comparison, I use the elasticity estimates relative to the range of 0.0 to 0.2 implicit in the traditional analyses of the energy growth enthusiasts. A summary of the different estimates appears in table 1.

The aggregate elasticity estimates are consistent across studies and over estimation periods. The elasticity estimates reinforce the conclusion that there is a large potential for cost-effective energy conservation, and the slow adaptation to reach that potential is far from complete.

Alternative Retrospective Scenarios

To illustrate the separate effects of prices and economic activity, I focus on the assumption of a 15 percent rate of adjustment and compare counterfactual hypotheses of no energy shocks with the actual history. A scenario that assumes economic growth at the 1960–72 rate of 4 percent a year and constant real energy prices after 1972 can be compared with one that substitutes the actual energy prices but continues to assume the historical growth trend. This comparison isolates the cost-effective conservation implied by the model. When the second scenario is compared in turn with a third one assuming the estimated demand and the actual economic growth, the difference can be attributed to the performance of the economy, rather than the effects of prices. The small residual would be assigned to errors or the effects of omitted factors.

The results of these comparisons appear in figure 8, which shows that by 1982, 72 percent of the drop in nonelectric energy demand and 29.5 percent of the drop in electric demand can be attributed to the actual as opposed to the assumed prices. This is the cost-effective energy conservation, which represents only part of the eventual adjustment one can expect in the gradual replacement of energy-using equipment. Given the greater relative increase in nonelectric prices, there is a correspondingly greater impact on nonelectric energy demand. And given the slow adjustment process, more conservation can be expected.

Poorer performance of the economy receives credit for the remaining differences (29.5 percent for nonelectric and 75.9 percent for electric energy) between the second scenario and the third one of estimated demand and actual prices and economic activity. Finally, the differences between the estimated demand and actual demand, measured as a percentage of the gap between the actual and the historical forecast, are −1.5 percent for nonelectric energy and −6.9 percent for electric energy.

My baseline forecast after 1972 at historical economic growth rates and constant energy prices does not reproduce the historical growth trend in energy demand. In particular, at its historical growth rate of 7 percent a year, electric energy demand would have had an additional 1.8 quads, a 20 percent increment, in 1982 compared with the prediction of the model for the first scenario. This residual could have been assigned to a time trend or other factors. But my data do not support any estimate of a significant time trend after accounting for the changes in prices and economic activity. In the present case, the explanation of the discrepancy is in the assumption of constant real prices at 1972 levels. The trend was actually one of a declining real price of electricity relative to the price of nonelectric energy. Such a scenario continued beyond 1972 would reproduce the historical 7 percent growth rate for electric energy demand. This is another illustration of the ability of the sparse model to explain the aggregate energy data for this tumultuous period.

My dissection of energy demand can be compared with the similar

Figure 8. *Actual and Estimated Demand for Electric and Nonelectric Energy Compared with Historical Growth Trends, 1961–82*

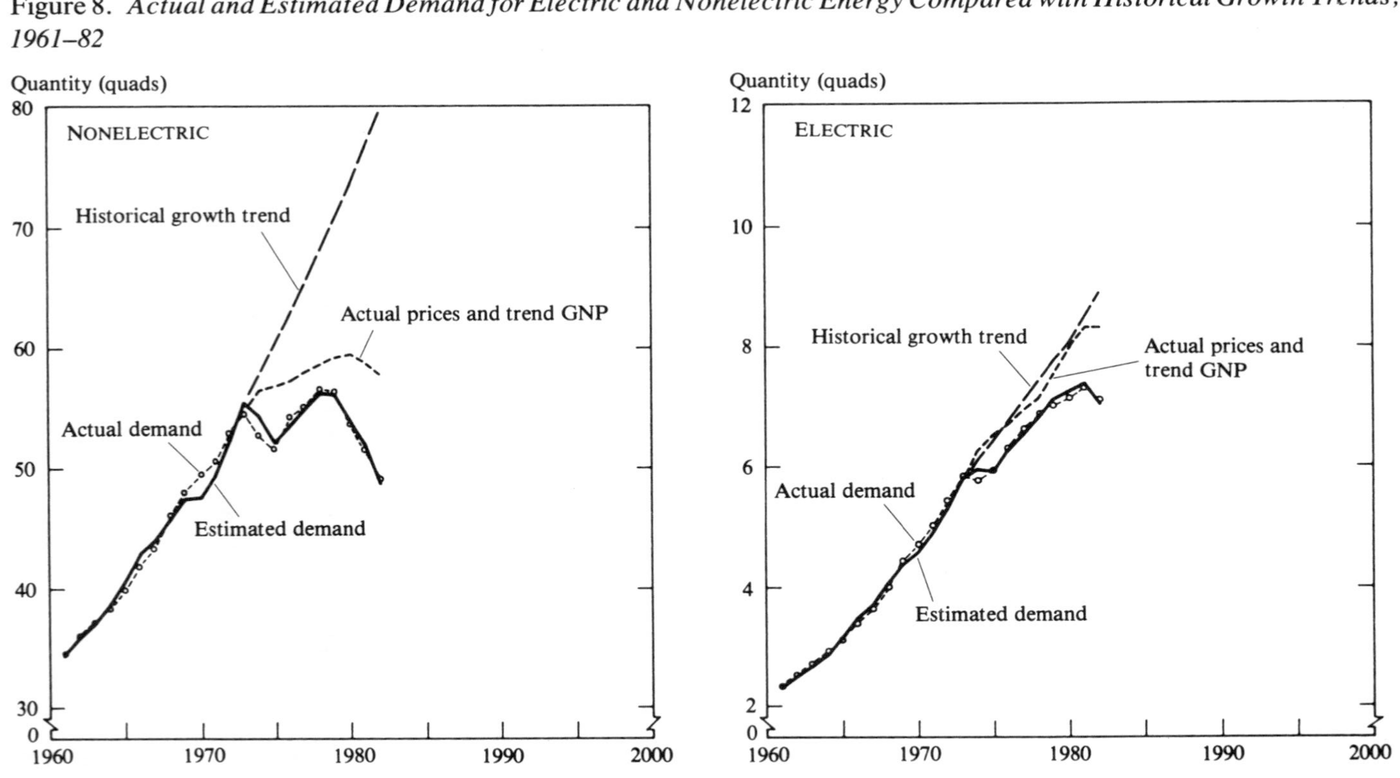

Sources: Same as figure 5.

Table 2. *Comparative Estimates of Total Primary Energy Demand under Varying Scenarios*
Quads

Scenario	Estimate: Hogan	Estimate: Hirst and others
Historical economic growth and constant real energy prices	102.1	102.1
Historical economic growth and actual energy prices	83.5	91.9
Actual economic growth and actual energy prices	74.1	79.1
Actual energy demand	74.1	74.1

Sources: Author's estimates and Eric Hirst and others, "Recent Changes in U.S. Energy Consumption: What Happened and Why," *Annual Review of Energy*, vol. 8 (1983), pp. 193–245.

analysis prepared by Hirst and others, who tackled both the top-down and bottom-up explanation of the changes in energy demand.[23] They considered total energy measured in terms of primary input, as opposed to my use of delivered energy separated by nonelectric and electric forms. As a rough approximation, my energy demand figures can be connected to primary inputs by assuming a 33 percent efficiency in electricity production. With this conversion, one can compare the data for 1981, the last year in the Hirst data, for the four scenarios: (1) estimates with historical economic growth and constant real prices, (2) estimates with historical economic growth and actual prices, (3) estimates with actual growth and actual prices, and (4) actual energy demand. Both analyses assign about the same impact to the changes in economic growth, but, in partial disagreement with Hirst, my study attributes a 50 percent larger impact to changes in energy prices and leaves little to time trends or other factors (see table 2).

The chief causes of this difference in the estimation of the price effects may be in the aggregation conventions. Hirst uses total primary energy as the demand quantity. Because of the difficulties during a period of relative price changes, my aggregation stopped at nonelectric and electric energy. Furthermore, Hirst used the Btu-weighted average as the

23. See Hirst and others, "Recent Changes in U.S. Energy Consumption." Another interesting study is A. J. Viscio, Jr., "United States Energy Demand: Conservation and Recession Effects, 1973 to 1982," *Journal of Energy and Development*, vol. 8 (Spring 1983), pp. 231–46. Viscio applies the Texaco energy demand model to isolate the effects of price and income in reducing energy and petroleum demand.

Figure 9. *Actual and Estimated Demand for Electric and Nonelectric Energy at Selected Rates of Growth, 1961–2000*

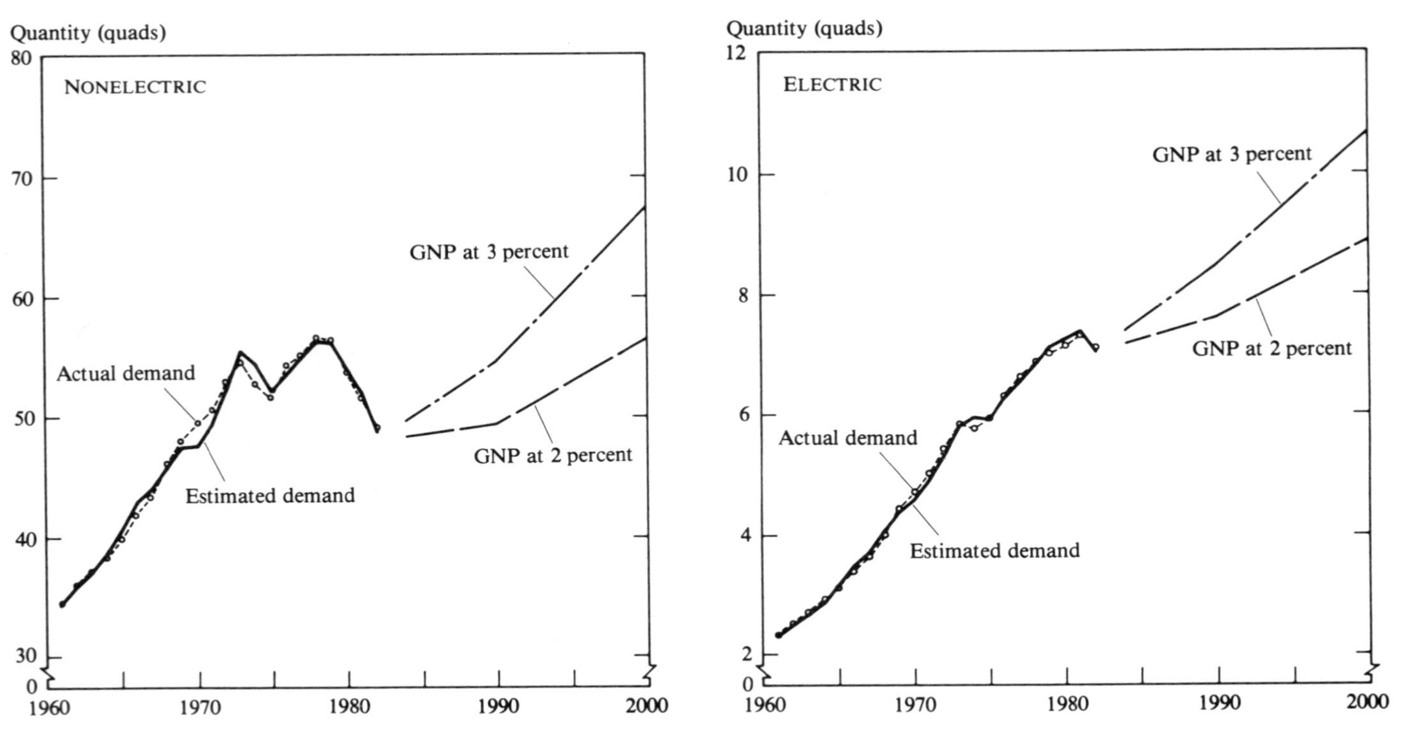

Sources: Same as figure 5.

measure of energy price, as opposed to an index such as the Tornquist approach applied here. Considering the investigations in the Energy Modeling Forum study, one would expect both these differences in approach to lead to lower estimates of price effects than those found with my model.

The implications of these different estimates will become more important in the long run. But the differences are not as important as the similarities. In explaining the experience since 1972, both studies agree that there has been a significant improvement in energy efficiency that can be attributed to a cost-effective response to higher energy prices. At least half, and possibly more, of the adjustment from the historical trend can be explained by the effects of prices alone. And both studies endorse the related view of slow adjustment to a long-run equilibrium. Therefore, the future evolution of energy demand should display a continued improvement in energy efficiency, even without further increases in energy prices. For this forecasting purpose, my model of electric and nonelectric energy can be applied to a few possible scenarios for the coming decades.

Alternative Future Scenarios

Given the soft oil market after 1980, there have been few predictions of an early repetition of the oil shocks of the energy decade. Although prices might fall, or stabilize only in nominal terms, the simplest assumption to use in investigating the trend in energy conservation is that energy prices will remain constant at 1982 levels. The chief uncertainty of the near term is the degree and duration of economic recovery, which will drive the immediate movements in total energy demand. To bound this uncertainty, I consider two cases of 2 percent and 3 percent annual growth in GNP between 1982 and 2000. With these assumptions, my model can be used to forecast a range of possible demands for electric and nonelectric energy use. Figure 9 presents these cases along with the historical and estimated energy demand for the period from 1961 to 1982.

As is shown, the continued inroads of energy conservation should have a major effect through the next two decades. In the case of 2 percent annual growth in GNP over eighteen years, nonelectric energy demand would not regain its historical peak level in this century, and electricity consumption would enjoy only modest growth compared with historical standards. Without any structural change in the energy economy, but only a shift in relative prices, there would be a significant and prolonged change in energy efficiency.

In the absence of structural change, in the sense that the same model applies over the full period from 1960 to 2000, the perception of energy conservation could be altered substantially if there were further movements in energy prices. For instance, with every drop in oil prices there are fresh reports of the consumer surge to larger cars, threatening the automobile industry's ability to meet average fleet fuel economy standards. This rapid fluctuation in consumer preferences is consistent with the implicit symmetry of my basic model of energy demand. If prices change again, there would be a slow adaptation to a new long-run equilibrium target, and energy consumption could increase.

Perhaps the most intriguing notion is the possibility of future erosion of the price difference between electric and nonelectric energy. A large part of the electricity price increase has been due to the addition of capital-intensive plants with front-end-loaded rate making. The result is a sharp increase in real prices, followed by a gradual decline if no further plants are brought on line. Over the near future, utilities will be working off excess capacity, not introducing new plants. Hence the amortization of the rate base coupled with a gradual rationalization of the fuel mix could lead to real reductions in electricity rates. While the lower relative rates would not necessarily be enough to recreate the rapid growth of the 1960s, a 2 or 3 percent difference between the rate of change of electricity prices and the price of nonelectric substitutes could have as much as a 20 percent impact on the demand for electricity at the turn of the century.[24] Therefore, the historical shift toward electrification of the economy could continue hand in hand with the improvements in energy efficiency.

My simple three-sector model of the energy economy lends itself to many possible analyses of the gradual unveiling of future energy demand. But these need not be pursued further to accomplish the main purpose

24. The importance of the changes in relative prices is often overlooked. For example, a report reviewing the major low-energy demand forecasts found that these forecasts typically assume significant increases in energy prices, but fail to notice that the assumptions would imply a decrease in the relative price of electricity. Hence electric demand would be underestimated and nonelectric demand overestimated in the total energy mix. See Putnam, Hayes, and Bartlett, *Alternative Energy Futures: A Review of Low Energy Growth Forecasts and Least-Cost Planning Studies,* rev. ed., prepared for the U.S. Department of Energy (Cambridge, Mass.: Putnam, Hayes, and Bartlett, 1983).

of this study, which is to isolate the energy conservation evident in the aggregate data for the United States. The historical backcasts, the comparison of structural parameters, and the simple forecasts all reinforce my straightforward interpretation of the data. In the long run there is substantial flexibility in the choice of energy use patterns. Energy efficiency in the economic sense can be explained by reference to the incentives provided by prices for nonelectric and electric products. And the economy adjusts slowly over many years in approaching the long-run target. The aggregate data since the first oil shock are consistent with this hypothesis, and the strength of the conclusion increases steadily as more data accumulate.

Conclusion

Despite the appeal of engineering analyses, international comparisons, and long-run econometric models, for many observers the most comprehensive, relevant, and persuasive evidence of the energy conservation reality would be the revelation of energy efficiency increases in the aggregate statistics for the United States. By now a mountain of detailed studies and computers full of accumulating statistics confirm what every new car buyer knows about the potential for energy conservation.

One need make no appeal to structural change in the aggregate data: the period before the oil shocks is consistent with the decade of turmoil after the oil embargo. And one need look no further than a simple economic explanation of energy choices: prices and economic activity can explain the movements in energy demand within a framework of slow adaptation driven by the turnover of the capital stock of energy-using equipment.

Nearly a decade after the first oil shock, the 24 percent reduction in the ratio of primary energy to GNP is more than the tip of a conservation iceberg. But further conservation can be expected as the cost-effective response to high energy prices. With no more than real energy prices sustained at the 1982 level, the same proportional improvement in energy efficiency could be obtained by the end of the century. And there should be even greater shifts in the mix of demands for energy products. The energy decade launched the improvements in energy efficiency and established energy conservation as a central feature of the evolution of the economy.

Appendix

This appendix summarizes the principal data, methods, and results used to aggregate and describe the short-run adjustments in the energy economy.

Data Aggregation

The Tornquist or translog index provides an estimate of the price of the aggregate good as a function of that price in a base period and the changes in the prices of the goods that make up the aggregate. The approximation, which is exact in the case of a translog cost function, applies a linear logarithmic estimate built on the changes in the logarithms of the prices.[25]

$$\ln P_1 = \ln P_0 + \sum_i \left[\frac{s_{i1} + s_{i0}}{2}\right]\left[\ln P_{i1} - \ln P_{i0}\right],$$

where

P_t = price of aggregate good in period t;
P_{it} = price of input good i in period t;
s_{it} = value share of input good i in period t.

I estimated the corresponding quantity of the aggregate output good as the ratio of the value of the inputs and the price of the output.

Using these definitions, I applied the aggregation formulas to the data in the Department of Energy State Energy Consumption Data Base for 1960–80, with 1972 selected as the base year in the index formula. This data base provides a convenient record over a long enough period to

25. See the Energy Modeling Forum 4 Working Group, "Aggregate Elasticity of Energy Demand," for a discussion of the use of alternative index formulas. For a different perspective and an investigation of several variants applied to the analysis of short-run data, see the work in David L. Greene and others, *Estimating the Total Impact on Energy Consumption of Department of Energy Conservation Programs,* ORNL-5925 (Oak Ridge, Tenn.: Oak Ridge National Laboratory, 1982). See also Reister, "Energy Conservation: The Post-Embargo Record," for a further discussion of alternative index numbers and the use of Btu-weighted averages.

address the issues of structural change in the aggregate model of the energy economy.[26]

The gross national product and GNP deflator data are from the Department of Commerce. The energy data for 1981 and 1982 were not available. Therefore I used the DOE *Monthly Energy Review* and *1982 Annual Energy Review* to estimate the aggregate quantities for the national totals. I applied the ratio method to determine the change from 1980 in these publications and then applied this ratio to the aggregate estimates obtained from the State Energy Consumption Data Base.

The resulting data for the translog indexes appear in table 3. For purposes of comparison, table 4 summarizes the same information calculated with the conventional Btu-weighted averages.

Energy Economy Model

For a description of the long-run substitution among energy and other goods, I adopted a translog approximation of a three-sector model including nonelectric energy, electric energy, and other inputs to the economy.[27] Hence I assume that the long-run cost function for gross output in period t takes the form of:

$$\ln P = \alpha_0 + \sum \alpha_i \ln P_i + 0.5 \sum\sum \beta_{ij} \ln P_i \ln P_j + \sum \sigma_i \ln P_i t + \sum \omega_i \ln P_i \ln Y,$$

where t indexes time and Y is the gross output.[28] With constant returns

26. The quantity data are from the DOE, EIA, *State Energy Data Report, 1960–1980,* DOE/EIA-0214(80) (DOE, July 1982), pp. 15–18. The price data are from the DOE State Price Data Base, computer listings dated February 24, 1982. The data are given for individual product and state classifications, but there are fewer price categories than quantity categories. Therefore I assigned the price for the closest substitute to the categories for which there was no independent data. The data include a Btu-weighted average price by state and for the nation for each fuel. I used the national averages as the input data to the translog index formula to aggregate across thirty-seven product and sector categories into total nonelectric and total electric energy.

27. The accounting system applied here is a variant of the accounting scheme applied in William W. Hogan and Alan S. Manne, "Energy-Economy Interactions: The Fable of the Elephant and the Rabbit?" in Charles J. Hitch, ed., *Modeling Energy-Economy Interactions: Five Approaches* (Washington, D.C.: Resources for the Future, 1977), pp. 247–77. Also see Robert S. Pindyck, ed., *Advances in the Economics of Energy and Resources,* vol. 1: *A Research Annual* (Greenwich, Conn.: JAI Press, 1979), pp. 7–26.

28. The translog model of long-run substitution has been used in many studies. It provides a tractable yet flexible functional form, and its properties are well understood. For a recent thorough discussion see Pindyck, *The Structure of World Energy Demand.*

Table 3. *Translog Indexes for Energy Quantities and Prices and Gross National Product, 1960–82*

	Nonelectric		*Electric*		*Aggregate energy*		*GNP*	
Year	*Quantity*[a]	*Price*[b]	*Quantity*[a]	*Price*[b]	*Quantity*[a]	*Price*[b]	*Quantity*[c]	*Deflator*[d]
1960	34.054	2.946	2.220	13.948	33.476	3.922	737.200	68.700
1961	34.506	2.917	2.349	13.496	34.238	3.866	756.600	69.330
1962	36.057	2.846	2.530	13.200	36.018	3.776	800.300	70.610
1963	37.210	2.794	2.733	12.623	37.600	3.682	832.500	71.670
1964	38.435	2.736	2.947	12.113	39.250	3.588	876.400	72.770
1965	39.876	2.715	3.143	11.602	40.991	3.531	929.300	74.360
1966	41.917	2.631	3.421	10.944	43.454	3.399	984.800	76.760
1967	43.518	2.604	3.655	10.516	45.438	3.340	1011.400	79.060
1968	46.288	2.502	4.024	9.950	48.692	3.201	1058.100	82.540
1969	48.267	2.445	4.417	9.393	51.416	3.103	1087.600	86.790
1970	49.630	2.445	4.730	9.082	53.575	3.067	1085.600	91.450
1971	50.624	2.451	5.016	9.155	55.346	3.071	1122.400	96.010
1972	53.035	2.385	5.444	9.235	58.479	3.023	1185.900	100.000
1973	54.709	2.528	5.849	9.161	61.033	3.144	1254.000	105.690
1974	52.931	3.360	5.801	10.465	59.461	4.012	1246.000	114.920
1975	51.807	3.472	5.973	11.108	58.992	4.174	1232.000	125.560
1976	54.448	3.553	6.300	11.353	62.033	4.272	1298.000	132.110
1977	55.197	3.728	6.621	11.902	63.656	4.471	1370.000	139.830
1978	56.623	3.683	6.872	11.957	65.577	4.433	1439.000	150.050
1979	56.661	4.467	7.007	12.058	65.739	5.136	1479.000	162.770
1980	54.010	5.446	7.198	12.548	63.588	6.046	1474.000	177.450
1981	51.728	5.787	7.378	13.211	61.510	6.421	1503.000	195.510
1982	49.064	5.074	7.168	14.015	59.040	5.918	1477.000	207.150

Sources: Aggregate indexes constructed by the author from U.S. Department of Energy, State Energy Consumption Data Base.
a. Quadrillion British thermal units (quads).
b. Translog price index in 1980 dollars.
c. Billions of 1972 dollars.
d. 1972 = 100.

to scale of output, invariance to the scale of prices, and aggregation to a single sector for goods, the symmetry and normalization conditions are:

$$\sum \alpha_i = 1,$$

$$\sum \beta_{ij} = 0,$$

$$\beta_{ij} = \beta_{ji},$$

$$\sum \sigma_i = 0,$$

$$\sum \omega_i = 0.$$

Table 4. *Btu-Weighted Averages for Energy Quantities and Prices, 1960–82*

	Nonelectric		Electric		Aggregate energy	
Year	Quantity[a]	Price[b]	Quantity[a]	Price[b]	Quantity[a]	Price[b]
1960	35.820	2.801	2.351	13.172	38.171	3.439
1961	36.191	2.781	2.465	12.863	38.656	3.424
1962	37.709	2.721	2.654	12.583	40.363	3.369
1963	38.923	2.671	2.842	12.139	41.765	3.315
1964	40.412	2.602	3.058	11.672	43.470	3.240
1965	41.926	2.583	3.255	11.201	45.181	3.204
1966	43.957	2.509	3.532	10.601	47.489	3.111
1967	45.143	2.510	3.751	10.247	48.894	3.104
1968	47.434	2.442	4.105	9.753	51.539	3.024
1969	49.286	2.395	4.483	9.255	53.769	2.967
1970	50.563	2.400	4.751	9.043	55.314	2.971
1971	51.076	2.429	5.013	9.161	56.089	3.031
1972	53.035	2.385	5.444	9.235	58.479	3.023
1973	54.568	2.534	5.845	9.168	60.413	3.176
1974	52.507	3.387	5.821	10.430	58.328	4.090
1975	50.236	3.581	5.961	11.131	56.197	4.382
1976	52.921	3.656	6.331	11.298	59.252	4.472
1977	53.456	3.850	6.648	11.855	60.104	4.735
1978	54.468	3.828	6.885	11.935	61.353	4.738
1979	54.667	4.630	7.058	11.970	61.725	5.470
1980	51.477	5.714	7.147	12.637	58.624	6.558
1981	49.300	6.072	7.326	13.305	56.626	7.008
1982	46.760	5.324	7.117	14.115	53.877	6.485

Sources: Same as table 3.
a. Quadrillion British thermal units (quads).
b. Translog price index in 1980 dollars.

Assuming cost-minimizing behavior, the value share equations satisfy:

$$S_i = \alpha_i + \sum \beta_{ij} \ln P_j + \sigma_i t + \omega_i \ln Y,$$

where S_i is the share of expenditure on input i. Applying the symmetry and normalization conditions, these equations reduce to:

$$S_1 = \alpha_1 + \beta_{11} \ln P_1 + \beta_{12} \ln P_2 - (\beta_{11} + \beta_{12}) \ln P_3 + \sigma_1 t + \omega_1 \ln Y,$$

$$S_2 = \alpha_2 + \beta_{12} \ln P_1 + \beta_{22} \ln P_2 - (\beta_{12} + \beta_{22}) \ln P_3 + \sigma_2 t + \omega_2 \ln Y.$$

Using the standard interpretation of GNP as the value added or payments to capital and labor, I constructed the value of gross output Y by applying the GNP deflator as the price of aggregate output. With prices measured in real terms, this is equivalent to setting the price of output equal to unity. Then the value of gross output is equal to GNP plus the real value of energy inputs. I have no independent measure of the price of capital and labor for the three-sector model. Therefore I used the translog index, with an output price set to unity, to calculate price P_3, given the nonelectric and electric prices, P_1 and P_2, as the inputs. This is equivalent to measuring the input of capital and labor in terms of "efficiency units."[29]

Adjustment Dynamics

The assumed dynamic model is a partial adjustment process. In each period, the efficiency of inputs versus output adjusts by a fraction of the difference between the long-run equilibrium and the current configuration. I denote the adjustment fraction as λ. With the notational convention of uppercase letters to denote the long-run value of output price (P), input quantity (X), and value share (S), and lowercase letters to denote the observed values of the same variables, the principal dynamic equation is:

$$\frac{x_{it}}{Y_t} = \lambda \frac{X_{it}}{Y_t} + (1 - \lambda)\frac{x_{it-1}}{Y_{t-1}}.$$

From this dynamic equation one can obtain the corresponding representation in terms of the share equations. Here I assume all prices are nominal in order to be specific about the several normalizations involved. Multiplying the dynamic equation by the ratio of input and output price and rearranging terms obtains:

$$s_{it} = \lambda \frac{P_t P_{it} X_{it}}{p_t P_t Y_t} + (1 - \lambda)\frac{p_{t-1} P_{it} P_{it-1} x_{it-1}}{P_{it-1} p_t p_{t-1} Y_{t-1}}.$$

In real terms this is equivalent to:

$$s_{it} = \lambda \frac{P_t}{p_t} S_{it} + (1 - \lambda)\frac{P_{it}}{P_{it-1}} s_{it-1}.$$

29. Alan Manne suggested the practice of measuring the rest of the economy in terms of efficiency units in order to avoid the necessity of assembling independent data on the value-added components. In a single-equation model of the goods sector of the aggregate economy, this is both necessary and feasible since the price of output is also interpreted as the inflation index for the conversion from nominal to real prices. Hence one can normalize on the price of output as the measure of the real price of goods. Of course, this procedure precludes any analysis of the changing productivity of the components of value added. In my terms, I treat energy as an intermediate product consumed by the goods sector. Hence the value of gross output is the sum of value added and the cost of energy.

One can obtain an estimate of P_t/p_t, the ratio of the long-run and short-run output prices, evaluated at the current prices, by exploiting the value identity between inputs and outputs. It is known that:

$$p_t = \sum P_{it} (x_{it}/Y_t)$$

and

$$P_t = \sum P_{it} (X_{it}/Y_t).$$

Substituting the fundamental dynamic equation into the first of these value identities and using the second obtains:

$$\frac{P_t}{p_t} = \frac{1 - (1 - \lambda) \sum \frac{P_{it}}{P_{it-1}} s_{it-1}}{\lambda}.$$

This gives the final form of the equations to be estimated:[30]

$$\tilde{s}_{it} = \left[1 - (1 - \lambda) \sum \frac{P_{it}}{P_{it-1}} s_{it-1} \right] S_{it} + (1 - \lambda) \frac{P_{it}}{P_{it-1}} \tilde{s}_{it-1}.$$

Estimation

With the exception of the parameter λ, the final dynamic equation in the long-run shares S_{it} and the predicted shares $\tilde{s}_{it-1}$ is linear in the parameters to be estimated. As discussed in the text, I apply a priori judgments to limit the range of possible adjustment rates and pick a set of values for λ. In addition, I introduce two extra parameters to benchmark the initial value shares for the dynamic recursion. Therefore, when I fix the adjustment rate, I can transform the dynamic equation

30. The characterization of the dynamics of energy adjustment has received increasing attention in recent years. My own study in "Dimensions of Energy Demand" focused on the post-embargo data through 1978. For a further discussion of alternative approaches to the characterization of dynamics, see Berndt and Field, eds., *Modelling and Measuring Natural Resource Substitution*. However, note that my form of the naive model takes a different approach and may circumvent the problems described by Berndt and Field. In particular, I posit the adjustment process as applying to the input-output coefficients and then derive the corresponding adjustment equations for the value shares. Berndt and Field considered the direct application of the naive model to the value shares, which one would expect to have unsatisfactory results if prices are changing and shares are evaluated at the current prices. For a comparison of alternative vintage capital and dynamic adjustment models applied to California data, see Ahmad Faruqui, "A Vintage Adjustment Model of Industrial Energy Substitution," *Resources and Energy*, vol. 5 (September 1983), pp. 285–301.

Table 5. *Parameter Estimates, by Selected Adjustment Rates, for Sample Periods 1960–82 and 1960–78*[a]

Equation	*1960–82*			*1960–78*		
	10 percent adjustment rate	*15 percent adjustment rate*	*20 percent adjustment rate*	*10 percent adjustment rate*	*15 percent adjustment rate*	*20 percent adjustment rate*
LAMBDA	0.10000E+00	0.15000E+00	0.20000E+00	0.10000E+00	0.15000E+00	0.20000E+00
	(0.00000E+01)	(0.00000E+01)	(0.00000E+01)	(0.00000E+01)	(0.00000E+01)	(0.00000E+01)
*ALPHA*1	0.54945E−01	0.28779E−01	0.15824E−01	0.51385E−01	0.23827E−01	0.96561E−02
	(0.92755E+01)	(0.76662E+01)	(0.48959E+01)	(0.40861E+01)	(0.29129E+01)	(0.14527E+01)
*ALPHA*2	0.37151E−01	0.32982E−01	0.30211E−01	0.40203E−01	0.33075E−01	0.29285E−01
	(0.44483E+01)	(0.68092E+01)	(0.75778E+01)	(0.46017E+01)	(0.58456E+01)	(0.64606E+01)
*BETA*11	−0.98123E−02	0.70439E−02	0.15464E−01	−0.29774E−02	0.10038E−01	0.16885E−01
	(−0.23882E+01)	(0.26254E+01)	(0.67196E+01)	(−0.27822E+00)	(0.14457E+01)	(0.29956E+01)
*BETA*12	0.50500E−02	0.98568E−02	0.12202E−01	0.37110E−02	0.10715E−01	0.14229E−01
	(0.25704E+01)	(0.85259E+01)	(0.12581E+02)	(0.10342E+01)	(0.46267E+01)	(0.76551E+01)
*BETA*22	−0.63992E−02	−0.74900E−02	−0.77134E−02	−0.71046E−02	−0.78708E−02	−0.81596E−02
	(−0.15322E+01)	(−0.30820E+01)	(−0.38503E+01)	(−0.17129E+01)	(−0.29138E+01)	(−0.37348E+01)
*SHARE*1	0.71388E−01	0.71031E−01	0.70814E−01	0.71320E−01	0.70860E−01	0.70546E−01
	(0.69041E+02)	(0.64478E+02)	(0.53650E+02)	(0.62666E+02)	(0.59356E+02)	(0.50584E+02)
*SHARE*2	0.21155E−01	0.21242E−01	0.21272E−01	0.21193E−01	0.21221E−01	0.21230E−01
	(0.44053E+02)	(0.47620E+02)	(0.42604E+02)	(0.44647E+02)	(0.43975E+02)	(0.40155E+02)
*ELAS*11	−0.11215E+01	−0.81752E+00	−0.66566E+00	−0.99825E+00	−0.76353E+00	−0.64004E+00
	(−0.15136E+02)	(−0.16896E+02)	(−0.16039E+02)	(−0.51722E+01)	(−0.60976E+01)	(−0.62964E+01)
*ELAS*12	0.11311E+00	0.19980E+00	0.24211E+00	0.88966E−01	0.21528E+00	0.27866E+00
	(0.31925E+01)	(0.95830E+01)	(0.13841E+02)	(0.13748E+01)	(0.51543E+01)	(0.83126E+01)
*ELAS*21	0.28458E+00	0.50268E+00	0.60911E+00	0.22383E+00	0.54163E+00	0.70107E+00
	(0.31925E+01)	(0.95830E+01)	(0.13841E+02)	(0.13748E+01)	(0.51543E+01)	(0.83126E+01)
*ELAS*22	−0.12683E+01	−0.13178E+01	−0.13279E+01	−0.13003E+01	−0.13351E+01	−0.13482E+01
	(−0.66930E+01)	(−0.11951E+02)	(−0.14609E+02)	(−0.69097E+01)	(−0.10893E+02)	(−0.13601E+02)
ELASAG	−0.10061E+01	−0.63609E+00	−0.45105E+00	−0.92485E+00	−0.57107E+00	−0.38799E+00
	(−0.14615E+02)	(−0.14232E+02)	(−0.11789E+02)	(−0.51985E+01)	(−0.49516E+01)	(−0.41583E+01)
Adjusted R^2	0.98987E+00	0.99397E+00	0.99396E+00	0.98955E+00	0.99032E+00	0.99100E+00

a. In the equations, 1 = nonelectric and 2 = electric; for example, *ELAS*21 is the elasticity of electric demand with respect to nonelectric price. Numbers in parentheses are *t*-statistics.

into the standard linear format with the dependent variable $\tilde{s}_{it}$ as a linear function of the parameters and the data.

I numerically executed this recursion to obtain twenty-three observations for each of the two share equations. This step eliminates the need to rely on the observed value of s_{it} as a lagged variable in the estimation equation. In order to give approximately equal weight to the errors in both equations, I scaled the electric equation by the ratio of the nonelectric and electric value shares in 1972. In the final adjustment of the data, I applied the Cochrane-Orcutt procedure for serial correlation in each equation.[31] This left forty-four observations for the pooled equations.

The estimates of time trend and output scale coefficients, σ and ω, were small in magnitude and statistically insignificant.[32] Therefore I dropped these parameters and concentrated on the estimation of the eight parameters λ, α_1, α_2, β_{11}, β_{12}, β_{22}, S_{10}, and S_{20}. In addition, I calculated from these structural parameters the standard formulas for the own and cross-price elasticities of nonelectric and electric energy and from these computed the price elasticity of aggregate energy assuming a proportional increase in the price of the two component energy products.

Finally, I estimated the equations for both the sample periods 1960–82 and 1960–78. The results appear in table 5 for three different values of the adjustment parameters.

Comments by Sam H. Schurr

What is mainly involved in Hogan's underlying mechanism is the substitution of other factors of production for energy, which permitted an increased level of economic output to be achieved with a constant level of energy use.

31. For a description of the corrections for serial correlation, see Robert S. Pindyck and Daniel L. Rubinfeld, *Econometric Models and Economic Forecasts*, 2d ed. (McGraw-Hill, 1981).

32. Alan Manne notes that there have been intense debates over the appropriate value of the income elasticity—as well as over the price elasticity of demand for energy. He further observes that my results do not require complicated hypotheses such as nonunitary income elasticities of demand or "structural" shifts to a low-energy service economy. This observation could be important in projecting 1990 demands under the assumption of constant or declining real oil prices.

In addition to the substitution among factors of production, he also finds a substitution among fuels, in particular the gradual electrification of energy demand in all sectors but transportation. And he tells us that the long-run adjustments are yet to come as new energy-efficient capital equipment replaces equipment installed during an altogether different energy regime.

I want to examine the past decade within the context of a much longer time period than Hogan employs and to offer another interpretation also based on the aggregative evidence on energy use in the United States.[33]

A substantial decline in the ratio of energy use to GNP is *not* a new phenomenon in the United States. There have been different eras in the energy-GNP relationship over the past one hundred years. There was a period of rising intensity that ran from the late nineteenth century until about the end of World War I. Then there was persistent decline in energy intensity running from World War I until about the 1950s. This was followed by a period of relative stability in energy intensity running from the 1950s to the 1970s. Finally, there is the most recent period of decline in energy use relative to GNP.

The other thing I want to consider is a comparison of energy intensity with the concurrent behavior of total factor productivity for those different eras—that is, overall national output in relation to the combined inputs of labor and capital. Particularly significant is the period from 1920 to 1953, in which energy intensity declined persistently while total factor productivity rose at quite substantial rates. Also significant is that during the period from 1953 to 1973 total factor productivity increased rather sharply without any increases in energy intensity relative to GNP. The most recent period of 1973 to 1981 shows, to be sure, the decline in energy intensity that Hogan describes. But it also shows the other side of the coin—that productivity has been behaving very poorly during this period of time.

The question that I want to raise is whether the simultaneous occurrence of rising economic productivity and declining or stable energy intensity, which characterized practically the entire period between World War I and the decade of the 1970s, should be regarded as a curiosity, or whether there were fundamental forces at work that are quite reasonable and important to understand.

33. The data referred to in these remarks are contained in Sam H. Schurr, "Energy Use, Technological Change, and Productive Efficiency: An Economic-Historical Interpretation," *Annual Review of Energy*, vol. 9 (1984), pp. 409–25.

It is generally taken for granted that the rise in overall productive efficiency requires a substitution of energy and machines for labor, so why did the intensity of energy use decline while overall productivity rose? One might have expected energy intensity to have risen during these years.

The truth of the matter is that the intensity of energy use did rise, but it did so relative to labor and capital inputs. Between 1920 and 1973 the ratio of energy use to worker hours more than doubled, and in relation to capital it increased by about 50 percent. Yet energy declined relative to output, and the reason is that, as a result of the leverage on overall productive efficiency exercised by technological advance during this period, final output grew faster than energy consumption.

So in this period the substitution among production factors ran just the opposite of factor substitution during the decade that Hogan has been telling us about. Energy was substituting for labor and capital rather than the other way around, but at the same time energy intensity, measured in terms of the ratio between energy use and GNP, was declining. It is very important not to lose sight of that part of the historical record.

History shows that energy conservation can result from factor substitution running in two opposite directions: labor and capital being substituted for energy, as in the 1970s, or energy being substituted for labor and capital, as during much of American history. The latter mechanism works as a result of technological advance that leads to an increase in output greater than the expansion in energy inputs required in the substitution process. Such technological progress has occurred when energy supply circumstances have been favorable. Under such circumstances the rise in factor productivity has also yielded a decline in energy intensity, with no special efforts being made to economize on energy use.

The situation that the United States faces at the present time is one in which renewed growth in total factor productivity is perhaps the most urgent national need. If energy conservation comes at the cost of overall productive efficiency, it would be a poor bargain. In the past the United States has been able to achieve both simultaneously. It has not been able to do that during the past decade.

I would therefore dissent from what I take to be Hogan's implication that energy conservation during the past decade has been shown to be consistent with the efficient operation of the economic engine. It all depends on how broad your definition of efficiency is: efficiency in energy use alone, or efficiency in the combined use of production factors.

Comments by Francis Bator

The two-part message of the Hogan paper is that the mills of Adam Smith grind gradually but powerfully—gradually, not slowly. There is a difference.

In economists' jargon, the long-run, full-adjustment, equilibrium-to-equilibrium elasticity of demand for energy compensated for changes in output—that is, changes in the per unit output of energy played against changes in the price of energy—is much closer to 1.0 than to zero. Opportunities for induced innovation, pure increases in energy efficiency, substitution of capital and labor for energy along the production function, and technology and fuel substitution—all lead to what Hogan called lots of flexibility, but it takes a long time to get there. This is in part because the vehicle for the large amount of flexibility is the efficiently gradual replacement of the capital stock.

I find Hogan's message cheerful in three respects. For one thing, it doesn't require that economists swallow hard. It fits our intuition of the way the Lord made the world. A second, less parochial, respect is that the fit of the theory to the evidence described, not to received doctrine, seems to be remarkably good. And the evidence is not just Hogan's evidence, as he points out. International cross sections, engineering studies, interstate cross sections, and long-run studies in equilibrium situations all point to the same result. The third cheerful aspect is that adjustments are possible. There has been a very large and sudden deterioration in the terms on which the United States can purchase fuel. A world in which technology and tastes allow lots of room for substitution and for economizing on energy is a less uncomfortable world than one that has fixed coefficients, no give, and little room for adjustment in technology or preferences.

I have one question: Will the relationships and trends Hogan describes hold up outside the specific range of energy price changes that he considered? If there is another 50 percent increase in the index for the price of energy between 1985 and 1987, will the proportional response be roughly the same as the response to the two price shocks in the 1970s?

Indeed, will what is still to come in response to the 1979 shock mimic what happened in response to the first shock?

One can think of a number of reasons why adjustments might get harder and harder. Would it be as easy to go from the present generation of Toyotas, for example, to proportionately lighter, more fuel-efficient cars as it was to go from eight-cylinder Cadillacs to Toyotas? Hogan's central thesis focuses on evaluating change that moves from one kind of machine to another kind gradually, with the replacement occurring primarily as a function of the age of the machine. But another scenario is possible. Machines that have easily available substitutes that use less fuel get replaced quickly. But machines with no substitutes reasonably available in terms of cost are replaced slowly. This might produce a situation where substitution keeps getting harder and harder.

A second question concerns symmetry. Suppose the real price of oil were to drop steadily for a period of three, four, or five years. Shifting back to wasteful use of fuel might happen a lot faster than the move to energy efficiency. This would be partly because of a preference for a known technology rather than a search for unknown ways of doing things. And it may be partly because the use of lighter and less fuel causes the economic life of the stock to become shorter. Say the real energy price trend keeps going up but with large fluctuations, each lasting several years: the price would swing above its trend and people would start substituting and economizing, but very slowly. But when the price swings down, they would substitute very fast and as a result there would be a kind of ratcheting effect and disequilibrium that could be very uncomfortable. I am not suggesting that I wouldn't like the price of oil to drop, but at least it is an interesting question of influence.

My last point is a plea. The great puzzle in macroeconomics is what happened to average labor productivity after 1973, and why. In 1973 there was a sharp reduction in the trend rate of growth in output per worker hour, cyclically corrected. There was another sharp break in 1979 that coincided—both in the United States and the rest of the industrial world—with large oil price increases and the subsequent adjustments. There is no conventional cost accounting or growth accounting explanation for more than half of the two-point drop in this trend rate of growth in labor productivity.

Martin Baily connects energy price and capital by positing that the large energy price increase resulted in a rapid obsolescence of the existing capital stock and therefore a large reduction in the use of that obsolescent stock. As a consequence, the flow of capital services relative to the flow of labor services and output dropped very sharply. Baily's theory may explain some portion of what happened to average labor productivity. But it is certainly not clear.

My plea is this: Economists working on energy should devote more analysis to that third factor. Instead of having a capital-labor lump, energy economists should separate the two because work on the energy substitution front at a disaggregated level may begin to tell more about what happened to productivity. At the moment, all we can say is that it is the residual.

MERTON J. PECK *and* JOHN J. BEGGS

Energy Conservation in American Industry

SUBSTANTIAL increases in the prices of energy in the last decade have changed significantly the competitiveness of many production techniques and technologies. This essay sets out to assess the adjustment to this new price regime by U.S. manufacturing firms.

Conservation is a common term, yet it is a misnomer for the adjustment process. If the price of a factor of production rises, there will be attempts to reduce the use of that factor—energy, in the present case. That is a less dramatic view than the frequently encountered rationing theme found in the popular literature on energy conservation, which draws its motivational force from past wartime and embargo experiences. While the ability of the economy to respond to a sudden curtailment of oil supplies is a serious issue, the political vulnerability of oil supplies is a more narrow issue that can be addressed by quite specific policy instruments targeted at oil imports.

From the viewpoint of the firm, energy conservation is little different from other forms of cost reduction. But from the viewpoint of society, a special concern for energy derives from the possibility that energy prices are not set at levels that fully reflect resource scarcity. How and why this may occur has been explored extensively in the literature of energy economics and is not restated here. We remain agnostic on the extent and source of the gap between the social and private prices for energy and on whether or not the gap should or can be closed by removing

James Dana, Emily Gilde, Fred Rockefeller, and Emanuel Thorne provided research assistance, and Virginia Casey, Blanche Collins, and Lorraine O'Donnell provided secretarial assistance. A grant from the AMAX Corporation to the Yale Economics Department provided financial support. The staffs of the U.S. Department of Energy and trade associations gave valuable advice.

government controls on energy prices. Nor do we need to take a position on whether there might be a special instability in energy prices.[1]

The possibility that energy prices for the 1970s have been less than the social cost to the U.S. economy of using energy, however, gives energy conservation a greater significance in policy discussions than the conservation of other inputs. The two central issues pursued in this essay—the record of energy conservation by American industry, and the barriers to further progress—are then more than a study of business efficiency.

Conservation is taken here to mean a reduction in energy costs per unit of output of a given industry, rather than the technical definition of energy consumption based on British thermal units (Btus) per unit of output. By our definition, then, increasing fuel efficiency or fuel saving (using fewer Btus per unit of output) and fuel switching (using less-expensive fuels) equally qualify as conservation since both actions reduce the cost of energy to society. We stress the concept of energy costs because it measures the use of the scarce resources of an economy in production, whereas Btus are a physical measure of energy that does not reflect the scarcity of the fuel source and neglects major differences in the costs of extraction and distribution of fuels. To be sure, through the 1970s energy prices, particularly those of oil and natural gas, were controlled. Errors arising from the use of imperfect prices are still much less than those from the use of measures that implicitly give each energy source the same scarcity value.

We also stress energy consumption relative to the output of a given industry because the emphasis in this paper is upon the response of individual manufacturing firms that are users of energy. Our definition explicitly excludes the conservation options open to society by switching demand from more to less energy-intensive products, not because it is unimportant, but because we are specifically interested in the behavior of individual firms in making the same products with less energy.[2] Our

1. Implicit in this essay is the view that the weakening of oil prices that began in 1983 does not signal a return to the pre-1973 energy abundance.

2. We also exclude from our analysis energy embodied in products, such as in chemical feedstocks. Energy embodied in products has an entirely different set of substitution possibilities than energy used as a fuel. The traditional inclusion of petroleum feedstocks in industrial energy consumption is arbitrary. After all, the energy represented by lumber is never counted as industrial energy consumption. In addition to changes in the consumption pattern of consumers of energy, two other industrial energy conservation measures are excluded from the essay: cogeneration and the use of scrap. See National Academy of Sciences, National Research Council, *Energy in Transition 1985–2010:*

definition of conservation is more circumscribed than in the essay by William W. Hogan in two respects: (1) our definition does not, as his does, allow for energy savings from changes in the composition of output, and (2) our focus is more on the shorter-run changes than on the long-run changes Hogan emphasizes.

For a business firm, each input to production is a cost item that can be economized. The historical record of energy saving before 1972 shows that it was part of the continuing cost reduction effort of manufacturing firms even when real energy prices were stable or falling. The sharp rise in energy prices after 1972 accelerated the pace of energy cost reduction, and it is this accelerated trend that is examined here.

A statistic that captures the effect of conservation measures is the percentage difference between the costs of the actual energy used and the costs that would have been incurred without fuel saving and fuel switching. The estimates derived below are that for 1981 fuel saving reduced energy costs by 18.0 percent and fuel switching increased energy costs by 3.8 percent, compared with what they would have been if the 1972 level of fuel efficiency and the 1973 fuel mix had continued through 1981.[3] Thus total gains from conservation were 14.2 percent; that is, without the adjustments industry made after 1972, energy costs in 1981 for the U.S. industrial sector would have been 14.2 percent higher. The increase in energy costs due to fuel switching is at first surprising, but that outcome turns on the regulated price structure in energy and increased industrial use of electricity, a point discussed below.

Any estimate depends on the assumptions, definitions, and data that are used, and there are alternatives to those used here. A difficult problem always encountered in estimating conservation arises from the fact that energy consumption depends on the level of economic activity; a recession year has a different level and mix of energy consumption than a boom year. Estimates of industrial energy conservation should reflect the long-term behavior of American manufacturers, not the current state of the business cycle. Yet the years 1972–81 are not a long enough period to make conservation estimates that are entirely free of cyclical influences.

While business cycle effects ought to be set aside in a statistical

Final Report of the Committee on Nuclear and Alternative Energy Systems (Washington, D.C.: NAS, 1980), pp. 96–88.

3. The careful reader will note we have combined 1972 and 1973 numbers. This was done for reasons of data availability. It does not change either the direction or general magnitude of the combined savings.

estimate of conservation, the discussion of energy policy is better informed by highlighting the impact of the recession and slower economic growth on energy consumption. Indeed, our estimate (discussed below) is that if the economy had maintained the growth rates and output mix of 1953–72, industrial energy consumption would have been 23.8 percent greater in 1981. Thus slow growth and conservation are of nearly equal importance in reducing industrial energy consumption.

A return of higher economic growth could result in sharp increases in energy prices and substantial dislocation in energy-intensive industries.[4] For these industries prospects are bleak in an era of high economic activity because the cheaper ways of conserving energy have already been utilized. Additional conservation measures involve investment in capital equipment. While capital projects become more viable with economic recovery, the energy-saving effect is delayed until new equipment is in operation. There is a paradox here. Economic recovery initially increases energy usage, but in the longer run, by encouraging modernization of capital equipment, it eventually accelerates the rate of energy conservation.

A net conservation saving of 14.2 percent may seem a modest response to the 117.5 percent increase in the real price of energy from 1972 to 1981.[5] Yet one of the themes of this essay is that it is difficult and expensive to conserve energy. These difficulties are examined in some detail for steel, cement, and aluminum. All three industries use large amounts of energy per unit of output, so that firms in these industries have an active concern with energy conservation. The three are also representative of the larger Standard Industrial Classification (SIC) two-digit sectors of primary metals and stone, clay, and glass, and these two sectors account for 31 percent of all energy (in Btus) consumed in manufacturing in 1979.[6] While all three industries are examples of energy-intensive industries, each faces a different set of economic and technical constraints in achieving energy conservation.

Steel illustrates how the general economic conditions facing an industry constrain energy conservation. The U.S. integrated steel in-

4. The sharp price increases reflect the short-run price inelasticity of energy. In the longer run, energy supply, particularly of coal, appears to be sensitive to price increases.

5. This is the real price increase for the fuels consumed by industry. The real price index is based on the weights and prices per Btu used in table 4 and the GNP deflator.

6. Calculations based on data reported in U.S. Bureau of the Census, *1979 Annual Survey of Manufactures: Fuels and Electric Energy Consumed* (Government Printing Office, 1981), p. 16.

dustry had partially completed a modernization process when the slowdown of the 1970s hit the industry with great intensity. Modernization, if completed, could reduce energy use per unit of output by 15 percent by the end of the decade.[7] Yet additional modernization would require a major increase in the profitability of the industry, which, in turn, needs the higher prices and output possible with greater protection from import competition. The higher steel output, however, would require more energy, which would offset to some degree the conservation gains. To further complicate the analysis, the steel industry is now composed of two distinct sectors, rapidly growing mini-mills relying on electric furnaces and integrated mills relying on blast furnaces. The proportion of steel output from the two sectors also has a significant impact on energy requirements, a point discussed below. Decisions in the steel industry have enormous consequences for overall energy consumption, because steel accounts for about 12 percent of industrial energy consumption.[8] Policy decisions about this industry, however, turn on much broader considerations than energy conservation alone.

Cement has a more successful record of energy conservation. Since 1978 the industry has had an annual fuel saving rate of 2.0 percent, well over its historic rate, and has made a major transition in its fuel sources from natural gas to coal. This has taken place despite slow market growth. The explanations are twofold. Because energy costs are high and the product is uniform enough to make small price differences significant, a cement producer has strong incentives to reduce energy costs below those of competitors. Equally important has been readily available alternative technology that has made fuel saving and fuel switching relatively inexpensive. The lesson seems to be that competitive conditions and technology of a specific industry can be such that significant energy conservation occurs even in the face of depressed demand.

In contrast, aluminum is an industry that has shown much less response to energy price increases than cement, even though energy costs are of comparable importance and output has grown significantly from 1972 to 1980. Again both institutional factors and technology explain the conservation response. Long-term electricity contracts have shel-

7. American Iron and Steel Institute, *Steel at the Crossroads: The American Steel Industry in the 1980s* (Washington, D.C.: AISI, 1980), p. 61.

8. For sources of statistics cited here for steel, cement, and aluminum, see the discussion below.

tered aluminum from the immediate effect of the sharp price increases in energy, and also there are few readily available technological possibilities for energy savings in aluminum smelting. The record of aluminum is a reminder that technology can be a sharp limitation on what is possible in energy conservation.

The Overall Record, 1972–81

Savings in energy costs have been obtained from both fuel saving and fuel switching. Estimates of those savings are discussed below, followed by a more qualitative examination of the process of energy conservation.

Fuel Saving

Table 1 reports the index of energy consumption for 1972–81 together with two indexes of industrial production. While over the decade the trend in energy consumption is down and the trend of output is up, annual energy consumption is strongly influenced by fluctuations in economic activity. In 1975, for example, there was a sharp but short recession, with output returning to its 1973 level by 1976; in 1980 and 1981 the recession was less sharp but longer.

Recessions have offsetting effects on energy consumption per unit of output. Postwar recessions have had a disproportionate impact on energy-intensive industries, of which steel and cement are leading examples, because capital goods output and construction have fluctuated more sharply than other sectors of the economy.[9] Thus the shift in output mix during a recession reduces energy consumption more than the fall in industrial output. During a more prolonged recession less-efficient plants are closed, further reducing energy consumption. These energy-saving effects are offset by the rise in energy use per unit of output caused by overhead uses of energy that do not decline proportionately with output.

The 1970s was also a decade of slow economic growth. The last

9. Robert Marlay has developed a shift factor that measures the change in the mix of industrial output either toward or away from energy-intensive industries. The shift factor is based on the behavior of the index of production and energy consumption of 442 mining and manufacturing industries. His shift factor reduces energy consumption significantly in recession years. See Robert Marlay, "Briefing Materials on Trends in Energy Use," U.S. Department of Energy, Office of Planning and Analysis (DOE, 1982).

Table 1. *Index of Energy Consumed by the Industrial Sector Compared with Two Indexes of Industrial Production, 1972–81*
Index, 1972 = 100

	Indexes		
Year	*Energy consumption*[a]	*Industrial production*[b]	*Industrial production at 4 percent growth rate*[c]
1972	100.0	100.0	100.0
1973	105.3	108.7	104.0
1974	101.9	108.4	108.2
1975	93.6	98.0	112.5
1976	99.1	108.2	117.0
1977	100.5	115.6	121.7
1978	101.3	122.6	126.5
1979	103.3	128.0	131.6
1980	95.8	123.0	136.9
1981	90.6	126.4	142.3

a. For 1973–81, calculated from industrial consumption as reported in U.S. Department of Energy, Energy Information Administration, *Monthly Energy Review* (July 1982), p. 23, after subtracting petroleum used as feedstocks. 1972 data obtained from the Department of Energy.
b. Federal Reserve index of production for manufacturing and mining as reported in Robert Marlay, "Briefing Materials on Trends in Energy Use," U.S. Department of Energy, Office of Planning and Analysis (DOE, 1982). The index excludes natural gas and electric utilities.
c. A continuation of the 4 percent growth rate for 1953–72 in the Federal Reserve Board index of industrial production as reported by Marlay, "Trends in Energy Use."

column of table 1 shows what output would have been had the growth rates of the 1950s and 1960s continued after 1972. Had energy efficiency been unchanged and this higher level of output achieved in 1981, energy consumption would have been 12.6 percent greater than it actually was.

In addition to the lower energy consumption caused by lower industrial output, slower growth also has had a disproportionate effect on the energy-intensive industries. These industries supply inputs for investment goods and consumer durables whose demand grows even more slowly than other sectors in a slow-growth era.[10] Higher energy costs also raise the relative prices of energy-intensive industries, further reducing their growth of demand. Our subsequent calculations demonstrate that for 1981 the shift of output away from energy-intensive industries reduced energy consumption by 11.2 percent from the level that would have prevailed with the 1972 mix of output (see table 2). Thus

10. Marlay's shift factor (see ibid.) reduces energy consumption every year since 1972 except 1973. Thus the 1970s exhibit a secular trend away from energy-intensive industries in addition to a cyclical pattern.

Table 2. *Estimate of 1981 Fuel Consumption at 1972 Fuel Efficiency*

Sources of reduced 1981 fuel consumption	*Percent*
Shift in the output mix[a]	11.2
Historic trend of fuel saving[b]	10.3
Accelerated fuel saving[c]	18.0
Total increase in 1981 energy with 1972 efficiency and output mix[d]	39.5

a. Estimated using factors developed by Robert Marlay to measure the structural shifts in energy use in the mix of industrial output toward or away from energy-intensive industries. See Marlay, "Trends in Energy Use." Since Marlay uses 1972 efficiencies, his shift factors overstate somewhat the energy savings accounted for by shifts in output mix. The calculation in the table is stated as a percentage of 1981 actual energy consumption.

b. The 0.8 annual rate of the reduction in fuel per unit of production from 1953 through 1972. The estimate is by Marlay and reported in "Trends in Energy Use." The calculation here applies the historical trend to the index of energy at 1972 efficiency, and that saving is quoted as a percentage of 1981 actual energy consumption.

c. Calculated as a residual.

d. The difference in what 1981 energy consumption, stated in Btus, would have been without the improvements in energy efficiency after 1972, and actual energy consumption, expressed as a percentage of 1981 consumption. The total decrease in energy consumed per unit of industrial output between 1972 and 1981 was 28.3 percent, calculated from the indices of energy consumption and production in table 1.

1981 energy consumption was 23.8 percent less than it would have been because of the combined effects of overall lower output (12.6 percent) and a lower proportion of output from energy-intensive industries (11.2 percent). Less energy consumption, however, is not the same as fuel saving since it is achieved by producing less rather than by obtaining greater efficiency.

ESTIMATING FUEL SAVING. Fuel saving is estimated as the difference between actual 1981 fuel consumption and what fuel consumption would have been if that output had been produced with 1972 fuel efficiency. Comparisons are influenced by the level of economic activity in these two years. With only a nine-year record, the best that can be done is to caution that the results are sensitive to the business cycle. Both 1972 and 1981 were years of economic slack, so the measurement can be considered, in old-style business cycle terminology, as being from trough to trough.[11]

Table 2 reports our estimate of fuel saving. It is important to underline exactly what the gross fuel saving of 39.5 percent represents. It is what Btu consumption would have been in 1981 if the 1981 industrial output had been produced with the 1972 fuel efficiency, expressed as a percentage of 1981 fuel consumption. Assuming no change in fuel prices or fuel

11. The slack, however, was more marked in 1981, a year in which unemployment was 7.6 percent, compared with 5.6 percent in 1972. *Economic Report of the President, February 1982*, pp. 266–67.

mix, fuel costs would have been 39.5 percent higher for American industry without the post-1972 efficiency gains.

The table also shows estimates of two sources of fuel savings. The shift in output mix away from energy-intensive industries accounted for 11.2 percent of the difference between 1981 consumption at 1972 efficiency and actual consumption, again expressed as a percentage of 1981 consumption. There was an annual trend in energy saving from 1954 through 1972 of 0.8 percent, even though real energy prices were generally declining or stable.[12] The extrapolated effect of this factor from 1972 to 1981 is 10.3 percent, again expressed as a percentage of 1981 consumption. Excluding those savings as a post-1972 price response implies that without the higher prices the pre-1972 trend of improving energy efficiency would have continued. The trend in energy efficiency could have declined without the 1972 oil shock, because the slower growth after 1972 might have led to a lower rate of investment, and fuel saving partly depends on modernization of capital equipment. To ignore the historic trend, however, would assign all of the post-1972 fuel savings to new conservation efforts. Since our objective is to explain energy-conserving activity by individual producers, the table also separates out the savings in energy caused by shifts in the output of the economy.

After deducting the fuel saving from the shift in output mix and the historic trend, the remaining 18.0 percent is the accelerated post-1972 fuel saving reported earlier as the fuel-saving component of conservation.

ALTERNATIVE ESTIMATES. Two careful studies of industrial energy conservation have been done by Robert Marlay and by a group at the Oak Ridge National Laboratory (see table 3).[13] Both are based on Btus rather than dollar energy costs. These two studies estimate the percentage saving of Btus in 1980 or 1981 relative to a base case, defined as the energy consumption that would have occurred if the economy had continued its 1972 growth and if the output mix and energy efficiency had remained unchanged. The percentage difference is then divided between slower output growth, changes in product mix, and efficiency improvements, which in turn are divided between those attributed to the

12. The cumulative effect of the trend is stated in a way to be additive to the effect of the shift in output mix. It is calculated as 7.4 percent, with a downward adjustment to reflect the application of the trend after adjustment for the output mix.

13. Robert Marlay's work is reported in "Trends in Energy Use." The Oak Ridge study is in Eric Hirst and others, *Energy Use from 1973 to 1980: The Role of Improved Energy Efficiency*, ORNL/CON-79 (Oak Ridge, Tenn.: Oak Ridge National Laboratory, 1981).

Table 3. *Comparative Estimates of Industrial Energy Conservation*
Percent

Sources of reduction	*Marlay study*	*Oak Ridge study*
Slower growth in industrial output	11.0	14.2
Changes in product mix	6.5	5.8
Efficiency improvements		
Historical trend	5.7	5.1
Accelerated efficiency	2.7	1.9
Total	25.9	27.0

Sources: Marlay, "Trends in Energy Use" (for 1981, with 1972 as the starting point); and Eric Hirst and others, *Energy Use from 1973 to 1980: The Role of Improved Energy Efficiency,* ORNL/CON-79 (Oak Ridge, Tenn.: Oak Ridge National Laboratory, 1981), p. 33. Calculations are for 1980. Figures are rounded.

accelerated gains in energy efficiency since 1973 and the historical trend. Their estimates of energy savings associated with changes in output mix and historic trend are not very different from ours, once allowance is made for the differences in the way these results are stated. Our estimates show a larger total fuel saving and hence more conservation gains, largely because these two studies are based on an unrevised series of industrial energy consumption statistics and the three studies all have slightly different beginning and ending years.[14]

The Industrial Energy Efficiency Improvement Program also reports estimates of conservation based on questionnaires filled out by corporations consuming more than 1 trillion Btus annually.[15] Between 1972 and 1980 the responding corporations reported energy efficiency gains of 17.7 percent.[16] This result appears roughly consistent with our estimate

14. In the spring of 1982 the Energy Information Agency of the U.S. Department of Energy substantially revised its industrial energy consumption statistics. For 1973 the total industrial energy consumption was increased from 29.4 quads to 31.9. Thus there was a much sharper decline in energy consumption in the revised series, which our estimates reflect. Comparisons are from U.S. Department of Energy, Energy Information Administration, *Monthly Energy Review* (May 1981), p. 23 and (July 1982), p. 23. Another difference from these two studies is that our estimates exclude petroleum for industrial feedstocks, which was a large and increasing share of consumption. In 1972 feedstocks were 8.3 percent of industrial consumption; in 1980, 12.5 percent. See U.S. Department of Energy, Energy Information Administration, *State Energy Data Report, 1960 through 1980* (DOE/EIA, 1982), p. 17. Of course, these calculations are sensitive to the accuracy of the feedstock consumption estimates.

15. U.S. Department of Energy, *The Industrial Energy Efficiency Improvement Program: Annual Report to Congress and the President 1979,* p. 5. The approximately 1,000 reporting corporations accounted for an estimated 53 percent of the energy consumed in industry in 1979.

16. DOE, *The Industrial Energy Efficiency Improvement Program: Annual Report to Congress and the President 1980,* p. iii.

of fuel saving of 18.0 percent for 1972–81. The consistency is fortuitous and reflects offsetting differences. Our estimate assumes a kilowatt-hour of electricity represents 10,000 Btus, reflecting the Btus lost in electricity generation and transmission, whereas the energy improvement report uses a conversion factor of 3,412 Btus that excludes Btus utilized by the electric utility to deliver Btus to industry.[17] The energy improvement data does not fully adjust for changes in overall output mix, nor is there a deduction for the historic trend. Finally, the energy improvement data covers only half of industrial consumption.

Fuel Switching

The second source of conservation gains is from switching among fuel sources. As indicated above, fuel switching has not been a source of measured conservation gains. Table 4 shows the fuel mix consumed by industry in 1973 and in 1981.

The share of oil consumption did not change, despite its sharp price increase. Surprisingly, coal consumption fell from 13.6 percent to 10.9 percent, despite having the lowest price increase of any fuel and the lowest price per Btu in 1981. The decline in coal consumption can be explained in part by a decline in steel output, for coal consumption by coke plants, used almost entirely by the steel industry, fell by 35 percent from 1973 to 1981.[18]

The share of electrical consumption increased from 25.3 percent

17. For the chemical and petroleum industries, electricity consumption is converted at 10,000 Btus per kilowatt-hour in compiling the energy improvement data. For other industries the conversion factor is 3,412 Btus per kilowatt-hour.

18. Calculated from data in DOE, EIA, *Monthly Energy Review* (July 1982), p. 62. We harbor some doubts about the accuracy of the coal consumption data. About half the coal used in industry goes to the steel industry, and the decline in that industry offers a ready explanation for the pattern of reduced industrial coal consumption over the study period. A year-by-year examination of the data is less convincing. Steel output increased 13.2 percent from 1972 to 1973 while coal consumption remained unchanged. Steel output again *increased* 7.4 percent from 1975 to 1977, while coal consumption for the period *fell* by 5.8 percent. Why should there be a fall in consumption of the fuel that has experienced only modest price increases? Continuity of supply is assured by the common practice of stockpiling before labor contract negotiations, and there is no threat of supply interruptions from international political events. The cost of meeting pollution control measures may be important, yet these have apparently been overcome by the cement industry. There remains a serious possibility that some as yet undetected systematic reporting bias (as was found in the petroleum data) remains in the Energy Information Administration coal statistics.

Table 4. *Change in Industrial Energy Costs Due to Shifts in Fuel Mix, by Type of Fuel, 1973–81*

	Share of total industrial Btus (percent)		*Price (cents per million Btus)*	
Fuel type	*1973*	*1981*	*1973*	*1981*
Electricity[a]	25.3	33.3	110.0	281.7
Natural gas	32.6	27.5	34.2	171.2
Coal	13.6	10.9	62.3	120.8
Oil	28.5	28.4	74.4	421.3

Sources: Percentage share of fuel type calculated from data in DOE, EIA, *Monthly Energy Review* (July 1982), p. 23; prices calculated from data in John G. Myers and Leonard Nakamura, *Saving Energy in Manufacturing: The Post-Embargo Record* (Ballinger, 1978), pp. 38–40; and U.S. Bureau of Labor Statistics.
a. Includes hydroelectric, electricity sales, and electrical energy losses.

in 1973 to 33.3 percent in 1981. Simultaneously, electric utilities shifted their own consumption of fuel from oil to coal. Oil consumption by utilities fell by about 1.4 quads from 1973 to 1981, whereas coal consumption increased by about 4.0 quads.[19]

Table 4 suggests that using coal directly is cheaper per Btu than using coal indirectly through consuming electricity. That suggestion, however, ignores the fact that utilization of coal directly by industrial firms requires greater operating and capital costs for transportation and handling facilities, coal-fired boilers, and environmental safeguards than increasing the consumption of electricity. Many aspects of coal utilization have economies of scale, and it is more economical to concentrate the utilization of coal in steam plants generating electricity and rely on the electricity for the distribution of energy. But using coal to make electricity does involve significant energy losses in generation. About 70 percent of the Btus of fossil fuels are lost in electricity generation.[20] It is for this reason the price per Btu of electricity is significantly higher than when coal is used directly.

The share of natural gas declined from 32.6 percent in 1973 to 27.5 percent in 1981, even though in 1981 natural gas ranked well below both electricity and oil in price per Btu. As indicated earlier, the price of natural gas has been kept down by regulation. Regulation has also involved rationing to industrial users by various federal and state agencies since 1971. The curtailments became substantial in 1974 and

19. Calculated from data in DOE, EIA, *Monthly Energy Review* (July 1982), p. 25.
20. DOE, EIA, *Monthly Energy Review* (May 1981), p. 27.

peaked in 1977, when curtailments reached 25 percent of interstate natural gas pipeline requirements.[21] Given the uncertainty of supply, manufacturing firms shifted away from natural gas despite its continuing low price. A further factor was the anticipation that natural gas prices would increase should pending legislation decontrol its price.

The total effect of fuel switching between 1973 and 1981 was to raise fuel costs by 3.8 percent (comparing the 1981 fuel costs with what they would have been if the 1973 mix of fuels had been consumed). As table 4 indicates, considerably more electricity was used, which is more expensive per Btu than either natural gas or coal, whose shares of consumption fell. Only the substitution of electricity for oil reduced fuel costs. The 3.8 percent estimate is a conservative one since it implicitly assumes that the change in fuel mix did not alter relative fuel prices. Without a shift in the fuel mix, the price of oil and natural gas would have probably been higher and the price of electricity lower.

This 3.8 percent increased fuel cost, when subtracted from the 18.0 percent reduction in fuel costs achieved by using fewer Btus, results in a net energy cost saving of 14.2 percent: this is how much higher fuel costs would have been in 1981 without the post-1972 changes in both fuel usage and efficiency. This seems an unspectacular response to a real price increase of 117.5 percent.[22]

The Process of Energy Conservation

More energy conservation is, of course, technically possible. Energy conservation measures can be divided into two categories: (1) house-

21. Calculated from U.S. Federal Power Commission, "Fourth Quarter 1976 Report of Actual Monthly Curtailments Based on FPC Form No. 17," FPC News Release 22929, February 22, 1977; Federal Power Commission, *Statistics of Interstate Natural Gas Pipeline Companies, 1973;* and Federal Energy Regulatory Commission Form no. 16 filing.

22. This statement means, of course, that the price elasticity from 1972 to 1980 is low. The implied elasticity for the 14.2 percent saving is −0.12. This is lower than that found by other researchers. The Oak Ridge study found a fuel price elasticity of −0.12 to −0.24, and the Stanford University Energy Modeling Forum, reviewing various models, found the average price elasticity was −0.5. These results, however, are for price elasticity with respect to GNP, not just the industrial sector. See Hirst and others, *Energy Use from 1973 to 1980,* pp. 50–51. The implied elasticity here is not the true price elasticity of economic theory, but rather a specialized conservation price elasticity. It measures the use of fewer Btus in producing a given physical output.

Table 5. *Capital Spending on Energy Conservation, Regulation Compliance, and Energy as Share of Shipment Value, 1980*
Percent

Industry and SIC level	*Energy conservation*	*Safety, health, and pollution regulation*	*Energy costs as share of value of shipments*
20 Food and kindred products	5.1	4.7	1.3
22 Textile mill products	6.1	13.1	3.0
26 Paper and allied products	5.7	8.2	6.0
28 Chemicals	7.3	11.2	5.5
29 Petroleum	3.4	5.0	2.5
30 Rubber and miscellaneous products	3.8	11.2	n.a.
32 Stone, clay, and glass	4.8	8.6	7.5
33 Primary metals	6.0	13.3	6.0
34 Fabricated metals	4.4	4.5	1.9
35 Machinery except electrical	2.8	5.0	n.a.
36 Electrical and electronic equipment	2.5	3.8	n.a.
37 Transportation equipment	2.5	5.3	n.a.

Sources: For energy conservation and safety, health, and pollution regulation, see U.S. Department of Energy, *The Industrial Energy Efficiency Improvement Program: Annual Report to the Congress and the President, 1980* (DOE, 1981), p. 12; for energy costs as a percentage of value of shipments, see DOE, *The Industrial Energy Efficiency Improvement Program, 1979*, p. 8.
n.a. Not available.

keeping measures requiring no major investment or changes in the production processes or the product; and (2) energy-oriented investment measures requiring the spending of capital funds to change significantly methods of production or products to save energy.

By the 1980s additional housekeeping measures were not an important source of further conservation gains. A Department of Energy study concludes:

> In looking to the future, the prospects for continued energy efficiency improvements in the energy-intensive industries are viewed as less promising. It is anticipated that the rate of improvement in the energy-intensive industries will decline unless a general transition is made to capital-investment-based strategies (i.e., more substantial industrial investments in energy-efficient process equipment.)[23]

Energy-related investment has not taken a large share of capital spending. Table 5 indicates the share of 1980 capital spending, by industry, that is termed energy-related. The table also shows for comparison the share of capital spending that is largely mandated by safety,

23. DOE, *The Industrial Energy Efficiency Improvement Program, 1979*, p. 7.

health, or pollution regulations as well as energy costs as a percentage of industry's value of shipments, a proxy for sales. Even in the energy-intensive sectors such as primary metals or stone, clay, and glass, capital spending on energy conservation is at most 6 percent of all capital expenditures.

Among those concerned with energy conservation, it is often said that energy saving is not given sufficient priority in spending. And yet energy saving investment seldom provides a significant cost saving. Table 5 shows that at the two-digit level in the SIC system, energy costs as a share of the value of shipments are frequently 7.5 percent or less. For many industries, then, energy costs are still only a small percentage of their total costs, ruling out widespread investment in the energy area that will yield major cost savings.

The Steel Industry

The steel industry is the largest industrial user of energy. In 1978, a relatively good year for steel, the industry accounted for 12.5 percent of the energy consumed in the industrial sector.[24] With this importance, the old saying, "As steel goes so goes the nation," is applicable to energy consumption. Improving energy efficiency in steel is a problem of obsolete capital rather than the availability of energy-saving technology. In the late 1950s the steel industry began modernizing to reduce costs, one major item being energy. In the 1970s modernization almost ceased as recessions and slower economic growth reduced steel consumption and import competition became extensive. As of January 1979 the U.S. industry had a third of its capacity in plants over twenty years old and as a result used 25 percent more Btus per ton of steel than the more modern Japanese industry.[25]

The steel industry is composed of two distinct sectors, the mini- or market mills and the large integrated mills. The latter sector uses the traditional production processes—large blast furnaces converting iron

24. Calculated from the Bureau of the Census, *1979 Annual Survey of Manufactures: Fuels and Electric Energy Consumed,* pp. 16, 24. Steel is defined more specifically as blast furnace and steel mills (SIC 3312). The blast furnace and steel mill portion of the steel industry is the most energy-intensive of the various components.

25. AISI, *Steel at the Crossroads,* pp. 11, 21. The basic oxygen furnace process can use less scrap than the open hearth process. Energy calculations are determined by the proportion of scrap used. The estimates here have not been adjusted for scrap content.

ore to steel—and it consists of the large established companies such as U.S. Steel. The major prospect for energy saving in this sector rests with the completion of various modernization measures. Yet further modernization is unlikely under the present economic conditions of the industry. To improve economic conditions would require major changes in government policy with respect to capital costs, import competition, and environmental regulations. Energy saving for the U.S. economy could also be achieved by allowing the U.S. integrated steel industry to contract its size by closing less-efficient plants. Steel imports could then supply the output that would otherwise come from the inefficient domestic plants. The choice between these alternatives turns on policy issues other than those of energy conservation, despite the importance of steel as an energy consumer.

Another prospect for energy saving lies in the shift of steel output to the mini-mill sector, which uses less energy than the integrated industry. Fuel switching, so important in the cement industry, has been relatively minor and limited to the substitution of fuel oil for natural gas as an ignition fuel.[26]

Energy Saving in the Integrated Steel Industry

As with most other energy-intensive industries, steel has a history of improving fuel efficiency. The gains came from three distinct changes: (1) reduced coke consumption from better charge preparation and fuel injection processes, (2) the development of continuous processes for casting and rolling, and (3) finishing steel by using the hot metal directly from the steel furnace so as to eliminate reheating of the metal.[27] The last two measures require significant capital investment, and as of 1981 the transition from the older processes to the newer ones was incomplete. The prospects for further energy saving are largely in the further utilization of processes introduced earlier.

Modern blast furnaces, in which iron making takes place, have a 15 percent lower energy consumption than the existing average for U.S. plants. About two-thirds of these energy savings are from design im-

26. Interviews with staff of the American Iron and Steel Institute, June 1982.

27. The Ford Foundation Conference Board, *Energy Consumption in Manufacturing* (Ballinger, 1974), pp. 417–18, 436–39. From 1947 to 1972 energy utilization per ton of steel declined at an average annual rate of 1.2 percent, compared with 0.8 percent for all manufacturing.

provements, and the remaining one-third comes from lower coke consumption per ton of iron production. In 1979 blast furnaces accounted for about 50 percent of energy consumption in the industry, so the 15 percent lower energy consumption would be a saving of 8 percent of the total energy consumption of the steel industry. The full savings can only be realized by modernization during the periodic relining of existing furnaces. Retrofitting of basic oxygen furnaces with more waste gas recovery would save about 3 percent of the energy now used in iron and steel making. Total replacement of primary rolling with continuous casting would result in a saving of about 5 percent of the energy used in steel production, partly from less use of energy in the process itself and partly from higher yields of the finished product. However, the technology for continuous casting of all grades of steel has not been commercially proven, and there are substantial technical problems in retrofitting existing U.S. plants. Potential energy savings from the hot rolling of steel are about 5 percent of the energy consumption in the production of steel. Again, hot rolling can be most easily introduced in the construction of new plants.[28]

Though there are possibilities for realizing energy savings in existing plants, most measures require new construction or major renovation, making the energy-saving measures just discussed (a total of about 20 percent) largely dependent on capital investment.

There are two aggregate estimates of the saving in energy costs to be achieved by the replacement of existing plants by new construction. Robert W. Crandall estimates potential savings at 20 percent, and the American Iron and Steel Institute estimates 35 percent.[29] Both estimates are consistent with this discussion. Given the differences in assumptions, a range of potential energy savings of 20 to 35 percent is not surprising

28. Ironmaking requires coke, which is produced by heating a coal charge. Coke plants consume about 10 percent of the total energy used in the steel industry. Energy saving in coke production can be achieved by more efficient ovens, heat recovery, and other measures. None of these provide possibilities for major energy saving. The energy savings discussed above were assigned to various steps by the authors based on data in AISI, *Steel at the Crossroads*, pp. 85–87.

29. Robert W. Crandall, *The U.S. Steel Industry in Recurrent Crisis: Policy Options in a Competitive World* (Brookings, 1981), pp. 84–85; and AISI, *Steel at the Crossroads*, p. 64. The AISI states, "Realization of this potential will require that steel production facilities be totally upgraded to the best available technology. This would require an extensive and complex program of facility improvement and replacement, retrofitting in some cases, individual process improvement in other cases, and complete plant replacement in still other cases."

and is in line with the difference between energy consumption in the U.S. and Japanese steel industries.

Prospects for Increased Investment

It is unrealistic to contemplate the total replacement of present plants with new ones. Over a ten-year period the phasing out of open hearth steel making, an increase in continuous casting, and the replacement of about half the present coke ovens would reduce energy consumption by about 15 percent per ton.[30] But the measures would require a doubling of capital expenditures in the steel industry over the 1978 level.

The economic return to society from the energy savings alone with the above modernization can be estimated as follows. The ten-year program would save 15 percent, beginning with 1.5 percent in the first year and increasing an additional 1.5 percent each year. The energy saving is measured relative to a 1978 consumption of 2.98 quads; thus a 15 percent reduction in consumption would save 0.447 quads when the modernization is completed.[31] The modernization program involves capital expenditures of $28.4 billion (in 1980 dollars) over 1978 levels of capital spending.[32] Assuming that the expected life of these capital improvements is twenty years, the stream of returns to society in the form of energy savings and the costs of the modernization program can be discounted to determine the internal rate of return that equates the present value of savings to the present value of the investment. The real rate of return so calculated is 7.6 percent. This seems low relative to the cost of capital to society, particularly given the risks involved and the generous estimate of the dollar amount for energy savings. This calculation illustrates that large-scale capital-intensive energy-saving measures are seldom cost effective for either society or a business firm, if only the savings from energy conservation are considered.

Modernization, of course, yields benefits other than energy saving.

30. This program is described in AISI, *Steel at the Crossroads*, pp. 31–41.

31. Ibid., p. 61. To make a generous estimate of dollar savings, energy savings are costed in terms of lower oil imports.

32. The $28.4 billion estimate represents the ten-year sum of approximately $2.84 billion annually over the 1978 level of capital expenditures. This allows for no expansion of the industry. See ibid., pp. 40, 44. The 1978 numbers have been converted to 1980 dollars by the use of the GNP deflator for gross private domestic investment. Conversion of Btus to barrels of oil was based on a conversion factor of 5.8 million Btus per barrel and the 1980 price of imported oil at $33.89 per barrel.

For example, there would be a marked improvement in the labor productivity of the steel industry. And yet it should be recalled that, even if energy and labor utilization are inefficient in existing plants, those plants may still remain competitive because their operation does not require capital expenditures. Crandall summarizes the economics of old versus new plants as follows:

> The capital charges for a new mill are staggering when compared with the cost of maintaining old equipment. In the past decade the steel industry has been spending $25 (in 1978 dollars) a finished ton of capacity to maintain and refurbish its plants. . . . Assuming that $30 a net finished ton is sufficient to maintain viable facilities in their current condition, the incremental capital requirements per ton are $131 less than those required by a new plant. Obviously the operating costs savings over an average plant do not offset this monumental difference, regardless of one's assumptions about energy and labor usage.[33]

It seems agreed among industry experts that an extensive modernization program requires changes in government policy to permit higher profits. This could be achieved by higher depreciation allowances, modifications in government occupational safety and environmental regulatory programs to reduce their cost, and greater protection from import competition.[34]

Crandall estimates that without a change in policy domestic steel capacity will decline by 10 percent over the next decade.[35] Closing the less-efficient plants would raise energy efficiency, but, more significant, a smaller steel industry would consume less energy. An interesting question, well beyond the scope of this essay, is whether it is better to import energy in the form of Japanese steel or OPEC oil.

The more energy-using techniques required by environmental regulations will offset future improvements in energy efficiency. An American Iron and Steel Institute–sponsored study estimated that the phasing in of additional environmental requirements could increase energy consumption 7 percent by 1983.[36] If environmental controls have an impact of this magnitude, the industry will be hard-pressed to maintain any net energy improvement. Environmental requirements also have an

33. Crandall, *U.S. Steel Industry*, p. 85.

34. See AISI, *Steel at the Crossroads*, p. 3.

35. Crandall, *U.S. Steel Industry*, p. 153. The AISI forecasts a loss as high as 13 percent of capacity by 1988 without changes in present policies. Calculated from data in AISI, *Steel at the Crossroads*, p. 40.

36. AISI, *Steel at the Crossroads*, p. 64. Interviews at the Environmental Protection Agency suggest that the additional energy requirement as calculated by the industry may be overstated.

impact by mandating certain capital expenditures. The primary metals sector spent 13.3 percent of its 1980 capital expenditures to comply with safety, health, and pollution regulations, more than any other industry and about twice the percentage of capital spending it devoted to energy conservation (see table 5).

Mini-Mills

While the prospects for energy savings within the integrated industry are bleak, they are considerably brightened by the growth of mini-mills—those with an annual capacity of 300,000–600,000 tons. Mini-mills use electric furnaces to convert steel scrap into steel. The electric furnaces are more energy intensive than the traditional blast furnaces that convert iron into steel. Nonetheless, considering the total process from iron ore to steel, including the coke ovens and the making of iron, the mini-mills, relying entirely on scrap, turn out to be the most energy efficient of all the three ways of producing steel. Electric furnaces use only 8.28 Btus a ton, compared with 19.38 for open hearth furnaces (using 45 percent scrap) and 20.28 for basic oxygen furnaces (using 30 percent scrap).[37]

Mini-mills have low capital costs: in 1980, for example, capital costs were $545 a ton of mini-mill capacity, compared with $743 a ton for roundout basic oxygen furnace capacity (additions to existing plants) and $1,287 a ton for basic oxygen furnace Greenfield capacity (entirely new plants).[38] The relative operating costs of mini-mills vary significantly with the price of scrap. Over the last twenty years the price of steel scrap has declined relative to the price of iron ore and steel, although the scrap price has been quite volatile on an annual basis. Two factors lie behind the downward trend in relative price. The shift to basic oxygen furnaces has reduced the demand for scrap by the integrated industry because basic oxygen furnaces typically use less scrap than the open hearth process. The increasing reliance on imports has also added to the supply of scrap, since the industry abroad has been taking back less scrap (as U.S. scrap exports) than it has been bringing in (as imports of finished steel). Increased imports of such items as automobiles also add to the

37. As reported in Joseph C. Wyman, "Steel Mini-Mills—an Investment Opportunity," in Shearson Loeb Rhoades, *Steel Quarterly* (November 20, 1980). p. 22.
38. As quoted in ibid., p. 21.

scrap supply. There is a good prospect that the price of scrap will at least maintain its position relative to the price of steel and iron ore.[39]

The mini-mill or electric furnace proportion of U.S. domestic steel has risen steadily from 6 percent in 1954 to about 27 percent in 1980. This growth reflects the continuing profitability of firms operating mini-mills, with a return on assets from 1970 to 1979 of about twice that of the integrated steel industry.[40] If this percentage continues to grow, it will reduce the energy requirements of domestic steel production. There is, however, another paradox here. If imports of finished steel and indirect imports of steel in the form of such products as automobiles are restricted, the growth of scrap supply will be reduced, which will retard the growth of the more efficient mini-mills.

For both the mini-mills and the integrated steel industry, the prospects for energy conservation are intertwined with future public policy for the U.S. steel industry. This policy, of course, depends on many considerations other than energy conservation. Thus the steel industry is a striking example of the proposition that the outlook for energy conservation cannot be separated from developments in general economic policy.

The Cement Industry

Cement has a more successful history of energy conservation than steel. Part of the explanation lies in the fact that energy costs are a large fraction of the selling price of cement. Over the postwar years energy costs averaged 19 percent of the selling price, and the industrial sector of stone, clay, and glass (which includes cement) ranks first in energy costs as a percentage of the value of shipments among the various industries shown in table 5. Still, there were variations in energy costs over the postwar period: Btu consumption per ton of cement declined at varying rates, from 9.04 million Btus in 1947 to 7.43 in 1962, remaining

39. Ibid., p. 19, has an extensive analysis of the future availability of scrap and concludes that even with a major growth in mini-mills "it does not appear that a scrap 'shortage' as such is in the making." There are some factors, such as the adoption of continuous casting, that would reduce the supply of scrap, but other technical changes—apart from the use of basic oxygen furnaces—increase it.

40. Average net return on assets for 1970–79 for fourteen companies that operate mini-mills was about 17 percent, compared with about 4 percent for six large integrated steel companies. Ibid., pp. 4, 7.

at about that level until 1974, and then declining from 7.36 in 1974 to 6.87 in 1980.[41] The record after 1977 demonstrates significant energy conservation, which occurred when the cement industry was in the doldrums, with production in 1980 about 10 percent less than in 1972.

There are several factors contributing to the energy conservation record of the cement industry. First, because fuel costs were more important here than in other industries, the oil shocks hit the industry hard. The industry used considerable natural gas but was given a low priority in the regulatory curtailments, forcing an acceleration in its shift to coal. Second, cement is sold largely on a price basis, making costs of competitive significance. With energy costs reaching 25 percent of the mill value in 1974, a 10 percent saving would lead to a 2.5 percent cost reduction. Though not all the energy saving need be passed on in price reductions, the potential for such price reductions would give a firm a competitive advantage.[42] Third, the technology was available for energy saving and permitted the substitution of coal for oil and natural gas. Finally, the cement industry has a history of fuel switching and fuel saving that goes back well before the 1972 oil shock and gave the industry experience in adjusting to higher energy prices.

The conservation record can be divided into the now-familiar categories of fuel saving and fuel switching. We estimate that fuel saving reduced 1980 energy costs for the cement industry by 8.7 percent from what they would have been with 1972 fuel efficiency, expressed as a percentage of 1980 fuel costs. Fuel switching reduced 1980 fuel costs by 17.2 percent from what they would have been with the 1972 fuel mix, again expressed as a percentage of 1980 fuel costs.[43] The total conservation effect was then 25.9 percent, a much better showing than for the industrial sector as a whole.

41. This estimate is based on data from U.S. Bureau of Mines, *Minerals Yearbook*, vol. 1: *Metals and Minerals*, annual eds. 1963–80; and, before 1963, Bureau of Mines, *Annual Report*, annual eds. 1947–62.

42. Since cement is a nearly perfectly homogeneous commodity, prices are a prime competitive weapon. This is reinforced by institutional practices of selling construction cement primarily on a bid basis, rather than by long-term contracts. Lower production costs allow the firm to trade off higher transportation costs and hence enlarge its market.

43. The calculation follows the same procedure as in table 4. Price data are from John G. Myers and Leonard Nakamura, *Saving Energy in Manufacturing: The Post-Embargo Record* (Ballinger, 1978), pp. 38–40; and U.S. Bureau of Labor Statistics. Fuel consumption by type of fuel is based on data from U.S. Bureau of Mines, *Minerals Yearbook*, vol. 1: *Metals and Minerals*, annual eds. 1963–80.

Table 6. *Fuel Sources for the U.S. Cement Industry, by Fuel Type, Selected Years, 1947–80*
Percent

	Fuel Type			
Year	*Coal*	*Oil*	*Natural gas*	*Electricity*
1947	59.6	8.8	20.2	11.3
1955	47.3	11.7	30.4	10.6
1960	43.6	5.3	38.1	13.0
1968	40.9	6.3	37.2	15.6
1972	30.3	12.9	39.3	17.5
1980	60.8	5.2	12.8	21.2

Source: U.S. Bureau of Mines, *Minerals Yearbook*, vol. 1: *Metals and Minerals*, annual eds.

Fuel Switching

Table 6 shows the fuel mix for certain key years. The consumption of electricity, used to drive fans, motors, and other equipment, rose steadily from 1947 to 1980. But among the other three fuels—coal, oil, and natural gas—there were striking changes in the proportions of fuel used. These three fuels are used in kilns as a heat source, and the production process can use any of these three. Cement is produced by grinding limestone, together with small quantities of clay, iron ore, sand, cement rock, and oyster shells. The mixture is fired in a kiln to produce small pellets called clinker, which is ground with gypsum to make cement. Heating the kiln requires large amounts of energy.

The shifts among fuels shown in table 6 are largely in response to relative prices. Thus the shift away from oil between 1955 and 1960 was in response to rising oil prices. The shift away from coal between 1968 and 1972 was in response to environmental regulations about the burning of high-sulphur coal that in turn caused a rapid rise in the price of low-sulphur coal. The increasing reliance on natural gas until 1972 reflected its low price until that time.

The post-1972 changes continue the history of responding to relative fuel prices. Oil, as table 4 indicates, increased almost sixfold in price per million Btus from 1973 to 1981; it supplied a smaller percentage of fuel by 1980 than at any time in the postwar years (table 6). The same is true of natural gas. The natural gas price increase was less marked than for oil (fivefold), and so one might not expect as sharp a decline, particularly since natural gas (unlike coal) is most often sold under long-term contracts rather than on a spot basis. However, regulatory authorities enforced substantial rationing of natural gas in order to ensure continuity of supply to household buyers.[44] The result was a fear by cement firms of disrupted fuel supplies (which implied a high shadow price for natural gas) and higher prices with deregulation. Both were factors in the switch away from natural gas. Cement was particularly hard hit because kiln heating was classified as a boiler fuel use, the lowest priority in the rationing of natural gas. Coal, whose price only doubled, returned in 1980 to its 1947 role as a fuel source. Conversion was expensive; an industry source estimates that conversion of a typical cement plant to coal costs about $10 million. Despite that, conversion did occur rapidly, so that by 1981 only 5 percent of U.S. clinker capacity was fueled by natural gas and none by oil.[45]

Fuel Saving

Much of the reduction in fuel consumption has occurred when new plants were built. The 1950s, characterized by rapidly expanding markets and the need for greater capacity, provided the opportunity for firms to install larger and more-efficient plants.[46] The acquisition of this additional capacity, together with a slowing in the rate of growth of demand, led to low levels of utilization of capacity in the mid-1960s. By 1966 new plant construction had fallen to record low levels. The slowdown in the introduction of new capacity explains, in part, the low rate of improvement in Btus per ton of output during the late 1960s and early 1970s.[47] Although important dimensions of industry performance are linked to capacity utilization and subsequent investment patterns, the gestation

44. An example of the sharp impact of rationing is the experience of a Texas company, Kaiser Cement and Gypsum Corp., which had a noninterruptible contract for supply of natural gas to its San Antonio, Texas, plant. A state regulatory agency in Texas established a system of priorities, superseding the contract and greatly reducing the plant's supply of natural gas.

45. Portland Cement Association, *U.S. and Canadian Portland Cement Industry: Plant Information Summary, December 31, 1981,* vol. 1 (Skokie, Ill.: PCA, 1982), p. 2.

46. Of the clinker production capacity available in 1981, almost 35 percent was constructed in 1956–65, whereas 27 percent was constructed in 1966–75. Retirement of oil equipment means these numbers understate the differential. Ibid., p. 8.

47. Detailed analysis of the role of capacity utilization is complicated, as there also can be significant movement in clinker inventories. Variations in the level of capacity utilization also alter the pattern of plant use. When utilization rates are low, firms close their less-efficient plants, thus causing an increase in average measured energy efficiency. This phenomenon may explain part of the apparent significant energy efficiency gains between 1979 and 1980.

lags in the planning, design, and construction phase make precise measurement of this linkage difficult. Because the physical capital employed in cement plants is remarkably long-lived,[48] its retirement through depreciation did not provide an important source of opportunities for new plant construction in the late 1960s.

Cement is made by two distinct processes—wet and dry—each with quite different energy requirements. In the wet process the ground raw materials are fed into the kiln as a slurry, whereas in the dry process they are fed into the kiln as a dry mixture. The wet process requires about twice as many Btus per ton of clinker output as the dry process in order to evaporate the moisture from the slurry before calcination can begin. The new dry process incorporates preheaters, which begin the calcining reaction by heating the feed before it enters the kiln. This allows the kiln time to be reduced, resulting in less heat loss.

Energy saving since 1966 has come about largely by the replacement of wet-process cement plants with new large dry-process plants. There is a substantial difference in energy efficiency between plants that have recently been closed and those that are newly constructed or modernized. The highest energy consumption for the new plants is a third below the best of the retired plants, demonstrating the limits that can be achieved in energy conservation without new investment.[49]

According to industry sources, the conversion of a typical wet-process plant to the dry process is estimated to cost $100 million, ten times that of conversion from oil or natural gas to coal. Hence the extent of process conversions can be expected to be much less than for fuel conversions. Still, the extent of the change is striking. From 1979 to 1981, 26.6 million

48. As of 1981 the average age of plants based on clinker capacity was nineteen years. When based on number of kilns, the average age jumps to twenty-six years. Portland Cement Association, *U.S. and Canadian Portland Cement Industry*, p. 8.

49. Our emphasis on the two processes differs from the view of Myers and Nakamura, *Saving Energy in Manufacturing*, p. 89. They assert that "nearly all the gains in energy conservation have been won by improvements within each process rather than by the rise in the importance of the dry process, which uses less energy. For example, if the 1976 output had been produced with the same proportions of wet and dry process plants that prevailed in 1966 . . . total energy use would have been less than 1 percent higher in 1976 than the actual amount." Such calculations fail to distinguish the two very different sources of increased energy efficiency for each process. In the case of dry-process technology, the efficiency gains are being effected by modification of existing technology (such as preheaters and precalciners) and construction of new, more-efficient plants. On the other hand, the average efficiency gains currently achieved in wet-process plants reflect primarily the retirement of old, small, inefficient plants, rather than modernization of existing plants.

tons of new dry-process capacity was built, amounting to 30 percent of the 1981 capacity. Overall capacity is down slightly, so that the new capacity has been matched by the retirement of wet-process plants.[50]

The 1970s were not years of great prosperity for the cement industry. Production declined by 10 percent as the demand for cement was reduced by the slowdown in public works and construction. There was no overall capacity expansion to permit modernization via expansion. We think that the importance of energy costs to the industry has necessitated the significant response in both fuel and process conversion.

The cement industry was affected by environmental regulations in ways similar to those affecting steel. Low-sulphur coal requirements in 1970 not only hindered the transition to coal after 1973, but also caused the industry to make a false start in 1970–73 by initiating a rapid movement out of coal and into oil. Industry sources identify environmental regulations as a major factor contributing to the industry's increase in electricity use of 8 percent a ton between 1972 and 1980.[51] The control of air and water pollution has required electricity-using precipitators, bag houses, and other devices, as well as new operating procedures.

Barriers to Further Energy Conservation

Despite recent achievements, there are further opportunities for energy conservation. International comparisons show that U.S. industry used more Btus per ton than other major producers (see table 7). Yet comparisons must recognize that national differences in energy efficiency are accounted for in large part by factors external to the cement industry.

The geographic dispersion of the United States is one such factor. Economies of scale, a major source of energy saving, are limited by transportation costs. More densely settled nations, such as Japan and West Germany, can build larger and more-efficient plants without the cost advantages of scale being offset by transportation costs. An examination of regional differences in energy efficiency within the United States indicates the same pattern, with greater energy efficiency in more

50. Portland Cement Association, *U.S. and Canadian Portland Cement Industry*, p. 2.

51. Portland Cement Association, "Energy Report: U.S. Portland Cement Industry" (Skokie, Ill.: PCA, July 1981), p. 1.

Table 7. *Comparative Energy Efficiency in the Cement Industry, by Country, 1973–76*
Million Btus per ton

Country	*1973*	*1976*
Austria	4.57	4.57
Canada	n.a.	6.35
Germany	4.47	4.11
Italy	4.47	4.25
Japan	5.25	4.84
Spain	5.80	5.43
Sweden	6.39	5.93
Turkey	5.75	5.25
United Kingdom	6.85	6.39
United States	7.47	7.30

Source: International Energy Agency, *Energy Conservation in Industry in IEA Countries* (Paris: OECD, 1979), p. 45. Converted from Btus per metric ton to millions of Btus per ton.
n.a. Not available.

closely settled eastern and Great Lakes regions than in the Rocky Mountains, northwestern, and north central regions.[52]

Cheaper ways to transport cement would allow geographically expanded markets. To date, relatively little use has been made of water transportation, though new production facilities located on the Mississippi River are utilizing inexpensive barge transportation. This represents an important development, since rising gasoline prices tend to shrink further the size of markets that are economically accessible by road transport.

The current gap between best practice and actual practice promises further conservation gains as modernization proceeds. Dry-process suspension preheater systems have the greatest potential for major energy savings relative to the traditional wet processes. In 1980 the average fuel efficiency of U.S. cement plants was 5.92 million Btus per ton, indicating that additional fuel savings of 30 percent could be achieved with the general use of best-practice technology.[53] Gains cannot be made quickly. While 41 percent of existing plant capacity still uses wet-process equipment, the large stock of inefficient plants will be modified and phased out only over many years.[54] Furthermore, not all

52. Ibid., p. 3.
53. Ibid.
54. Portland Cement Association, *U.S. and Canadian Portland Cement Industry,* p. 2.

the raw materials located near cement plants and their market are suitable for use in the dry-process technology.

Aluminum Smelting

The aluminum smelting industry converts bauxite into alumina and then alumina into aluminum ingot. The industry has used the same two key production processes since its founding: the Hall-Héroult reduction process for aluminum, discovered in 1886, and the Bayer process for alumina, discovered in 1888. Unlike the dry process for cement, no distinct new process has come along to create a sharp reduction in energy consumption.

Instead the gains in energy efficiency have been achieved with a succession of improvements in the Hall and Bayer processes that reduced energy consumption between 1947 and 1972 by about 35 percent a ton.[55] These have been primarily in the reduction process, the most energy-intensive stage. Perhaps the most significant have been the increase in the size of reduction cells and the increase in the amperage of electric current flow in the cells.[56] Other significant changes include (1) improved electrodes that reduce resistance between cathodes, anodes, and the molten metal; (2) the addition of lithium in the reduction process; (3) the trend to use of prebaked anodes in place of the earlier Soderberg anodes; (4) increased delivery of molten aluminum to fabricating plants, saving on the energy required for remelting; (5) improved heat and electrical insulation to reduce direct energy loss; and (6) use of computerized controls to maintain optimum spacing of the electrodes in the reduction cells.[57]

55. Calculation based on Btus per ton of primary aluminum as reported in U.S. Bureau of Mines, *Minerals Yearbook,* vol. 1: *Metals and Minerals,* annual eds. 1946–80. The energy data contains an unknown amount of systematic bias due to the established practice of converting hydroelectricity and thermal electricity to Btu equivalents, the former being converted at 3,412 Btus per kilowatt-hour, and the latter at 10,300 Btus per kilowatt-hour. Some of the reduction in energy use shown in industry-level data may be attributable to the greater use of hydroelectricity, particularly in the Northwest.

56. By 1960 new cells were drawing from 130,000 amperes to 140,000 amperes, compared with 80,000 amperes to 100,000 amperes for cells being installed in the early 1950s. Modern cells draw over 200,000 amperes.

57. This listing is based on discussions with Richard B. Pool, director of energy and regulatory affairs, Kaiser Aluminum and Chemical Corporation, December 1983.

Some of these technological changes could be economically retrofitted in existing plants, but others could be economically applied only in new plants. Aluminum has been one of the U.S. economy's fastest-growing industries, with its output increasing almost eight times from 1947 to 1972. This rapid growth has called for continuing investment in new plants, with each succeeding generation of plants embodying greater energy efficiency. This contrasts with the steel industry, where demand growth since 1965 has been too modest to lead to the extensive construction of new plants.

From 1972 to 1980 there was a market slowdown in capacity expansion: only one new smelter was built during this period, in contrast to almost one a year from 1947 to 1972. As a result, the annual rate of improvement in energy efficiency fell from about 1 percent for 1947–72 to about 0.5 percent for 1972–80.[58]

An additional factor in the slowdown in the rate of improvement in energy efficiency is that government-mandated environmental control measures have required additional energy consumption. Industry sources put the Btu requirements of such regulations at 1.3 percent of the 1980 energy consumption. These requirements probably will not add much to energy consumption in future years, as most of the new environmental standards are now being met.[59]

Fuel switching has been very limited in this industry for technological reasons. The Hall process requires large inputs of electricity, and, as discussed below, the source of electricity has shifted from hydroelectric to thermal generation. Natural gas has also been used in the calcining of the alumina, for which it is an ideal clean fuel.

Electricity Costs

Electricity costs vary widely by location because electricity can be transmitted economically only for short distances. Electricity costs are a large share of the value of shipments, as shown in the table on page 88, and thus are a major factor in an aluminum plant's competitiveness.[60]

58. Computed from data in U.S. Bureau of Mines, *Primary Aluminum Plants, World Wide* (GPO, 1982); and U.S. Bureau of Mines, *Minerals Yearbook,* annual eds. 1946–80.

59. The Aluminum Association, *Energy Conservation and the Aluminum Industry* (Washington, D.C.: Aluminum Association, 1981), p. 4.

60. The costs shown are authors' calculations based on 1980 value of shipments of $1,432 per ton, energy consumption of 168 million Btus per ton, and 1 kilowatt-hour equal to 10,000 Btus.

Cost of electricity (cents per kilowatt-hour)	*Cost as percentage of value of shipments*
0.3	3.5
0.5	5.9
1.0	11.7
1.5	17.6
2.0	23.5
2.5	29.3
3.0	35.2
4.0	46.9
6.0	70.4
8.0	93.9

The location of an aluminum smelter involves a trade-off between power and transportation costs. Before World War II aluminum smelters were located largely in the southeastern part of the United States to take advantage of low-cost hydropower from the Tennessee Valley Authority (TVA). During and immediately following World War II, new smelters were located in the Northwest to use low-cost hydropower supplied by the Bonneville Power Administration (BPA). By 1950 half the smelting capacity was in the Northwest.

In response to the increased demand associated with the Korean War, there was a sizable increase in capacity. Low-cost hydropower was not available for this expansion from either the BPA or the TVA. The new capacity used instead thermal-generated power available in the Midwest from coal or in the Southwest from natural gas. The higher power costs of thermal sources were offset in part by savings in transportation costs to East Coast markets. By 1953, as the Korean expansion finished, the Pacific Northwest accounted for only 30 percent of U.S. smelting capacity.[61] The subsequent expansion of smelting capacity from 1953 to 1972 was again largely based on thermal power.

Technological Breakthroughs

Efforts have gone on for several decades to develop an alternative to the electricity-intensive Hall-Héroult process. Most of the effort has concentrated on bypassing the electrolytic reduction stage by obtaining

61. See Merton J. Peck, *Competition in the Aluminum Industry, 1945–1958* (Harvard University Press, 1961), chap. 9, for a discussion of the expansion of the aluminum industry in the 1950s.

aluminum directly from bauxite. The technical barriers are substantial, and development has been slower than many expected. Several pilot processes have proven to be technically feasible, but none have been able to match the costs involved in producing the metal by the Bayer and Hall processes.

Direct thermal reduction to produce aluminum was tried in Germany during World War II, but this process was not tested again until the late 1950s when Alcan built a pilot plant to test a monochloride process for producing pure aluminum.[62] Pechiney, the largest French producer, experimented with two quite different production methods: a carbothermic and a nitride process. Both the Alcan and Pechiney projects were canceled because the new processes could not achieve profitable operating levels. Other developments in the 1960s of the subhalide process and direct reduction also failed to achieve their early promise and were discontinued.

In the 1970s Alcoa established an operating facility using chlorine reduction, where aluminum chloride was electrolyzed in a closed cell. This process saved energy, labor, and capital, but has encountered major difficulties with plant corrosion. The apparent failure of the chlorine reduction process has come after Alcoa's fifteen years of research. The most promising recent development has been in still another approach, the partial carbothermic reduction of silica-rich aluminum ores in a shaft furnace with final reduction of aluminum silicon alloy in a submerged arc furnace. Even though the 1977 *Minerals Yearbook* indicated the development of this project would be completed by 1982–84, recent assessments indicate that "the extreme complexity of the reactions involved, and the severity of the conditions encountered, require extensive development which will take many years to accomplish."[63]

An overview of the record shows that major technical barriers have hindered the development of radical new technologies for aluminum production and will continue to do so. Perhaps more promising, at least for the immediate future, is the continuation of research to improve the existing technology of electrolytic reduction. Much of the effort has

62. In the first instance this was not to be a major energy-saving new technology, but was to create possibilities for subsequent redesigns of plant and equipment that could achieve important energy efficiency gains.

63. U.S. Bureau of Mines, *Minerals Yearbook, 1977,* vol. 1: *Metals and Minerals,* pp. 133–34; and Maxine Savitz, "Energy Conservation Policies," in Aluminum Association, *Aluminum Industry Energy Conservation Workshop VI Papers* (Washington, D.C.: Aluminum Association, 1981), p. 19.

focused on the materials and method of construction of the anodes and cathodes in the reduction cell. In the 1960s there was a movement to refractory hard-metal cathodes and to prebaked anodes, which saved electricity consumption and increased output from existing plants.[64] Recent improvements in the electrical efficiency of the Soderberg anode have been achieved by Japanese manufacturers, but pollution control requirements make it unlikely that U.S. manufacturers will utilize this process. Design of wettable cathodes and inert nonconsumable anodes to improve the electrical efficiency of the Hall cell has also been another area of research. Together these developments could reduce smelting power requirements by over 20 percent, but, as with so many previous promising projects, development is proceeding more slowly than was expected earlier.

Beginning in 1979, electricity rates to aluminum smelters rose sharply: for example, the BPA's rates increased ninefold from 1979 to 1984. The combination of these high rates and a downturn in demand has led to the closing of four of the nation's thirty-one aluminum smelters.[65] The aluminum industry has adjusted to high energy costs by reducing output and closing smelters—a response that saves energy for the nation but does not fit our definition of energy conservation.

The continuation of marginal improvements cannot offset the marked rise in electricity costs that the aluminum industry has experienced since the late 1970s. The low-cost locations for new smelters are now in Australia, Brazil, and Canada, countries with low-priced electricity. Not only will no new aluminum smelters be built in the United States, but it seems likely that even more existing smelters will close. The energy shocks have led to a decline in U.S. international competitiveness in aluminum production and the United States may become increasingly dependent on imports to meet its demand for aluminum ingot.

64. U.S. firms were quick to adopt the prebaked anode. By 1965 only 46 percent of U.S. capacity was still employing Soderberg anodes, while 64 percent of the free world capacity was still in this older technology. U.S. Bureau of Mines, *Minerals Yearbook, 1965*, vol. 1: *Metals and Minerals (Except Fuels)* (GPO, 1966), p. 186. Though all new production facilities are expected to use prebaked anodes, there can be considerable costs in converting existing facilities from Soderberg to prebaked anodes, and many older plants continue to use the Soderberg anode.

65. Bonneville Power Administration, *Selling Power: BPA's Direct Service Industries: Changing Conditions—Changing Needs?* (BPA, February 1985), p. 5. Data on plant closures obtained from *Metal Statistics 1984: The Purchasing Guide of the Metal Industries* (New York: Fairchild Publications, 1984), p. 18.

Conclusions

The conservation response of U.S. industry to the 1973 and 1979 energy price increases has been a modest one. The response, however, is consistent with the relatively minor role that energy costs represent for most industrial firms. The estimated overall cost of energy for 1981 was $79.1 billion, 4.0 percent of the manufacturing value of shipments for that year. It would have $11.2 billion higher without the accelerated conservation effort after 1973.[66]

In the long run, it remains to be seen how much the impact of higher energy prices can be ameliorated by altering and redesigning production technology to reduce energy consumption. As the discussions of the steel, cement, and aluminum industries show, the possibilities of energy saving vary among industries, depending on technology and economic conditions. In general, optimal economic scheduling for both the firm and for society dictates that the introduction of many energy-saving technologies be delayed until they can be introduced at the time of major renovations or construction of new plants and equipment. Since the average plant has a life of twenty years or longer, many of the new technologies warranted by the oil price increases of 1979 may not be applied until plant reconstruction in the later part of this decade or even the next one. By that time, the economy will be in the time period that William W. Hogan's essay examines, and the outlook for energy conservation becomes more favorable.

Comments by Robert W. Crandall

First of all, there are a few things that bother me about the aggregate saving estimate. One is the assumption that somehow there was a trend rate of growth that would have continued. Just recently I looked at auto fuel economy and found absolutely no trend for a substantial period before 1972 or a long period ahead of that. Second, it is not clear whether

66. Calculated from energy consumption by industry as reported in DOE, EIA, *Monthly Energy Review* (July 1982), p. 23; energy prices as shown in table 4; and value of shipments for manufacturing as shown in *Economic Report of the President, February 1982*, p. 289. The percentage applied to determine the effect of conservation is the 14.2 percent arrived at earlier in this essay.

the adjustment for the shift in output mix takes into account the fact that there were different trend rates of growth across the various sectors and whether that might have affected the calculation.

I am not sure that one ought to view the 18 percent estimate for post-1972 fuel saving as a terribly pessimistic number. It may well be that there was substantially more fuel saving. Also, the descriptions of the individual industries indicate to me that there are tremendous disequilibria and the potential for fuel saving here is much greater than what has been shown thus far.

In the steel industry there is going to be a sharp shift away from coke, hot metal, and basic oxygen furnaces toward scrap, maybe eventually direct reduction in this country. That shift is going to give much greater energy conservation than any improvements forecast in the coke oven, basic oxygen furnace, or blast furnace processes.

One of the important sources of conservation of energy comes from improving rolling mills. U.S. manufacturers will obviously replace many of their primary mills with continuous casters. But even finishing mills in the United States are much less efficient than in other parts of the world, particularly in Japan. Increasing the efficiency of the rolling mills reduces the amount of waste and scrap generated from those mills, which in turn reduces the amount of hot metal needed per ton of final steel production. That is going to generate further improvements in the next few years.

What has happened thus far in the steel industry is a dramatic change in market growth, which in turn will feed back on the technology and therefore on energy savings in future years in far more dramatic fashion than has happened thus far.

Comments by Dermot Gately

Peck and Beggs calculate an implied price elasticity of -0.12, which they describe as relatively low. This is an important reminder, I think, of the technological limits of reducing energy use in industry. Several factors, however, put this low price elasticity in perspective, some of which they have mentioned.

First, international comparisons are probably more appropriate for giving an indication of what the ultimate substitution or conservation possibilities are. They cite data from the steel industry that indicate that in Japan a ton of steel is produced with 25 percent less energy than in the United States. Perhaps that would be a better estimate or at least a lower boundary on what the ultimate conservation possibilities would be.

Second, Peck and Beggs observe that their price elasticities are quite low in comparison with an elasticity of -0.5 from a study by the Energy Modeling Forum. The EMF study referred to an elasticity response over a twenty-five-year period, so Peck and Beggs's estimate, although much smaller, is not surprising and is probably consistent with the EMF estimate. Moreover, the EMF estimate was an aggregate response, whereas Peck and Beggs's estimate is for just the industrial sector.

A third point involves the substitution of electricity for nonelectric energy and how this can confound results elsewhere, for example, Peck and Beggs's finding that fuel switching between 1972 and 1981 actually increased total fuel costs. This type of substitution is driven by wholly rational, nonprice considerations. Even though it is a small effect, it moves the elasticity calculation in the wrong direction. If one took account of that and measured it differently, my guess is that it would tend to increase the implied price elasticity.

ARNOLD W. SAMETZ

Financial Barriers to Investment in Conservation

THIS ESSAY attempts to assess whether there are barriers that prevent energy conservation investments from receiving financing in the same manner as other investments: are such investments being discriminated against by the financial community? I have sought the answer in two ways: by examining the application of traditional investment rules (such as net present value and payback) and by administering a questionnaire to officers in banks and other financial institutions. Both methods have led me to the same conclusion: the major barrier to energy conservation investment is its relative riskiness, which is a perfectly legitimate investment consideration. That is, I find no evidence that this type of investment is being discriminated against to a degree greater than is warranted by its risky nature.

The Capital Budgeting Framework

Financial barriers to energy conservation investment can best be evaluated within the traditional capital budgeting framework. Private expenditures for energy conservation projects—like any investment project of business or households—can be expected to be made only if they are "worth" more than they "cost." For example, if the current

I am indebted to my colleague Anthony Saunders, who reviewed the first draft of this paper, redrafted some parts, and commented critically on the rest. The final draft was edited by John Teall. For conducting the interviews, I am pleased to acknowledge the work of Edward Auden and Roberta Pitchon, and for handling the manuscript in its various stages, I salute Ligija Roze.

cash outlay on an investment is $10,000, the investment must promise a series of cash flows in return whose present value exceeds that $10,000 current cash outlay.

Those future cash inflows are subject to a double discount: they will be received only over a period of time, and they are not certain to be received. Thus the series of expected future return flows must be discounted or reduced for the delay (the interest forgone on alternative risk-free investment) and for the risk assumed (risk premium over the risk-free rate forgone). To calculate the present value of the expected payoffs on energy-saving projects for comparison with the present value or cost of the outlay, the future flows must be estimated and discounted at a rate that reflects the opportunity cost of capital, that is, the rate of return offered by investments of comparable time and risk patterns.

This hurdle rate or financial barrier excludes both noneconomic and public economic policy factors. In subjecting conservation investment to general analysis, this essay considers only private financial barriers, which may, however, be offset by public policy.

In sum, then, the basic capital budgeting rule—the net present value (NPV) rule—is that the difference between the discounted value of future return flows (benefits) and the initial investment outlay (costs) must be positive. In addition, when choosing among investment alternatives, the rule is to choose the one with maximum NPV. Obviously, the NPV rule is translatable into benefit-cost terms.

In terms of rates of return, the equivalent rule is to invest if the expected returns on the energy-saving equipment are at least equal to the rates of return available on equivalent investment in capital market instruments. This hurdle rate is, of course, a financial barrier; but the whole capital budgeting calculation—the NPV test—is also a hurdle. An investment project may fail the test not because the risk-discounted cost (or nonavailability) of funds is high, but because the expected cash inflows are small or slow relative to the initial cash outlay.

Assuming for the moment fully efficient financial markets and intermediation, the basic financial barriers to any investment, including conservation investment, must be found in the real interest rate level or in the discount for risk of expected return flows (such as energy savings payoffs). Both high real interest rates and riskiness present a hurdle, but these hurdles apply to all investment. Only to the extent that financing for conservation investment is singled out for discriminatory treatment is it considered a barrier for the purposes of this essay.

Risk Factors

The two principal determinants of the amount of future energy savings from conservation investment—the future price of oil and the productivity of conservation investment—are difficult to estimate. These significant uncertainties, when translated into discounts for risk on conservation investment, constitute a significant barrier to such investment. Energy savings are usually calculated on the assumption that oil prices will rise in the future. If oil prices rise more slowly than the overall rate of inflation, however, the savings will be either small or nonexistent. An additional risk, to the extent that the technology of energy-saving equipment is developing rapidly, is that money spent on this equipment now might have a greater productivity if invested in better equipment later. These combined risks strongly suggest the economic benefits of postponing conservation investment.

Thus, even if financial and economic markets were perfect, the relative riskiness of energy-saving investment would have to be considered as a normal financial hurdle. One of my main conclusions is that the risk-return relation is the major barrier at present, resulting from the application of traditional, evenhanded capital budgeting rules.

Financial Market Imperfections

On the other hand, because money and capital markets are *not* perfect, there are also purely financial barriers; but these are additive (and, I judge, subordinate) to the basic budgeting hurdles. There is evidence, of course, that financial markets are imperfect in that some interest rates are sticky, that capital rationing gaps exist, and that financial information is imperfect and asymmetric. But the pertinent issue is whether these factors raise barriers to energy-saving investment plans and implementation that exceed the average for all or alternative investment projects.

A general case can be made for the special significance of financial market imperfections in energy conservation investment.

1. Financial discrimination is known to be more prevalent against small businesses and consumers than against larger businesses; and an important feature of energy-saving investment is that it often involves smaller decisionmaking units.

2. Informational imperfections are known to be greater for longer

investment periods and more innovative production functions. These characteristics are descriptive of much of energy-saving investment.

But the significance of informational imperfections as a barrier should not be exaggerated compared with that of the overall capital budgeting decision to postpone investment in the light of future uncertainties. And similarly, financial market imperfections are unlikely to be as inhibiting to investment as above-average risk premiums, though they may be related, especially in a capital-rationing framework.

Strategic Factors

Significant, but less subject to quantification, are restrictions on the applicability of the basic accept-reject capital budgeting rule because of realistic and complex operational conditions facing investment decision-makers. *Strategic* capital budgeting requires joint investment portfolio decisionmaking, usually given fixed total funding, rather than single project decisions taken one at a time and financed one at a time. To cope with large corporations' long-term strategic planning, divisional project ranking, companywide discontinuous fund-raising, and other managerial operative rules, modifications of simplified NPV rules are common. For example, "defensive" projects to avoid possible great future losses (such as a market or resource base) can be subject to a relaxed NPV rule: current investment that is less than maximizing is adopted.[1] Or a company may specify the use of the current average cost of funds on outstanding capital structure in calculating the cost of capital, rather than a marginal cost linked to the specific risk characteristics of the project at issue. Here investments are treated as part of a package, usually with an overall dollar ceiling.

To what extent are strategic factors of special significance for energy conservation investment? Unlike financial market imperfections, which seem more applicable to household and small business investment, strategic factors seem more applicable, on structural and administrative grounds, to larger corporate investment decisionmaking. Larger corporations also are more apt to be characterized by interactive projects, formal capital structures, and "infinite" life; but presumably they are also more capable of calculating modified NPV rules. Small businesses

1. Conversely, if postponement is an important element in long-term investment planning, it can be wise to specify a NPV that is not just greater than zero but strongly positive.

(and households), more dependent on financing via bank loans, are more likely to evaluate investment projects one at a time.

Even though energy-saving opportunities stem from dynamic change in energy prices and energy technology and may involve investment in research and development and new production techniques, this is more a matter of calculating risk discounts than of managerial strategy.[2] But even highly innovative energy-saving investment is essentially cost-reducing investment, which, compared with revenue- (or capacity-) increasing investment or new product investment, is seldom considered "strategic." Cost-saving projects seldom are primary determinants of market share unless they also happen to be key to assuring energy supply. This suggests that the straightforward NPV approach is appropriate. But it also suggests that when capital is rationed cost-saving projects lacking absolute priority and urgency may be bypassed when strategic projects are numerous or large. Low-risk cost-reduction projects may be considered unacceptable if subjected to an overall or uniform opportunity cost of capital and forced to compete with high-risk high-return projects for funds. In contrast to the general applicability of options to postpone conservation investment, new product or venture investment often requires the strategic decision to invest *now*, even in the absence of positive NPV, because the investment now creates real options for profitable follow-up investments.

The Payback Rule and NPV Rule

It is common conservation economics to measure net benefits or profitability not by the NPV, but by simple, crude decision rules of thumb such as the payback period or the availability of funds. The payback rule evaluates an investment project by the test of whether the outlay is expected to be matched by return cash flows over a specified number of years, typically three to five. The available funds rule stresses whether funds are on hand or assuredly available, such as a line of credit. Both rules stem from the difficulties of estimating uncertain future net

2. Besides, this special riskiness of conservation investment that is attributable to the unpredictability of future energy prices is less imposing when evaluated within a portfolio framework. For example, if sharp rises in oil prices depress the economy and returns on average investment, energy savings or returns on conservation investment will increase. Such negative correlation adds to the attractiveness of conservation projects as part of a portfolio.

cash inflows and the fear of future financial stringency and capital rationing.

The typical payback application to energy conservation in determining whether to go ahead with the investment is to measure the annual expected savings (profits) from the project and to calculate the number of years it will take for the initial outlay to be recouped. A common statement is "this investment will pay for itself in $4\frac{1}{2}$ years." If that number falls within the rule of thumb set by the firm or household, the investment is deemed advisable. It is usually pointed out that the payback number not only falls within the generally acceptable range, but that special energy aspects lower the payback hurdle further.

However, the crucial question is how the average threshold payback period is determined in the first place and how it varies depending on the nature of the project. Even if based initially on NPV calculations and converted to payback form for simplicity and convenience, traditional industry or financial institution payback norms cannot yield correct signals when, as is usual, project risks and duration and opportunity costs of capital are diverse.

The realities of financial imperfections, interdependence, and uncertainty are handled better by adapting basic NPV rules than by using the payback criteria or other approaches. Neglecting to estimate future fund flow estimates and opportunity costs of capital does not avoid their consequences. The payback formula neglects both the discount for futurity of the returns received *within* the payback period and the uncertain returns that may be received in the years *after* the payback period. To find the true acceptability of such an investment one needs to know how long the *actual* life of the investment is likely to be and the rate at which to discount those future streams.

Consider, for example, this typical application of payback decision-making to solar water heater installation in households: a heater costs $2,400 and annual savings of heating costs are projected at $200, with a resulting twelve-year payback.[3] Some reasonable further calculations show a more appealing four-year payback by allowing for tax credits and fuel price changes as follows: (1) Since the $200 is a tax-free return in that it cuts costs rather than increases income, it increases pretax income, say, to $300, in a 33 percent tax bracket, improving payback to eight years; and (2) with fuel costs expected to rise at a real rate of 2

3. See Modesto A. Maidique, "Solar America," in Robert Stobaugh and Daniel Yergin, eds., *Energy Future* (Random House, 1979), pp. 191–97.

percent a year for thirty years, and with funds borrowed at current fixed interest rates, the payback would improve further to four years. Presumably, consumers' inability to perceive rates of return or improved cash flows obtained from cost-saving investments constitutes the critical obstacle to purchasing energy conservation services.

However, there are counterarguments: (1) Cost savings may be tax exempt, but reduced costs are less acceptable to lenders than increased revenues as sources of funds to repay loans; (2) interest rates on energy-saving term loans are likely to be variable or, if fixed, higher in an environment so inflationary that fuel costs are expected to rise faster than the rate of inflation; and (3) households may well have alternative investment opportunities (including alternative conservation projects) that have better yields or carry less risk.

Though there is a total absence of risk measurement in this payback application, there is in fact a surprisingly long list of risks to households in investing in a solar water heater:[4] (1) Dynamic technology risks are difficult to quantify due to lack of established records of installation, effectiveness, maintenance costs, life spans, and expected rates of improvement (and costs) of new models; (2) future savings flows are uncertain because of differential impacts of local climate and energy rates, and neither factor can be predicted precisely for the next eight years or so; and (3) the recent and expected future volatility of interest rates challenges all calculations of costs of financing and alternative returns from household financial savings.

Note that the market cost of funds is not considered in the payback decision. The emphasis on quick payback stresses instead the importance of the availability of funds (liquidity), both to the equipment business and to its household customers. Interest rates (and net returns) are slighted.

If capital constraints, rather than difficulties in calculating cash flow risks, are the rationale for using the payback criteria, the decisionmaker must be estimating future reinvestment needs and their rates of return. In general, even when funds are rationed, it is still necessary to rank projects. Risk estimates are necessary in that process even for unique strategic projects, for such projects also have mutually exclusive alternatives: investment now versus investment later.

Thus the best argument for the payback approach—aside from its

4. Many of the following points can be found in *Consumer Reports*, vol. 47 (May 1982), pp. 256–61.

convenience and simplicity—is that cash flows beyond a few years are so uncertain as to be unmeasurable and that liquidity problems are so significant as to dominate the firm's decisions. However, neither of these conditions can be said to be descriptive of energy-saving investment projects as a whole.[5]

But perhaps there is something unique about investment in energy conservation. Much of the conservation-based literature implies that (1) investment in energy saving is fundamentally different from investment in general, typically involving more categorical or absolute projects, and hence is less subject to risk-return measures; and (2) investors in energy-saving projects are different—less informed, more vulnerable to financial constraints and costs, and less rational—and hence more subject to exclusion from financial channels.

These implications explain why the financial analysis in conservation investment "manuals" does not calculate or suggest the need to calculate risk-adjusted discount rates, but rather uses crude payback formulas, and implicitly assumes that lack of promotion or shortage of capital will inhibit much of such worthwhile investment (such as in solar water heaters, which suffer from insufficient promised returns weighted for risk). By simultaneously overestimating expected returns and implying the need for promotion of projects or subsidies, this approach dilutes allocative constraints from both the benefit and cost sides.

In planning a survey of barriers to financing energy-saving investment, my colleagues and I included questions designed to probe these issues. We found no evidence of a selective capital shortage or a need for special financial analysis in connection with energy conservation projects. This is not to say that these projects did not face barriers of unusual risk or market imperfections, especially on the informational side for the more innovative projects. But the barriers did not appear to be primarily in the supply of funds,[6] and therefore there were no special grounds for stressing the quick recovery of initial investment. However, the novelty of energy-saving investment and the wide variety of investors do seem to put strains on financial institutional arrangements and data keeping. There also appears to be justification for modifying the NPV rule so as to increase the average current hurdle in order to allow for risk resolution over time for this type of investment.

5. Even if this were not so, it would be better to apply NPV, allowing for riskiness and illiquidity in the discount rate used.

6. These findings are quite distinct from issues of the private need and public benefit of subsidizing energy-saving projects for lower-income or all income groups.

Rules of Thumb versus an Adjusted NPV Rule

While the conservationist literature oversimplifies (and distorts) by emphasizing payback models and neglecting risk measurement, academic financial analysts overgeneralize the NPV model, seldom coming to grips with the need to cope with difficulties in forecasting cash flows and to specify methods of discounting for risk and sources of risk capital. Neither assuming that the funding problem is *the* problem nor assuming it away as *no* special problem is helpful to an evaluation of the nature and size of the financial barriers to energy conservation investment. My conclusion—that the problem is one of difficult risk estimation, especially on the demand side, rather than a specific capital shortage problem—is far more critical of conservationist literature than academic work; but applied academic analysis has not been very helpful.

Guidebook Rules of Thumb

It is commonplace for guidebooks to investment in energy conservation to ignore risk in the decisionmaking process or to dismiss it as relatively trivial in projects that are "obviously" energy saving. Considering only official publications by professional economists that present reasonably complex case studies of household and business energy-saving projects, with discounted cash flow calculations, one still finds the following typical errors:

1. The discount rate for households to apply to energy investment is often assumed to be a savings account rate,[7] as if the investment were risk-free, the borrowing rate were also at the risk-free level, and no alternative investment project need be considered. In other examples, household mortgage rates or tax-exempt rates are used as best alternative rates, again assuming implicitly equal risks to investment in energy conservation investment. A more appropriate discount rate to use for heat pump installations, for example, would be the expected return on Honeywell stock: at least it is more likely to reflect the price change and technology change risks of the investment.

2. It is stated that inflation trends suggest that "energy conservation investments that you can afford today will cost a lot more if you wait

7. Harold E. Marshall and Rosalie T. Ruegg, *Energy Conservation in Buildings: An Economics Guidebook for Investment Decisions,* U.S. Department of Commerce, National Bureau of Standards (Government Printing Office, 1980), p. 34.

until next year. In addition, energy saved today will represent greater dollar savings next year. Therefore if you have the money, it is probably worth your while to implement conservation measures as soon as you can."[8] There is a serious error in each sentence of this quotation: (1) Simple extrapolation of past inflation rates for conservation equipment is an especially risky forecasting method, but risk in any case is unavoidable, for future technology is also at risk; (2) the value of energy saved depends on future oil prices as well as on future energy equipment technology and prices; and (3) whether you have the money or not, you can borrow it; but in either case, you will pay (or forgo) a rate that discounts expected inflation.

The NPV Rule Modified by Timing

What these examples and the critique demonstrate is that the allowance for risk in the case of energy equipment investment by households or business, especially in the case of upgrading investment, was increasing during 1978–82 because future energy prices and energy technology seemed to be less predictable and interest rates were high in real terms. In short, the current risk-adjusted rate was high. Under these conditions, it is rational to postpone investment if it is expected that in time the technology may stabilize, fuel prices may vary at predictable rates, and real interest rates may fall back to historical levels.

The special riskiness of mutually exclusive energy investment alternatives leads to an increase in the value of the option to invest later versus the decision to invest now. This is not to say that more energy will not be saved by investment now; it is to say that the current project may not promise to yield a net return (after all costs) equal to the return offered by equivalently risky alternative investments.

Project timing is particularly important in retrofit forms of investment for two reasons: (1) The expected net savings (or benefits) from the new installation will be offset to some degree by the loss of the value of the option to invest later; and (2) there is a risk that the net savings may not be realized. These savings depend on such key variables as initial and expected costs and productivity of the equipment as well as current and future energy prices.

8. James E. Bailey and others, "Saving Money with Energy Conservation: Economic Analysis of Conservation Measures," prepared by the American Institute of Industrial Engineers for the U.S. Department of Energy, DOE/CS-xxx (1981), p. 39.

Postponement does involve forgoing expected net savings in the near future, but the funds can be invested *reversibly* in otherwise comparably risky financial instruments until there is less uncertainty in the particular irreversible cost-reducing investment. Thus it is very important in the case of energy conservation investment to calculate the expected savings properly using a risk-discounted hurdle rate, and to consider the value of the option to wait that will be given up in the act of investing irreversibly.[9]

There are, of course, a multitude of energy-saving projects that involve labor-intensive application of standard technology such as extra insulation and weather stripping. Such projects are unlikely to be inhibited by the value of waiting or by strategic investment considerations. However, neither are they likely to be subject to important financial constraints. Here, perhaps, the significant barrier, if any, is informational.

Capital Market Imperfections and the NPV Rule

If the assumption of perfect capital markets is lifted, how is the investment decision affected? More specifically, is conservation investment likely to be affected more or less than average investment when taxes and transaction costs are not zero; information is not costless to borrowers and lenders; and access to money and capital markets is not equal?

To illustrate the relative significance of these imperfections for conservation investment, I will consider these special attributes of energy-saving projects: (1) Net returns from these investments are cost reducing rather than revenue increasing; (2) investors (which include households, small businesses, and government) are highly varied and often of small size, making infrequent decisions; and (3) the risks of many sizable energy-saving projects are viewed as substantial by both lenders and borrowers.

The fact that the net returns from energy-saving investment are taken in cost-reducing form is important to households subject to significant

9. The value of the option to postpone investment was modeled and estimated in a recent paper. Simulations show that this option value can be significant and that for "surprisingly reasonable parameter values, it can be optimal to defer investing until the present value of the benefits from a project is *double* the investment cost." Robert L. McDonald and Daniel Siegel, "The Value of Waiting to Invest," National Bureau of Economic Research Working Paper 1019 (Cambridge, Mass.: NBER, November 1982), p. 3.

personal income taxation. The returns from the investment in a heat pump are not revenue producing and hence not taxable (though depreciation may be allowed), and interest on funds borrowed is also deductible. Since the household share in conservation investment is substantial, the cost-reducing aspect should be stimulating to such investment. However, lenders prefer revenue-producing projects for the assurance of additional cash flows to meet loan repayments. Imperfect information, transaction costs, and access to funding are all involved in this instance.

There is some evidence that business investment in new energy-saving projects is handicapped in traditional capital budgeting procedures by cash flow forecasts that are biased in favor of sales expansion projects. A study of one company, which compared the cash flow results of fifty projects with the forecasts of cash flows made in their respective requests for capital, showed that sales expansion projects' cash flows and therefore present values were overestimated by 40 percent. The forecasts for cost reduction (energy-saving) projects, on the other hand, underestimated cash flows by 10 percent. This says that managerial decisions are biased against cost-cutting projects in favor of sales expansion projects.[10] In addition, the fact that corporate taxation, unlike personal income taxation, is imposed on net profits also differentiates business investment in revenue-producing energy conservation from household investment in cost-saving energy conservation.

Lenders clearly are ill informed about the creditworthiness of new customers or small customers borrowing for novel purposes; rational responses for risk-averse lenders would be to raise the interest cost to such borrowers or to ration credit. Failure to raise the rate, but rather excluding the borrower, is rationing. The traditional reason for rationing has been the rigidity of rate setting due to cost stickiness, rate ceilings, and lags in general; clearly this has become less important. However, rates probably remain stickier for small customers than for large ones.

Rationing may be the result of asymmetrical information: the borrower knows the true riskiness of the loan (that is, the project) better than the lender, but the lender assumes that the borrower is likely to conceal adverse information. Thus, in the absence of a nonbiased (market) signal of loan quality, the lender will ration low-quality high-risk loans. An important signal of quality or risk is the size of the equity participation;

10. Joseph L. Bower, *Managing the Resource Allocation Process: A Study in Corporate Planning and Investment* (Homewood, Ill.: R. D. Irwin, 1972), pp. 11–12 and exhibit 1.

the larger the stake of the borrower, the less the risk faced by the lender. But such a signal would discriminate against the household and small business with limited and informal equity positions.[11] Furthermore, a borrower's willingness to pay high interest rates implies greater risk of default and possibly lower returns to the lender.[12] In other words, the better-quality borrowers may withdraw from the market if rates rise; the lower-quality borrowers may take greater risks to obtain higher returns in order to meet the greater borrowing costs.[13] On the other hand, some small or infrequent borrowers are willing to pay high bank rates because alternative sources of funds are not available to them.

Although many, if not most, energy-saving investments are relatively high-risk investments because of volatile energy prices, variable public policy, and rapidly changing energy technology, this risk is knowable to lenders as well as borrowers. It lacks the asymmetry described above and thus is likely to be matched by higher rates rather than by rationing.

However, many energy-saving investments in significant total amounts are made by small business and household units, which are subject to serious financial asymmetries and penalties or barriers. Transaction costs for long-term debt and equity are higher with smaller scales of borrowing, even in the absence of other imperfections. Per unit fixed costs and risks of new publicly marketed security issues are higher in smaller issues and are prohibitively high for the smallest ones.[14] Not only are flotation costs for new issues high, the costs of maintaining secondary markets in these smaller, unlisted issues are also high, as measured by the width of the bid-ask spreads of broker-dealers.[15] These costs should be reflected in greater required yields by the supplier of

11. Hayne E. Leland and David H. Pyle, "Informational Asymmetries, Financial Structure, and Financial Intermediation," *Journal of Finance,* vol. 32 (May 1977), pp. 371–87.

12. Joseph E. Stiglitz and Andrew Weiss, "Credit Rationing in Markets with Imperfect Information," *American Economic Revew,* vol. 71 (June 1981), pp. 393–410.

13. It is also possible that lenders can monitor borrowers' behavior via contractual restrictions. But design and enforcement of protective convenants is costly and is less applicable to smaller borrowers and in general to longer-term high-leveraged conservation projects.

14. Securities and Exchange Commission data show that the smallest class of issues has flotation costs of over 20 percent of gross proceeds compared with 3 to 4 percent for the largest new issues.

15. Of the stocks traded over the counter, 10 percent had spreads of 25 percent of the stock price. See Hans R. Stoll, "Dealer Inventory Behavior: An Empirical Investigation of NASDAQ Stocks," *Journal of Financial and Quantitative Analysis,* vol. 11 (September 1976), pp. 359–80.

funds. The de facto exclusion of small firms from the public securities markets confines them to local or regional financial intermediaries, which at least in some areas are less competitive and more expensive than those available to nationally diversified borrowers.[16] The smaller investor faces the financial barriers of premium rates at financial intermediaries and exclusion from public capital markets for all investment projects, including energy conservation investment.

The Cost and Availability of Funds

The simplistic hypothesis that credit availability is the principal barrier to energy-saving investment has been fostered by much of the conservationist literature. The more likely barrier to such investment, as I have already stated, is the nature of conservation investment projects—their returns and riskiness, as evaluated by capital budgeting rules. But it is difficult to separate general capital budgeting rules from specific financial constraints. Financial barriers can be offset by appropriate governmental subsidies and tax policies enabling investors to cope with the risks of investment.

Household Funding

One of the few studies to explore objectively the cost and availability of funds for energy-saving investment is by John Tuccillo.[17] Tuccillo examines the effect on various sources of finance and interest rates of mandatory energy standards to be imposed when residential properties are sold or exchanged over 1980–90. The overall financing to be required will be $1 billion a year. He finds moderate effects on interest rates and "very short-run" effects on the availability of the funds. These effects are short-term because total sources of funds are large and varied, credit is fungible, and financial channeling is flexible and responsive. There are varied sources of funding for retrofit projects for all classes of investors—mortgages, home improvement loans, tax credits, and grants. (And I

16. Bernard Shull, *Changes in Commercial Banking Structure and Small Business Lending*, Studies of Small Business Finance (Washington, D.C.: Interagency Task Force on Small Business Finance, 1981), p. 10.

17. "The Impact of Residential Energy Conservation Standards on Credit Markets," prepared for U.S. Department of Housing and Urban Development, no. 1344-04 (Washington, D.C.: Urban Institute, 1980).

would add personal loans and personal savings, which are the principal source of funding for do-it-yourself projects.)[18]

The basic question Tuccillo deals with is "the ability of the available sources to match up to the need of different income groups"; Tuccillo concludes that "there is at least one source tailored to each group of households."[19] The search for such sources may cause some short-run increase in sectoral interest rates. As a result of fund supplies shifting to meet these demands, availability will not be a problem and interest rates will fall back toward original levels, though aggregate levels will not, owing to increased aggregate demand, and some crowding-out will take place.

My surveys of financial sources for energy-saving investment confirm that neither availability nor cost of credit seems to be a major or special financial barrier. The existence of a sophisticated and competitive set of financial markets and financial institutions plus household self-finance and business internal finance assures a responsive pool of funds at competitive rates. Unlike Tuccillo's assumption that the demand for funds is assured by the mandatory standards in place, in the more general and overall case the failure to undertake such projects at predicted or desired levels must generally be attributed to unusual risks or other inhibiting factors.

Small Business Funding

The smaller business seems to face credit-rationing problems, especially during tight monetary periods. Small business finances itself with higher debt-equity ratios than other business, and its debt composition is more heavily weighted with short-term funds.[20] This "risky" capital structure is likely to inhibit term investment projects during a period of tight money, especially when bank term loans are relatively less available. Under these conditions, small business energy-saving investments are likely to be financed via the suppliers of the investment goods, such

18. Neil S. Mayer and John L. Goodman, "Constructing Longitudinal Data Files of Quarterly Residential Alteration and Repair Activity, with Illustrative Computations," prepared for U.S. Department of Housing and Urban Development, no. 1131-2 (Washington, D.C.: Urban Institute, 1979).

19. Tuccillo, "Impact of Residential Energy Conservation Standards," pp. 31, 46.

20. Victor L. Andrews and Peter C. Eisemann, "Who Finances Small Business Circa 1980," *Studies of Small Business Finance,* prepared by the Interagency Task Force on Small Business Finance (The Task Force, November 1981).

as trade credit, equipment leases, installment sales contracts, and captive sales finance companies. Larger businesses often serve as financial intermediaries, financing the smaller businesses. This shifts the external financing problem to larger business, for this era of tight money has also been a period when profitability and internal finance—so important to larger business finance—have been impaired. It therefore seems reasonable that larger business financing of its own energy conservation investment may be inhibited by its assumption of an above-average burden of financing smaller business at a time when internal financing is constrained.

Evidence of a general small business financial gap has been documented, but not for small energy-saving loans in particular. Indeed, the very tight money period of 1979–80 showed interest rates on large loans increasing faster than those on small loans. This is not to say that interest rates are not generally lower as the size of the loan is larger; but to the extent that this is due to lower transaction costs (or perhaps lower risk) per loan dollar, this is not a discriminatory gap.[21] However, in the current deregulated, volatile financial environment, banks make increased use of variable-rate (or shorter-term) loans, increasing both financial risk to the borrower and incentives to lenders to ration credit as the pool of satisfied borrowers becomes increasingly less risk averse or more prone to creative financing.[22]

Large Business Financing

Just as solar water heater sales are more inhibited by an insufficient stream of expected net cash returns when discounted for risk than they are by financial stringencies, so too is business cogeneration investment. Although there are serious organizational inhibitions and more complex financial requirements, the basic drawback to cogeneration projects is not capital shortage but risk and risk-sharing.[23]

This is evident, for example, from the way the fortunes of cogeneration projects fluctuate with cycles and trends in the pricing of fuel (oil or coal)

21. *Federal Reserve Bulletin,* vols. 65 and 66, various issues, table 1.34.

22. Stuart I. Greenbaum, George Kanatas, and Sudhakar D. Deshmukh, "Credit Rationing and Small Business Finance," *Studies of Small Business Finance,* prepared by the Interagency Task Force on Small Business Finance (The Task Force, July 1980).

23. Kidder, Peabody & Co., *Financial Considerations Affecting Implementation of a Large Multiparty Cogeneration Project,* prepared for Gulf States Utilities Company and Oak Ridge National Laboratory, ORNL/SUB-7913521/1 (1979).

and electricity. The weaker the investment flows, the more frequent are the complaints about average costing for electricity, although it is difficult to imagine any near-term change in this regulatory pricing policy.

The gist of the case is that major cogeneration projects generally are not undertaken because business chooses better alternative capital investments. This is not to say that cogeneration technology would not be attractive, given current energy costs and prospects, to initially establish optimal energy facilities. But the situation does not allow starting from scratch, and the path of energy costs over the next decade is far from certain, though they are likely to be higher in real terms at the end of the decade than they are today.

Attempts to explain away the lack of business investment in cogeneration as "benighted" or short-sighted behavior can be conveniently extracted from two *Harvard Business Review* articles that flatly reject the simple likelihood that cogeneration does not yet offer attractive risk-adjusted returns to private investment relative to alternative opportunities.[24] Hatsopoulos and others argue that average costing rather than marginal costing of electricity (or any energy source) makes alternative energy generation projects *seem* unattractive. Were electricity to be generally sold at replacement or avoidable cost rather than at the average of total historical costs (or were the price of oil to rise, say, 50 percent in real terms), cogeneration projects would be correspondingly more attractive. But this is not the same as to argue that in 1978 "many manufacturers set too high a return for these investments."[25] This statement presumes that the capital budgeting (NPV) method or its application in business is faulty. But neither the method nor its application make cogeneration (or other alternative energy sources) seem unattractive as business projects; they *are* unattractive, given current energy cost structures, the additional risks of complex contractual provisions, and the increasingly uncertain level toward which energy prices must rise (as is the time path toward any higher level). It is futile to speak of the "low risk of energy conservation projects" under these circumstances.[26]

24. G. N. Hatsopoulos and others, "Capital Investment to Save Energy," *Harvard Business Review,* vol. 56 (March–April 1978), pp. 111–22; and Robert H. Hayes and David A. Garvin, "Managing as if Tomorrow Mattered," *Harvard Business Review,* vol. 60 (May–June 1982), pp. 71–79.

25. Hatsopoulos and others, "Capital Investment," p. 111.

26. However, one could explore the net social benefits of such projects—that is,

Hayes and Garvin attack the NPV method for the current "decreased (private) willingness to invest" in new projects. The authors argue that along with increased use of NPV capital budgeting procedures, there has been a decreased growth of capital investment and research and development spending, and they state, "We believe this to be more than a simple coincidence."[27] A better example of attacking the messenger (or the medium) for bringing the bad news could hardly be imagined. The authors do not consider the possibility that the problem might be the obvious increased risk in the economy (energy prices) and financial markets (inflation and interest rates) and the consequentially increased rates at which new investment projects are discounted. Instead they call for managers to lower hurdle rates to match the declining profitability of company assets. They do not ask whether managers should, in the interests of owners, invest in other companies whose risk-weighted rate of return has not deteriorated, and do not see the advantage to the firm of postponing investments in view of current uncertainties. Rejecting the NPV approach, they conclude by terming capital investment "an act of faith."

Coping with Financial Barriers

The principal barriers to conservation investment are the risk-return structure of such investment in particular and the basic cost of funds for any or all investment. If it is public policy to reduce such real barriers, effective measures must focus on lowering the cost of finance or offsetting the risks of such investment via subsidy or tax programs. To deny or neglect unattractive risk-return ratios or to claim fund unavailability will not stimulate private investment in such activities. Our experience demonstrates that not too much should be expected even of direct tax or subsidy programs.

---

subsidies in the form of tax credits to raise private returns or sponsored financing to selectively lower the private costs of funds in order to induce the private sector to undertake such projects. Here the issues are the relative advantages of subsidies versus taxes and the relative benefits or costs of allowing uninhibited energy price rises to speed energy-saving behavior and the gradual closure of the marginal or average costing gap. The overall advantage of the price-increasing (tax or tariff) approach over the selective subsidy route is a matter of public policy rather than microeconomics.

27. Hayes and Garvin, "Managing as if Tomorrow Mattered," p. 71.

The Organizational Approach

To improve the delivery system rather than to kill the messenger is the more reasonable and workable approach taken by Roger Sant.[28] By concentrating on businesses already tied in to the energy delivery system—electric utilities, energy equipment makers, and energy services companies—Sant is able to show that marshaling lower hurdle rates, subsidized trade credit, and tax credit swapping will stimulate investment in conservation. This approach does not require artificially heightened returns or lowered risks or costs of finance. It simply allows utility-bound businesses whose basic investment opportunities are restricted to low "average" returns by regulation to choose alternative investments, which, though subsidized, yield greater returns than investments to increase energy supply capacity. These returns, although greater than utility-constrained returns, are *not* greater than the average return to nonregulated enterprise. To induce the latter to invest in large cogeneration investment projects requires that the hurdle rate be lowered by tax credit subsidies and risk reduction arrangements, such as those arranged by energy service companies. These financial and technical intermediary steps serve not to supply funds, but to share the cost of funds or the risks of future savings, thus helping energy-saving projects to pass the traditional capital budgeting tests. Here the potential drawback is that the public benefit from the subsidy may not be large enough to merit the public cost.

This organizational approach to overcoming the barriers to energy conservation investment seems workable; it neutralizes or offsets existing utility rigidities and imperfections instead of railing at them or wishing them away. Furthermore, it accepts the market return tests of investments by the nonutility sector instead of calling for faith, hope, or charity. The objective is the delivery of the *services* of energy at least cost rather than simply least-cost electric current or fuel.

It turns out that an organizational approach to institutional barriers also yields useful insights into the ways to get around those barriers. For example, the commercial bank may be ill structured to handle energy conservation projects; one can not usually phone the bank's loan officer in charge of energy-saving loans as one can the officer for energy supply

28. Roger Sant, "Coming Markets for Energy Services," *Harvard Business Review*, vol. 58 (May–June 1980), pp. 6–24.

loans. But banks are major financiers of energy services companies, energy equipment manufacturers, and utility firms.

At first glance or first survey, it seems that banks are not heavily involved in the energy-saving financing business. In-depth study indicates they are indeed involved, but largely indirectly, by various utility service company intermediaries the banks are financing. For example, as our surveys reveal, electric utilities financing residential retrofit at subsidized rates often borrow from the banks at commercial rates and pay the difference to the bank. Moreover, bank or holding company leasing affiliates finance major energy-saving equipment sales. Finally, energy service companies who "rent" energy services, while financing and assuming much of the risk of industrial energy-saving investment, are in turn financed by standard commercial bank loans. Similarly, the traditional long-term business financing institutions such as investment bankers and insurance companies have entered into consortia involved in the issue of industrial development bonds or the private placement of multicompany debt as parts of packages financing major cogeneration projects.

Tax Credits

The available data are too aggregated for direct tests of the effect of the tax credit for specific energy conservation investments. But it has been shown by regression models that three-fourths of household retrofit investment for 1978–80 was explained by claimants' income level, fuel bills, and climatic factors. Thus the maximum effect of *all* nonmarket factors, including the tax credit, could total 25 percent.[29] Other studies by the Department of Energy estimate that federal programs and tax credits probably account for "less than 5 percent of the overall increase in energy efficiency per unit of GNP."[30]

A National Science Foundation mail survey suggests that fewer than 8 percent of the 15 million people claiming tax credits would "definitely

29. Eric Hirst and others, *Household Retrofit Expenditures and the Federal Residential Energy Conservation Tax Credit,* ORNL/CON-95 (Oak Ridge, Tenn.: Oak Ridge National Laboratory, 1982); and James L. Sweeney, "The Response of Energy Demand to Higher Prices: What Have We Learned?" *American Economic Review,* vol. 74 (May 1984), p. 35.

30. Eric Hirst and others, "Recent Changes in U.S. Energy Consumption: What Happened and Why," *Annual Review of Energy,* vol. 8 (1983), p. 202.

or probably" *not* have invested without the tax credit.[31] The three-year cost of tax credits was $1.3 billion on $9.5 billion investment. Thus $0.76 billion in investments was almost surely stimulated; but the cost in lost tax revenue was $1.3 billion. Thus the bulk of the tax credits were likely windfalls rather than incentives. For the most needy (financially and in terms of need for retrofitting), tax credits are neither incentives nor windfalls. A recent review article summarized its principal conclusion in the title: *Studies on the Effectiveness of Energy Tax Incentives Are Inconclusive*.[32]

For emerging technologies rather than such well-established technologies as insulating, the tax incentive may be stronger; it is more likely to be business than household investment, and expected returns after tax have to be attractive to offset the extra risks involved.[33]

Subsidized or Zero-Interest Rates

There are no definitive studies of the net effectiveness of subsidized consumer loans to stimulate conservation investment. It is clear that high-income groups take advantage of low or zero-interest rates, but it is not known whether the energy price effects alone would induce conservation investment by this group.[34] For lower-income groups, the great opportunity cost of any increased current outlay, combined with ignorance or uncertainty as to lower future utility bills, limits their responsiveness. In any case, the poor are predominantly renters, or, if they are owners, have even more important housing expenditures awaiting finance.[35]

The case for concentrating conservation subsidies on low-income groups is heightened under current conditions of lessening need for additional utility capacity, especially in those areas with high marginal

31. Hirst and others, *Household Retrofit Expenditures,* p. 36.

32. General Accounting Office, 1982.

33. S. P. A. Brown and G. Anandalingam, "Economic Analysis of the Tax-Credit Incentives for Business Investment in Energy Conservation and Production," Brookhaven National Laboratory, BNL-51526, prepared for U.S. Department of Energy (December 1981).

34. Peter Lazare, "A Case Study in Utility Financing for Residential Conservation Measures," *Public Utilities Fortnightly,* June 4, 1981, p. 30.

35. John E. Bryson and Jon F. Elliott, "California's Best Energy-Supply Investment: Interest-Free Loans for Conservation," *Public Utilities Fortnightly,* November 5, 1981, pp. 22–23.

costs of additional capacity.[36] These costs are avoided as the high price elasticity for energy curtails the demand for energy without subsidy.

The conditions that made this subsidy so attractive—the average cost of electricity (and its price) greatly exceeded the marginal cost of increased supply—have been dissipated by the relative rise of utility prices vis-à-vis fuel prices and the consequent fall in both the avoidable cost and the need for new capacity. Not only is the gap between average cost (utility prices) and marginal costs (costs of additional energy) narrowing, but the relevant prices and costs are volatile. The volatility that unfavorably affects the demand for investment in conservation does the same for the demand for investment to increase energy supply.

Aggregate Evidence

Recent studies of energy consumption comparing 1950–73 with 1973–81 provide strong evidence that neither financial institutional barriers nor financial uncertainties are required to explain much of the remarkable change to more efficient energy use by consumers or businesses since 1973. Models applied to recent change reveal the major factors determining energy use. Hirst and others show that U.S. energy use at 74 quadrillion Btus (quads) in 1981 was twenty-eight quads below what the pre-1974 model would have predicted.[37] Of the twenty-eight quads, twelve were due to slower growth, but that leaves sixteen quads to be explained by factors that increased efficiency in energy use. Of these sixteen, eleven quads were due to higher fuel prices, leaving only five quads to nonmarket forces.

This residual suggests that all nonmarket factors—including all public or private conservation policies, information lacks, high financial costs, inertia, and institutional rigidities—explain only 31 percent of energy conservation. A similarly developed analysis by the Department of Energy found that for 1981 less than 5 percent of total energy conservation (0.85 quads) was attributable to federal programs and tax credits.[38]

36. Charles J. Cicchetti and Rod Shaughnessy, "Is There a Free Lunch in the Northwest? (Utility-sponsored Conservation Programs)," *Public Utilities Fortnightly*, December 18, 1980, pp. 11–15.

37. Hirst and others, "Recent Changes in U.S. Energy Consumption," pp. 199–200. Indeed, 1981 total energy use was slightly lower than it was in 1973, and per unit of GNP it was 18 percent lower. The question is what were the principal causes of this sharp increase in the efficiency of energy use.

38. U.S. Department of Energy, Office of Policy, Planning and Analysis, *Sunset Review*, vol. 2; *Program-by-Program Analysis*, DOE/PE-0040 (DOE, 1982), p. 185.

William Hogan's model of energy demand with and without the energy shocks finds the same effect of slower growth but a 50 percent higher price effect, leaving little influence attributable to any other factors (see his essay in this volume). (Of course this estimate includes only the direct effects of the program and does not include all programs. On the other hand, there is evidence that some of the effects of these programs stemmed from energy price increases.)[39]

Total conservation gains are likely to be sustained even if energy prices cease rising through replacement demand for cars, housing, and machinery with greater energy efficiency. For example, in 1981 not only did U.S. total energy use decline but "the effect of new car fuel economy improvements exceeded the effect of reduced travel."[40] Note that not only is the price effect on energy use the single most important determinant, but also that the adjustment is protracted. Hogan forecasts "the same proportional improvement in energy efficiency" by the end of the century even if energy prices are constant at the 1982 level.[41] (Furthermore, there is a very long-run adjustment factor of radical technological change in response to high, though not rising, energy prices.)

In sum, when one seeks to isolate and measure the major factors that explain recent off-trend energy uses in 1973–81 as compared with 1950–73, there seems to be little place for direct financial barriers (or their lifting) to play a major role.

Survey Methodology

An analysis and review of the literature suggests that unavailability of funds or discrimination in fund allocation are not the key financial barriers to investment in energy conservation. If this is so, what or where are the financial barriers? Because appropriately classified financial data were not available, surveys of financial institutions and intermediaries were carried out to elicit information about the barriers.[42]

39. David L. Greene and others, *Estimating the Total Impact on Energy Consumption of Department of Energy Conservation Programs,* ORNL-5925 (Oak Ridge, Tenn.: Oak Ridge National Laboratory, 1982); and Hirst and others, "Recent Changes in U.S. Energy Consumption," p. 240.

40. Hirst and others, "Recent Changes in U.S. Energy Consumption," p. 242.

41. See also Sweeney, "The Response of Energy Demand to Higher Prices," pp. 31–37. Sweeney expresses Hirst's and Hogan's work in terms of price elasticities.

42. Copies of the questionnaire and a list of those interviewed can be obtained from the author.

Initial Survey Plans

Surveys, unless persistently pressed forward, tend to be unsupportive of the intuitive view that restraint is primarily demand-based rather than supply-based. Our survey got off to a wrong start by following traditional patterns for surveys of financial institutions. The questionnaire was designed primarily with commercial banks in mind since banks are by far this nation's largest suppliers of funds; we expected to modify the questionnaire to suit other traditional lenders after gathering the funding records of banks.

This procedure did not work for what now seem obvious reasons:

1. Bank lending is organized primarily geographically or by standard industrial classification (SIC). When one asks for the "energy conservation" loan officer, either the answer is (with a few exceptions) that there is none or the interviewer is referred to the department for loans for increasing the energy supply (such as oil or coal).

2. Energy conservation loans are buried in the home improvement or housing loans area and in the business (equipment) term loan section, as well as in many other areas. Thus data are not readily available through any survey that is less than a complete audit of bank loan and investment portfolios.

Redesigning the Survey

Following this initial experience, the questionnaire was redesigned and redistributed to four industry groupings: (1) banks; (2) leasing companies, finance companies, and factor or trade credit companies; (3) utilities, equipment manufacturers, and energy service companies; and (4) investment banks, insurance companies, and venture capital companies. This procedure led to the principal patterns of energy-saving investment financing; but it also led right back to the banks. For example, leasing companies are often part of a bank holding company; energy services are heavily financed by banks; and utilities handle loans to their customers via their bank.

Thus it turns out that banks are probably a principal financier of energy conservation investment, as they are of business and households in general. But much of it is "intermediated" finance and the banks' lending for conservation purposes is hidden within the traditional bank organization. Quantification of these impressions, however, requires a major survey of the whole range of lending by banks and their subsidiaries.

The other principal source of finance for energy conservation investment, like all household and business investment, is equity finance, primarily internally generated funds. Again, except for new corporate equity issues where the prospectus (or debt indenture) for innovative issues specifies the use of funds, the use of equity funds is not publicly reported. A principal source of funds for equipment manufacturers and utilities is retained earnings. This internal equity funding is also a major source of financing for households: equipment down payments (or 100 percent cash purchases) do constitute equity funding—but again, not recorded as used for energy-saving investment expenditures. Similarly, much consumer spending for insulation and its installation is hidden in credit card purchases at home improvement centers or lumber yards and in unpaid do-it-yourself labor. It may prove easier to measure household retrofit activities on the "real" rather than the financial side, that is, total outputs by industry of the relevant materials and equipment less those going into new construction, compared with the pre-1977 patterns of new and old installations.

In any case, our questionnaires and surveying techniques had to be geared to overcome the fact that the two principal sources of finance of conservation investment—bank loans and equity finance—are not directly accessible.

A Few Provisos

Before investigating the evolution and recent record of energy-saving investment financing, several important provisos were discussed with the research assistants and interviewers and are implicit in the questionnaires that were used as guides in meetings with financial managers.

1. The financial and economic environment that has accompanied the energy revolution has not been conducive to investment in general. It is important to distinguish between general investment restraints and particular restraints on investment in energy-saving projects. Stagflation, with both high real interest rates and low real profit rates and hence relatively low internal financing, is a poor investment climate. It is important to identify the special conditions that make energy-saving investment either more or less depressed than average investment. The demand side is probably favored, for innovative cost-saving investments

are less penalized by recession than are mainstream investments aimed at sales or revenue increases.[43] On the funds supply side, the novelty of conservation projects adds to perceived risk on the part of the financial institution.

2. The financial environment has also become both more volatile and more innovative as a result of the combined effects of deregulation, technological developments, and unpredictable rates of inflation. The development of new financial instruments, markets, and institutions should help in financing innovative projects. However, the shift of interest rate term risk from lenders to borrowers has the opposite effect on the borrower side.

3. The task of surveying the barriers to financing conservation is much more difficult for the major traditional financial institutions because, as discussed above, they are not structured so as to reveal the extent of their energy-saving activities. Moreover, banks are increasingly engaged in financing various smaller specialized institutions, who in turn use the funds to finance energy-saving projects. Our survey information and knowledge of financial institutions' structure supports the impression that banks are far more active and important in financing energy saving than the conservation literature suggests. This impression is reinforced by the fact that as the principal financier of small business via revolving credit lines, banks would automatically become the financier of their energy-saving projects as well. Again, the loans would not be categorized as such.

4. Further, institutional surveys tend to neglect the primary significance in the United States of *internal* financing of all investment, and especially of energy-saving investment. Some 55 to 65 percent of industrial investment is financed internally, as is 30 to 35 percent of utility investment and 25 to 35 percent of household investment in durables when down payments and do-it-yourself labor are counted as equity.[44] Once again, specific data on the proportion of energy-saving investment financed internally are not available.[45]

43. From the consumer perspective, however, it is likely that recession and increased financial risk favor lowered consumption rather than increased investment; that is, consumers may opt to conserve energy by reducing consumption of heat rather than by investing to produce heat more efficiently. In either case, consumers' sensitivity to energy costs is demonstrated, as is their economic behavior in response to price signals.

44. Arnold W. Sametz, "Business Investment Demand," in Murray E. Polakoff and others, eds., *Financial Institutions and Markets* (Houghton-Mifflin, 1981), pp. 256–60.

45. For example, Mobil Oil reports that about 5 percent of its total investment ($100

5. The decentralized and diffused funding decisionmaking on both sides of the energy-saving lending contract is quite different from that for the energy supply-increasing business and its financiers. Oil and gas loan officers or investment bankers deal with major oil and gas corporations.

Information on the sources of finance of energy-saving investment is difficult to obtain, for the sources are so scattered: we were concerned with equipment, instrumentation, and small business retrofit, as well as household retrofit, and, in addition, large and small cogeneration projects (business and government) involving a vast variety of financial institutions and instruments.

Thus in our survey we were particularly alert to query the various specialized energy-saving financial institutions about their own sources of finance. More often than not the sources turned out to be banks, investment banks, or internal funds. This evidences the adaptability and flexibility of the financial market structure, even when it seems that the traditional financial institutions are neglecting new investment directions. However, it does require innovative entrepreneurial and managerial activity on the part of new institutions that can serve as integrating units, such as the energy service company, and the development of such innovative financial instruments as the leveraged lease. In short, financial intermediation has changed as radically as financial instrumentation, though less visibly so.

Survey Findings

Our survey was divided into specific questionnaires for several types of financial institutions: commercial banks, investment banks, insurance companies, pension funds, leasing companies, equipment manufacturers, utilities, and energy service companies. In general, the questions dealt with the institutions' organization for energy-saving lending or financing, the availability of credit, their loan or lease characteristics, how they made decisions about pricing and profitability, whether they

million over a five-year period) is specifically cost reducing (primarily energy saving), as distinguished from maintenance or expansion investment. Such investment is internally financed since it involves new parts, such as furnaces, in old refineries. It is unlikely that this $20 million a year is included in estimates of total energy-saving investment.

engaged in indirect or joint financing, what the barriers were to energy-saving investment, and what their future plans were in this area.

Commercial Banks

Difficulties in locating the appropriate bank department or official to interview taught our surveyors quickly that banks are not geared toward new-purpose financing except on a custom basis. They are structured to lend to new borrowers in old lines of activity and to make new-purpose loans to old borrowers or depositors. Banks have not been reorganized to promote or facilitate massive new-purpose lending to new customers; rather all the old categories have been stretched to accommodate the new types of loans. Personal loans, commercial and industrial loans, and mortgage loans are being made to finance energy-saving investments; but, with exceptions, the impetus comes from the demand side. Creditworthiness, not purpose, is stressed; and when a need for technical information and financial counseling has arisen, a variety of special-purpose independent financial institutions have been created (such as energy service companies and leasing companies), or nonfinancial institutions, including utilities and equipment manufacturers, have developed financing arms. In some cases, however, a few banks have hired energy-saving experts, but it has proved difficult to integrate them into the banks' structures.

As indicated, we revised our questionnaire to trace energy-saving loans to (1) the traditional bank loan categories, such as home improvement and construction loan departments; (2) bank financing of traditional business customers who in turn were financing energy-saving customers, such as utilities and equipment makers; and (3) bank financing of new bank subsidiaries, primarily leasing companies or new full-service energy-saving businesses. These bank financial activities add up to much of the energy-saving loans made. But the way in which these financial patterns have developed makes it difficult to describe them qualitatively, much less to quantify them. This is especially true with the vast expansion of credit cards and mechanized consumer deposit banking practices. The vast bulk of household borrowing (if not that of smaller businesses) is in overdraft or revolving credit form, with purpose unspecified and no bank personnel involved at any stage of the transaction, once credit lines have been established. In addition, this new financial technology makes it harder to distinguish between smaller business and household financing.[46]

Among the new specific energy-saving loan practices that we found at New York City banks were: (1) loans made at the behest of an old and important customer such as a utility; (2) FHA-sponsored home improvement loans and second mortgages; (3) loans that fell within established categories, such as equipment loans for new generators, reclassified as "asset-based loans," or construction loans for cogeneration plants, reclassified as "project finance"; and (4) loans stimulated by various tax incentives applicable to all investments, made by bank leasing subsidiaries. In addition, a variety of consortia to finance very large projects, such as combined cogeneration–waste disposal–housing projects, included bank participants through their new cross-departmental units—venture capital subsidiaries or revenue bond underwriting syndicates.

Savings Banks and Savings and Loan Associations

Thrift institutions are in a state of difficult transition that makes them currently unimportant even in the supply of traditional mortgage funds. It may be expected that they will emerge shortly as larger and more sophisticated multipurpose lenders to households and smaller businesses. As the thrifts match their increased sophistication to that of households, they might well become an important locus for energy-saving construction or equipment loans through the use of term loans and lines of credit to business as well as imaginative mortgage financing, including open-end mortgage forms with variable rates and flexible or low-transaction-cost second mortgages.

Investment Banks

In investment banks, as in commercial banks, there is no single department to survey for energy-saving investment activities. If a long-term or permanent financing of a major business or government project is a free-standing project, it can be found in the utility, public finance, or

46. The role of finance companies seems to be relatively unchanged in function and of diminishing significance relative to the banks. Some finance companies continue to make low-end high-interest personal loans and home improvement loans; however, the development of second mortgage lending in some quantity is new. Some commercial finance companies and factors continue to lend on receivables, but with no special discernible implications for energy-saving activities.

corporate finance group. But if an energy-saving investment is simply slated to use part of the funds raised through one of the perennial new corporate debt or equity issues for a long-standing customer, it will not be so easily traceable.

As is true of internal funds, the principal uses of most corporate (investment) finance are not specified in advance, if at all. Underwriters of a new Honeywell bond issue will not classify it, even in part, as energy-saving capital raising. In this sense investment bankers, like commercial bankers, are not structured to afford easy survey of their role in financing energy-saving investment.

However, when a corporate or local government's new issue involves multiple sponsors or is classified as "project finance," the energy-saving aspects are highlighted and detailed indentures are available.[47] Several large investment firms have been involved in major cogeneration or low hydroelectric or nuclear transactions involving utilities, companies using industrial power, municipal governments, and a managerial-equity group. Such public issues, requiring complex orchestration, are precisely what investment bankers and syndicate leaders are equipped to accomplish. One major $89 million transaction required contracts for the purchase and sale of electricity and steam by an electric utility and a paper company to a housing project; provision of disposal services by the utility to the project; and financing by an issue of $58 million in solid waste disposal revenue bonds, $8 million in HUD funds, and $23 million in new equity funds. Note the complex arrangements and business risks involved in contracting future energy or steam prices and dealing with regulatory bodies, as well as the implicit technological risks and the financial risks involved in multiple sourcing.

Investment bankers are in constant contact with their customers, providing counsel or offering suggestions. One large firm has an "alternative energy group" that seeks out new connections proferring novel leasing arrangements or packaging limited partnerships to supply the requisite equity base. Several investment bankers have arranged for the financing of hydroelectric projects by private placements with insurance companies for electric utilities.

There is a large role for equity financing in complex cogeneration

47. "Project finance" is large, multipurpose, multifunded financing that is referred to in terms of its purpose rather than its financiers. The project is designed to be freestanding or legally separated from the bank and other financing institutions involved; that is, it is "off-balance sheet."

projects as stand-alone projects, for the risk in such projects is considerably higher than the average utility financing. Industrials have financed one-third of their cogeneration projects from internal funds.

Finally, major investment bankers serve a fairly narrow universe: little financing under $5 million and nothing but the highest-rated customers, who therefore are often capable of financing themselves. Smaller and less highly rated businesses will finance through the commercial banks.

Insurance Companies

Holding the largest portfolio of corporate bonds, insurance companies are important suppliers of funds for major energy-saving projects, especially for complex privately placed issues that require assured future commitments of funds. But the end use of the funds is not the prime concern of the insurance company; such issues tend to be evaluated by objective, comparative, credit-scoring techniques. But, like the banks, insurance companies are shortening their loans and exploring new lending and equity projects. They are negotiating ten- to fifteen-year project financing, cogeneration loans with equity warrants, and flexible-rate intermediate-term utility construction mortgage loans.

At the other extreme, as insurance companies move increasingly into equities, and especially to owning buildings, they become involved in energy-saving activities for their own properties. For example, one company has used an energy management corporation to audit and advise about the energy operations of its buildings. Investment here is internal in source and subject to traditional industrial capital budgeting tests.

Pension Funds

For the most part, pension fund investment policy resembles that of insurance companies. But when the pension fund is that of an energy company and is internally managed, its interest and expertise in selecting energy-saving investments is likely to be heightened. Most pension funds set aside a small portion of their very large funds for venture capital investment; some funds are among the biggest suppliers of leveraged lease debt, which is often part of the financing of large energy-saving projects.

When surveyed, several insurance and pension fund officers reported their difficulty in quantifying loans for energy conservation purposes. One stated:

While we do loan directly to various utilities and participate in project financing which may contain specific components related to energy conservation, the uses of the proceeds from any of our loans are not specifically identified. The proceeds from these loans are often used for more general corporate purposes such as the borrower's overall capital expenditure program or to refinance floating rate bank debt which, in turn, may have been incurred for a variety of purposes. In these cases our lending decision is based on the general credit of the proposed borrower and our assessment of that company's ability to service the loan in accordance with its terms.

The preceding discussion dealt with more traditional financial institutions. There is another group of financing businesses that have a special interest and expertise in energy-saving investment. Their financial operations are usually quite small in contrast to the traditional financial institutions. However, information about energy conservation investment is more readily available for this group.[48]

Lease Arrangements

Lease arrangements have proven particularly adaptable to financing energy-saving investments. Tax aspects and custom-tailored "loan" arrangements explain much of the overall attractiveness of leasing, especially for energy-saving applications where there are various special tax deductions, allowances, and credits. Moreover, leasing, in lieu of borrowing and buying, allows the lessor (owner) to take the deductions (or to split them) while the lessee uses the funds and pays rent as a fixed charge instead of interest. So long as the lessee or funds demander can make less than full use of the tax privileges (such as a utility or small business with lower tax rates than the lessor), both sides can gain by leasing rather than borrowing. (Of course, their mutual gain is at the expense of the government, which presumably allows this only if it increases expansion of investment in desired directions.)

Especially attractive to energy-saving applications are the following aspects of leasing:

48. Useful leads to nontraditional financial sources were found in Martin Klepper, Joseph Sherman, and Megan Carroll, *Innovative Financing for Energy Efficiency Improvements: Phase I Report* (Washington, D.C.: Lane and Edson, 1982).

1. Leases from equipment makers can include obsolescence or maintenance provisions that reduce the technological risk to users.

2. Leases can easily be custom-made, that is, arranged to fit the needs of the lessee—such as an intermediate-term, fixed-rate loan that may be hard to arrange at banks.

3. Furthermore, through leveraged leasing, the lessor can raise funds by borrowing against the leased asset and promised lease payment and by selling equity in the lease payments after debt service.

Leasing arrangements are particularly attractive to new and smaller potential borrowers without established credit lines at a bank. But leasing can be risky to the lessor if provisions protecting against tax-change risk and technological risk are not carefully drawn. If they are, as is usual, the lessee is well informed of those risks. But leases are always riskier than loans that are not made for 100 percent of equipment cost. Unless the leasing company is well diversified, its basic interest-equivalent fees should be higher than the loan interest would be.

Plainly, leasing is attractive to both large companies (for tax reasons) and small ones (for convenience and risk avoidance) in the market for energy-saving assets. Institutions that compete with banks in supplying funds attempt to make it easier to lease rather than to borrow and buy. Banks have found it easier and more effective to add leasing subsidiaries to compete for this business than to alter their lending arrangements, so long as tax-burden swapping is so freely allowed. Investment bankers and insurance companies have also gotten into the burgeoning leasing business; some use leveraged leasing, which involves raising fresh debt and equity funds.

A large diversified lessor with over a half-billion dollars in outstanding leases in turn has a subsidiary that was established to finance energy management systems sold by the parent. Here the leasing technique finances not just the energy-saving equipment but the whole management package; the lease payments are set at less than the energy savings. The parent company itself is financed externally by banks (loans), insurance companies (private placement of debentures), and commercial paper issues, as well as internally through the cash flow from receivables.

The largest tax-oriented leasing company in the United States benefits from its operational parent company's tax status and internal funds, but its primary sources of funds to finance its billions in outstanding leases and total receivables are sales of its own bonds and commercial paper. This giant lessor is interesting for the size and variety of its leasing deals and for the way it operates with the more traditional financial institutions. Like investment bankers, it syndicates very large cogeneration and hydroelectric projects. It works with equipment manufacturers to design, build, maintain, and finance energy-savings projects from start to finish. It is also planning leases with "shared savings" provisions so that the rent payments will be based on a percentage of the expected saving. Here the risk and the returns are being shared, as in some energy service company arrangements.[49]

The leasing company clearly is a new financial institution comparable in size with more traditional giants; for energy-saving investment it is of prime significance, for both equipment purchasers and major energy generation plants.

Equipment Manufacturers

With the relative advantage of leasing equipment over borrowing and buying, some equipment makers, in the old tradition of providing trade credit to customers, will now arrange leases. Of course, they in turn finance themselves through commercial banks or investment banks, as they do when they finance receivables by term borrowing, or through internal funds. But other firms prefer equipment buyers to borrow elsewhere and pay the seller or to arrange leases through a leasing company or bank subsidiary. Manufacturers generally do not choose freely to enter the finance business beyond the normal extension of trade credit; rather, they finance only if financial intermediaries do not. Thus as leasing companies develop and banks get some of the business via financial leasing companies, manufacturers reduce their bank financing.

Public Utilities

Subsidized audits and loans for household energy-saving expenditures are sponsored by public utilities under federal and state laws. These arrangements essentially provide incentives for households to retrofit and reequip residences modestly to conserve energy at the immediate expense of other households: *all* rates rise to pay the subsidy to the retrofitters amounting to the difference between the (lower) average cost of capital that the retrofitter pays (as interest) and the higher avoidable

49. Major pension funds finance the lessor's leveraged lease debt. They have their own energy venture group to take equity positions in leases such as leveraged leases.

marginal cost of capital (bank rate) that the utility is allowed to add to its rate base. In the long run, all ratepayers may benefit more or less by the reduced need to expand utility capacity; but the retrofit subsidy will not be equalized.[50]

The energy service company approach attempts to stimulate similar energy-saving investment by commercial and industrial business, not by subsidizing or lowering financing cost below market rates, but by reducing the investment risks and (like leasing arrangements) by allocating tax privileges to those best able to benefit. But there the cost of reduced risk is in the shared saving forgone beyond the value of the shared risk to the customer.

Public utility energy-saving services, as noted, utilize private financial companies (banks) to finance private contractors to install insulation, weatherization, and heating equipment authorized by law. The utility reimburses the bank for the difference between the subsidized rate and the rate negotiated between the bank and the utility for such guaranteed loans; the subsidy and audit costs plus contractor supervisory costs are added to the rate base in lieu of the expensive new electric capacity that would have to be added if energy use were not so curtailed.

Quite apart from the justice of the subsidy allocation, which in part depends on uncertain needs for and costs of future energy capacity, there is the issue of whether the increased risks the truly subsidized household is taking are worth the near-term utility bill savings. Even at zero interest rates, it is not always wise to borrow funds if the mandatory use of those funds involves uncertain returns *and* if the repayment of the principal adds uncertainties to future cash flow allocations. What is clear is the addition to the national welfare in terms of environment and energy security, but which particular households are net beneficiaries is not clear.

Energy Service Companies

The energy-saving investment promoted by the energy service companies, including a variety of cogeneration projects, can involve larger investment volumes than state- or federally subsidized plans involve. But there is probably a cost, perhaps a large one, to the shared savings

50. Currently, capacity is not a major issue in the Northeast. But in the Northwest and Southwest it is cheaper to invest a dollar in energy saving than in energy increasing.

agreement that is the only unique feature of the energy service company that is not available through one or another of the currently available financial and energy management agencies discussed above.

The guarantee that utility bills will be lower with no investment expenditure by the business, hospital, or office building does not demonstrate that this is the optimal path for the energy user. If the share of savings forgone (return) exceeds the user's costs of alternative handling (such as owning or leasing) of the energy-saving investment, the energy service company arrangement will not be best. Moreover, there are a variety of risks that should be considered: a private guarantee can never be a firm guarantee; assumptions about future technological change, fuel prices, and regulatory or tax practices are necessarily built into the cost of the package; there are serious monitoring costs for both parties to such a package; and there are certain to be inefficient and fly-by-night firms in the business.

But there are also first-rate companies in operation with satisfied customers willing to pay the cost of the management-finance-maintenance package. Such firms benefit from specialized but diversified operations and from financial economies of scale; their customers benefit from early energy-saving installations and from delegating specialized operations to experts while they concentrate on their own basic business operations.

Still it is well to remember from the viewpoint of this essay that it is not *financial* barriers that these companies are noted for overcoming. They finance their operations by leasing equipment, borrowing from banks, and joining in the use of subsidized funds from industrial development revenue bonds (through investment bankers), government agencies, and internal sources, such as parent companies.

Conclusions

Analysis of financial barriers to conservation investment seems in many respects to be similar to financial gap analysis of new and small business. The latter literature deals primarily with the monopoly power of lenders, credit rationing, and high unit-transaction costs for loans.

Even large companies when borrowing for new purposes face some of the same barriers listed. But in general the larger borrowers (who of course do not face the financial barriers of the small ones) in practice end up financing the smaller businesses themselves.

Except for higher unit-transaction costs for handling smaller financial packages, the barriers in the case of conservation investment might well be attributed to higher risk.[51] After all, the standard nondiscriminatory reason for higher interest rates (or reduced loan availability) is higher risk; and energy-saving projects are subject to the unusual risks of volatility of oil prices, conservation technology, and government tax and regulatory policy. And, of course, all these barriers or distinguishing characteristics are sharpened during periods of economic stagflation and monetary tightness and turbulence.

In my judgment, the barriers to financing energy investment are not seen as much in the volume of financing available for these purposes (including intermediated funds) as in the costs of those funds. But these costs are probably justified by the greater risks as well as monitoring and transaction expenses that are associated with loan purpose, novelty, and size. This is also to suggest that energy-saving investment is probably not too low by private market tests and that there is little evidence of market failure. This, of course, does not say that by public welfare tests the level is not too low.

I do not claim that the financial system is (or even could be) optimal for coping rapidly with serious structural shocks and the resultant need to finance new energy technology in all-size packages for all sectors of the economy. Just as everyone was pleasantly surprised at the sudden evidence of the energy price responsiveness of households and businesses as they curtailed demands for energy, so they may be surprised at the responsiveness of financial institutions and larger nonfinancial corporations in increasing the supplies of funds for energy-saving investment through new financial techniques and instruments, patterns of financial intermediation, and financial institutions.

But in contrast to data on barrels of oil and kilowatt-hours used, data on diverse forms of real investment in energy saving are difficult to gather together; it is even more difficult to estimate the net flows of funds

51. Small business is also more leveraged and less diversified than large business, so its cost of finance ought to be greater. Andrews and Eisemann, "Who Finances Small Business," tables 3 and 4. However, so too are experienced rates of return higher for small than large business. Richard Zock, "Small Business Access to Capital Markets through Pension Funds," *Studies of Small Business Finance,* prepared by the Interagency Task Force on Small Business (The Task Force, January 1982), p. 17.

into energy-saving investment, much less the channels followed by those funds on their way to the investment. Research into such financial data would seem to be the most-needed next step to advance understanding of the financial barriers to conservation. This would be a major project, involving the actual sources and uses of funds of households, small business, and corporate business and requiring the active cooperation of the Federal Reserve System and other government statistical and research organizations.

Comments by Edward H. Blum

To talk about an obstacle or a resistance or a barrier, you have to have a normative theory that says what you would have expected to see in the absence of any barriers. What is a barrier? How would you recognize it? What are the characteristics of a barrier? How would it show up in data? That definition has eluded people for quite some time. As a result there has been a lot of unfocused talk about removing barriers.

In the absence of theoretical structure, one resorts to anecdotal evidence. But the anecdotes clearly show that there has been removal of what one could say were barriers. For example, lenders who would not take into account the energy-conserving features of a home now are factoring that into their formula that computes how much income a person has to have to take out a mortgage. That is a step forward; that is a removal of a barrier that was there. It is occurring on a transient basis in a segment of the lending industry. There is still a segment of the lending industry that doesn't do that. It is important to take into account that these are institutions that take a long time to adapt.

Corporations definitely segment their investment decisions based on priorities. The budget process is a segmented allocation process in which optimization is done within segments. It can in practice be very difficult to compare investment decisions across segments.

In addition, there are larger costs and benefits outside the very narrow evaluation that is being done, such as whether the company will be in business two years from now. It may be very difficult to put a number on it, but the value of keeping the company in business is obviously extraordinarily high. If you recognize the importance of staying in business, then you would see why an investment that appears to have a lower rate of return now may in fact have a much higher implicit rate of return to the company.

I think it is worth summarizing two types of financing that are potentially important for investments in energy efficiency by households and small businesses. Households basically have three financing choices. They can buy something for cash; they can take out a loan; or they can try to arrange to buy the service benefits rather than the hardware itself. For example, until recently most people have not bought telephones, they have rented them. Today people are buying telephones now that that option has become available. They don't typically rent their furnace or their air conditioner in their houses. That is simply the way it is set up. There is no reason why the furnace or the air conditioner has to be any different than the telephone. Thus there has been the advent of "micro-utilities" that put heating and cooling equipment into a garden apartment development or an aggregation of houses. This is a new form of intermediary or institution growing up in response to a perceived need.

This new business entity reduces a form of financial barrier, whether it is totally financial or partially informational or inertia. It is difficult for an individual to decide to act. But it is easy if someone comes around and offers a yes or no decision. The individual doesn't have to go collect all the information, interview lots of salesmen, try to figure out who would install the equipment, and try to figure out how to pay for it.

Small businesses have essentially those same three financing options, plus the option of vendor financing. They go to somebody who wants to sell them something and say, "You don't have enough of a track record in this equipment for me to be able to project finance this and get a loan for it; if you really want to sell it to me, you are going to have to extend credit for it." The larger company helps finance the smaller company. That is called vendor financing or construction financing. This is fairly common, particularly during downturns in the economy when it is hard to make sales.

Comments by Perry D. Quick

A barrier can be either a shut door or a prohibitive cost. I can't discriminate between them. Nor can a potential investor in energy-saving capital. I could see a survey taker asking a bank loan officer,

"Have you a bias against energy conservation loans?" The loan officer will say, "No." "Well, do you make many of these loans?" He will say, "No." "Why not?" He will say, "We charge a very high price because we don't know or understand how these energy conservation loans work, and therefore not too many people come to us." Is that a barrier of access or a barrier of price? It is a barrier of some kind, and the policy question then is: is that barrier warranted or not?

The two sources of risk that Sametz has pointed out—technology risk and price risk—shouldn't necessarily lead to a big increase in the hurdle rate and therefore less attraction to energy-saving projects relative to other kinds of investment. Future improvements in technology, if they are properly accounted for in the opportunity costs of a new energy-saving investment, would reduce the initial price of that investment and could make it more advantageous to invest today than to wait until the future. The unpredictability of future energy prices, when considered in a portfolio framework, could lead to a reduction in the risk premium rather than an increase, because savings generated by energy conservation are negatively correlated with the return on the market portfolio.

Sametz talks about a strategic bias against conservation investment because it is cost reducing, as opposed to revenue increasing or investing in new products. He suggests that because they lack absolute priority and urgency, cost-saving projects may be bypassed when strategic problems are numerous or large and capital is rationed. Yet the recent press is full of stories about companies favoring cost-saving and efficiency-improving investments over market or product development, especially in a downturn.

Sametz also points out that the high cost of information discourages many potential investors from seeking information on energy conservation projects and that high transaction costs discourage them from going to the markets for financing. Information and transaction costs are a major difficulty for small investors generally, but I don't see these as compelling explanations for low investment in energy conservation relative to alternative investments.

He points to the same thing on the supply side. Financial institutions have a justifiable lender bias against new customers or small customers borrowing for novel purposes. This doesn't seem to me any more compelling than it did when looking at the demand side. Why would new customers or small customers be disproportionately investing in energy-saving conservation?

As to the novelty, Sametz asserts that lenders have a general bias against cost-saving projects, that somehow lenders have an impression that cutting costs won't generate cash flows as certainly as increasing revenues would. If this exists, it is a financial barrier. But I wonder which project a lender would favor given the choice between a cost-saving energy conservation project and a project to develop a new product or enter a new, uncertain market. Obviously, the relative attractiveness depends on the relative risk assessments of the firm and of the lender, and the lender may be more inclined to favor a conservation company trying to cut costs over a firm that is going for broke by entering a new market.

Sametz's survey results show that the number and diversity of mechanisms for energy-saving project finance is very large and broad. I find these results encouraging but not conclusive.

Existence of a set of diverse facilities for financing energy conservation planning should not be equated with broad access. It appears to me that traditional financial institutions have been slow to adapt their organizational structures in order to take advantage of the dramatic shift in investment opportunities brought about by changes in energy prices. Policymakers should be asking why the organizational shifts have not been equally dramatic. The explanations presented so far seem less than adequate.

ROBERT F. HEMPHILL *and* EDWARD A. MYERS

Electric Utility Conservation Programs: Progress and Problems

"SOME PEOPLE call it the 'soft path'—well, I call it soft-headedness!" said Marshall McDonald, president of Florida Power and Light Company, in a keynote speech to the 1979 American Power Conference, an annual gathering in Chicago of nuclear engineers, power plant salesmen, and other utility traditionalists. A mere three years later, Alvin W. Vogtle, then president of the Southern Company, the parent of Alabama Power Company, Mississippi Power and Light Company, Georgia Power Company, and Gulf Power Company, reported to stockholders at his annual meeting: "Our product is *not* really electricity; our product *is*, rather, the *satisfaction* of the energy-using customer."[1] He then went on to detail Southern Company efforts in energy conservation and alternative energy sources, truly a "soft path" approach. He could have noted that Georgia Power has set as an internal corporate goal the reduction of its residential demand growth rate to zero by 1990. The explanation given is clear and unapologetic: while the activities necessary to meet this goal will cost money, they will cost a lot less than the new power plant that would be needed in 1990 if the 3 percent average growth rate of earlier years were to continue. In almost every utility in the nation the advantages of a utility-sponsored conservation program are beginning to be understood and are gaining acceptance as a management priority.

The term *conservation program*, for the purposes of this chapter, needs to be carefully defined, since the popularity of the term *energy conservation* has led it to be applied rather broadly and with less than scientific precision. A utility conservation program is defined as activities that are aimed at all or a major subset of the utility's customers and have

1. Southern Company, *36th Annual Meeting of Stockholders, 1982,* p. 13.

the objective of shaping the pattern of consumption or demand to the utility's ability to supply power with minimal impact on the customers' quality of life. All or most of the costs of these activities are included in the utility's operating costs. Freezing in the dark, rolling blackouts, or other extreme options are not included, but our definition does include:

—Educational activities, including advertising designed to modify customer behavior as to the timing and amount of energy consumption.

—Conservation of energy: actions to reduce energy requirements through hardware and facilities alterations in homes, businesses, and factories and thus reduce consumption, both by active conservation (insulation, storm windows, high-efficiency appliances) and by passive conservation (increasing or decreasing the solar contribution to the facility's energy use).

—Load management: actions to reduce the demand on the utility system, both by eliminating loads that cause demand at peak and by activities that shift a customer's consumption from one time period to another. Peak shifting can result in aggregate consumption that is not one kilowatt-hour less than it would otherwise have been. However, because costs of generation to the utility can vary substantially within a twenty-four-hour period, especially at the margin, during times of lower demand or "off-peak" periods this consumption can be substantially cheaper to serve and often can be sold at a lower price. More important, the shift of on-peak loads to off-peak periods can lead to deferred construction of new power plants.

—Utility activities to improve the efficiency of their own systems: voltage standardization, circuit analysis, street light programs.

We have excluded research and development activities and omitted small or dispersed power generation not owned by the electric utility, such as cogeneration at industrial sites, small hydroelectric facilities, or wind machines. We have focused on electric utilities, since gas utility distribution systems buy their end product from pipelines, rather than manufacturing it themselves with expensive capital facilities.

Early Conservation Programs

Embryonic conservation activities initially were slanted principally toward reducing energy use. They most often took root in vestigial marketing or sales groups where they were nurtured by the few survivors of the headlong retreat from all-electric promotion that had been the posture of most utilities in the early 1970s. Utility managements were seeking demand-side relief from skyrocketing supply-side costs. Customer bills were soaring, reflecting fuel cost escalations and double-digit inflation. Companies that retained their ongoing marketing intelligence systems soon discerned a dramatic change in customer wants and needs. Surveys began to show that voluntary limitation on energy consumption was a practical possibility because customers were now seeking advice about how to hold their electricity bills at acceptable levels.[2] Thus the concept of energy conservation began to shinny up the corporate decision tree.

Almost concurrently, on the power supply side of the utility industry time delays, permit uncertainties, and inflation were driving *economy of scale* out of the generation engineer's lexicon. The wisdom of costly huge plant additions to serve peak loads began to be questioned. Managements directed their system planners to explore alternatives to conventional power plant construction, including new energy technologies, cogeneration, combustion turbines, and demand-side relief through peak load shifting. Load management started its parallel climb into the corporate conservation package.

The determination of final responsibility for all conservation programs still eludes some utilities because of these two such disparate origins. Many utilities met the problem by assigning all consumer conservation and load management opportunities to one department called "conservation" or "energy management" with basic marketing and customer service experience as the principal determinant. Other utilities still allow various departments to become involved in conservation, including system planning, power supply, advanced engineering, fuel supply, and customer service. Industry leaders, however, seem to have a single officer responsible for total conservation results.

As late as 1977, Carter administration witnesses had little factual evidence to offer when testifying in favor of the portion of the proposed National Energy Act that would require utilities to offer conservation audits to their residential customers. There were very few long-time conservation programs around, and those that did exist were still experimental and not at all well known. Since the imposition of the audit

2. Southern California Edison Company, "Evaluation of the Home Energy Analysis Program," *1980 Conservation and Load Management*, vol. 2 (Rosemead, Calif.: SCE, March 1981), p. V-71.

and other federal requirements, there has been a virtual explosion of such programs, but this fact may be one of the best-kept secrets in the entire utility industry. Consider just a few examples:

—The Tennessee Valley Authority (TVA) began its first conservation program in 1976 under the leadership of Chairman Aubrey J. Wagner. Under the subsequent chairmanship of S. David Freeman, these programs were greatly expanded. By the end of 1982 the TVA and its municipal and cooperative power distributors had conducted free energy surveys in the homes of 688,000 customers, 30 percent of all those they serve. Moreover, they have made zero-interest loans to more than 300,000 customers to enable them to take the actions recommended; over the life of the program more than $300 million has been loaned out.[3]

—Southern California Edison Company since 1978 has offered free water heater wrapping and low-flow shower heads to its electric water-heating customers. By the end of 1982 they had insulated 138,000 water heaters and put in 128,000 shower heads.[4] Among over one hundred customized programs, including low- and no-interest loans, is the "buy back" of second refrigerators. When customers donate their second refrigerator to charity, Edison pays the customers $25 and also pays the charity $5 per pickup and $20 for each "frost-free" (and therefore less efficient) unit it destroys. During 1981, 5,600 units were turned in; these had capacity savings for Edison at a cost of only $75–$100 per kilowatt, far less than new plants would cost.

—Houston Lighting and Power Company, serving a million residential customers in the fast-growing Houston area, recently offered residential customers investing up to $1,000 in conservation materials either low-interest loans, subsidized by HL&P through existing commercial banks, or 10 percent cash rebates.

—Carolina Power and Light Company canceled Harris 3 and 4 nuclear generating units and adopted a conservation and load management strategy totaling 1,750 megawatts that replaced the capacity the units would have added. The company stated that this decision reflected the fact that construction of new generating capacity would be prohibitively expensive and that conservation and load management would be more cost effective. Boston Edison Company has adopted a similar policy in the aftermath of the cancellation of Pilgrim 2, as has Public Service

3. Tennessee Valley Authority, "Monthly Report," May 1982; and telephone interview, January 1983.

4. Southern California Edison Company, *Conservation and Load Management: 1982 Program Results* (Rosemead, Calif.: SCE, 1983), pp. 27–28.

Electric and Gas Company of New Jersey following the cancellation of Hope Creek 2.

A recent survey of thirty-nine utilities came up with 105 different conservation, solar energy, and load management programs under way.[5] The variety is fascinating. For example, Duke Power Company discounts its electric rate for customers who buy or build new homes that meet prescribed conservation standards; Pacific Gas and Electric Company awards Blue Chip stamps to salesmen who sell high-efficiency air conditioners; Fire Sands Electric Co-op runs a lottery with cash and valuable items as prizes, open only to those who participate in its water heater cycling program; and Texas Power and Light Company awards its own employees with "points" that can be redeemed for gifts for encouraging their friends and neighbors to purchase energy-efficient appliances. Programs that provide cash rebates or low-interest financing for weatherization abound.

Since 1977 the Electric Power Research Institute (EPRI) has done an annual survey of these programs. Their 1981 survey has some significant data, especially when compared with the 1977 baseline. There were 871 projects under way, divided into four categories: solar end-use (363), communication and load control (210), conservation (207), and thermal energy storage (91). The conservation numbers should not be taken as all-inclusive; as the report notes, "The conservation listings . . . are not necessarily comprehensive. . . [They] do, however, provide a representative indication of utility activity in these areas." Excluding conservation, the growth of projects in one year (1980–81) represents a 42 percent increase, with solar end-use projects alone increasing by 62 percent. In load control, the 1977 EPRI survey reported 251,000 "points" (customer items of energy-using equipment such as air conditioners and water heaters) under control; by 1981 this figure had grown to 892,000, an annual growth rate of 37 percent. Perhaps of equal interest is the distribution of projects. The Northeast and the Southeast each had 18 percent of all reported projects, while the West (including California) had only 16 percent.[6]

In its survey of conservation programs, the EPRI report notes that

5. David R. Chamberlain and William A. Camp, "A Summary of Utility Incentives for Alternative Energy and Energy Conservation Programs," TVA Planning and Communications Office, July 1982.

6. Energy Utilization Systems, *1981 Survey of Utility Load Management, Conservation and Solar End-Use Projects,* vol. 1: *Survey Results,* EPRI EM-2649, prepared for the Electric Power Research Institute (Palo Alto, Calif.: EPRI, 1982), pp. S-5–S-11.

137 large investor-owned and 739 rural cooperative utilities were conducting energy audit or residential conservation service programs. The data are less precise for municipal utilities, but the figure appears to be around 1,200.[7] Overall it probably would be fair to say that more than three-quarters of the nation's households now have a free or very low-cost on-site energy audit of their house available to them. These numbers do not include figures for gas utilities.

Conservation versus Construction

Although utilities may indeed be investing money, time, personnel, and rhetoric in conservation programs, the real measure of commitment is the extent to which these programs are being maximized and whether they are reflected in company load forecasts and system planning as substitutes for new capacity. If, for example, a utility predicting 3 percent growth over the next ten years concludes that this will require 1,000 megawatts of new capacity, it can meet this need with 1,200 to 1,300 megawatts of new construction (allowing for the necessary 20 to 30 percent reserve), or with a conservation and load management program that will lower growth by 500 megawatts combined with a new construction program that is half as large. Are these trade-offs of conservation versus construction being made? This is a difficult question to answer. For the utility planner, it is not easy even to assign trustworthy numbers to each side of the equation. To make accurate predictions is a challenging technical task, and the best estimates of the future tend to be those based on some historical record. Conservation programs simply haven't been around long enough for planners to understand very well how they have worked and thus how they will work in the future.

The anecdotal evidence is abundant; many utilities have assigned a single point of officer responsibility and explicitly undertaken this course of action. As an example, when Southern California Edison Company planners examined price- and program-related energy reductions in their 1982 long-range forecasts, they came up with a projected 2.6 percent ten-year annual compound rate of growth in demand.[8] A conscious

7. Ibid., pp. 3–10.

8. Southern California Edison Company, *System Forecast and Future Generation Resource Program, 1981–2000* (Rosemead, Calif.: SCE, March 1981), as reflected in the SCE summer 1982 systems resource graph supplement.

decision was made by management to control the rate of growth to 2 percent through specific emphasis on additional load management programs. The goal of programmed reduction of 1,500 megawatts by 1992 was included in the system resource plan and assigned to the conservation group. Progress is monitored by senior management on a quarterly basis. Savings of over $1 billion in power plant construction deferred by achievement of the goal will accrue to the company's ratepayers.

To summarize how system planners are incorporating anticipated conservation achievements on a nationwide basis is even more difficult. There is no required reporting procedure nor any national planners' repository for load-forecasting data. To best answer the question would require an exhaustive examination of each company's specific procedures, which has not been attempted. Nor is a survey of vendors very helpful. Unlike contracts for specific plants, conservation equipment is not contracted for years in advance.

Almost every utility now acknowledges that future load growth will be lower than pre-1973 levels, no matter what assumptions are made about economic growth and real price increases. The price of a unit of electricity relative to the market basket of other commodities has changed, and consumers have adjusted their consumption and their attitudes to such change more quickly and more energetically than predicted by most academics, energy professionals, government officials, or any other energy experts (except for "extremists" like Amory Lovins). Even the Edison Electric Institute, ever-bullish on electricity sales predictions, now forecasts a kilowatt-hour growth of 3.5 percent a year, well down from the 6 to 8 percent of previous years.[9] Many utilities now believe growth will be somewhere in the 1 to 2.5 percent range, and could approach zero for some classes of customers. The experience of the early 1980s can hardly be reassuring to those seeking high electricity growth rates, for whatever reason, since electricity sales nationwide have been essentially flat during this period.

Not only are utility estimates of future sales down, orders for new plants are down significantly. No new nuclear plants have been ordered in this country since 1978, and half of those on order at the time have since been canceled or deferred. The situation on coal plants is little different. No new coal boilers were ordered by utilities in 1982. One can argue from this data that, whether sponsored by utilities or not, conser-

9. "34th Annual Electric Utility Industry Forecast," *Electrical World* (September 1983), p. 55.

vation, aided by price elasticity, is substituting for new electric generating plants at quite a remarkable rate.

Problems in Planning

Conservation programs present complicated planning challenges for utilities. Utility planning activities are critically important, since mistakes can have such long-lasting and expensive implications. Planners have an especially hard task in subtracting the potential results of utility-sponsored conservation programs explicitly from long-range system load forecasts. For any utility, the potential and persistence of conservation programs are uncertain, although the data base is growing. The actual amount of conservation that a given program will generate cannot be planned with certainty. The timing of any savings, the costs of the program, and the duration of its effects are not predictable. On the other hand, the same problems exist in predicting new power plant construction: how much will a plant cost, when will it be finished, and how well will it work? In either case, conservation or construction, performance improves when a single corporate officer assumes full responsibility for meeting the objective.

Another more subtle problem is assigning the cause of a given consumer conservation action. Very few utility conservation programs are mandatory in nature, and they generally do not require that participants take actions not in their own interest. Thus, when a homeowner requests an energy audit of his home, the utility provides it, and the homeowner acts on the audit recommendations, is this action prompted by the utility's audit program, or would other motivations, such as a recent increase in the consumer's electricity bill, have had the same result? If the action can be ascribed to the audit, then the utility can legitimately count it as part of the impact it is relying on from its conservation programs to displace new capacity. If the action is a price reaction, then it should be reflected in the load forecast, and, if the estimates of price response are correct, it already has been. The less direct (and generally the less costly) a utility program is (such as television advertising promoting conservation), the more difficult it is to separate price reaction from program impact. This leads to the "free rider" problem. The widespread provision of conservation knowledge by utilities will stimulate both price- and program-related action, and in-depth surveys over time should provide more precise information for utility planners' ability to answer this question in the future. Utility-controlled load-limiting devices do offer improved dependability for planning, but they also restrict customer freedom of action.

A related difficulty in assessing how much capacity replacement value to assign to a potential conservation program is that of predicting customer behavior. One thing that experience with these programs has demonstrated is the unpredictability of customer response. Any utility executive can cite several examples of programs that proved either much more effective, or, perhaps more frequently, much less attractive in action than anticipated. In Pacific Power and Light Company's conservation program in the Pacific Northwest, for example, homeowners were offered zero-interest signature loans to finance attic insulation, and no payments on the loan were required for ten years or until the house was sold. Nevertheless, 13 percent of those customers who asked for and received energy audits did not act on this generous offer.[10] Planners had anticipated that not everyone would be interested in the program, but not that anyone who went through with the audit would then turn down what was essentially "free" insulation. In another instance, the TVA offered free energy audits to residential, commercial, and industrial customers, with zero-interest loans for residential customers but only the most limited financing assistance for the others. This difference in subsidy led planners to expect residential customers to have a higher follow-through rate on recommended conservation actions than commercial and industrial customers. The actual result was a higher incidence of conservation action (75 percent) in the commercial and industrial sector than in the residential conservation program (60 percent), where customers had much more attractive encouragement.

The conclusion to be drawn from the utility experience to date is that to be successful in the conservation business utilities must understand their customers. As pointed out above, at one time almost every utility had a marketing department whose job was to stimulate sales of electricity as a means of holding down rates and improving corporate profitability. Due to the fuel shortages and high construction costs of the 1970s, many such departments had their missions redirected or were abolished. But utilities still do have a customer benefit to sell—conservation, and a mission—load shaping. Marketing expertise is very much needed. A

10. "Northern California Energy Conservation Baseline" (Bellevue, Wash.: GMA Research Corp., 1981).

utility with a conservation program, even a well-funded one, still needs to convince customers to invest some of their own capital, or at least their time, for their own benefit as well as that of the utility. The utilities that have realized the highest levels of conservation have backed up their programs with sophisticated efforts to understand their customers' needs and motivations. As yet few research analysts have supplemented attitude surveys with comprehensive end-use studies necessary to pinpoint cost-beneficial conservation opportunities.

Several trends in customer attitudes have been identified through retroactive surveys of early program participants and ongoing surveys of new participants.[11]

—Personal control and belief in the effectiveness of conservation actions are the most important attitudes in predicting intent to engage in conservation behaviors.

—Given a belief in the effectiveness of their actions, saving money and lowering the electric bill are by far the most important customer motivations to action, with "conserving energy," "improving the comfort of the home," and "increasing the home's value" all rating a good deal lower on the motivation scale.

—Adequate information from word of mouth, utility bill enclosures, or other media is considered necessary to prompt action.

—No-cost or low-cost loan programs, along with the expected monthly savings, are most frequently selected as "very important" in influencing participants to carry out energy survey recommendations, but an income tax credit is rated low in attractiveness.

—Probability of taking actions varies by demographic group (income, household size, length of residence, ownership status) and by appliance type (lights, air conditioning). To maximize program impact, program appeals should be designed to influence specific groups and aimed at particular appliances.

What has been slow to evolve is the resurgence of the marketing techniques once so skillfully applied to sell the all-electric concept. Top management still places heavy reliance on the econometric forecasts of system planners. Even when these forecasts reflect conservation an-

11. See, for example, Southern California Edison Company, *Evaluation of the 1983 Conservation Financing Program* (Rosemead, Calif.: SCE, February 1984), pp. 15, 17; and Marylander Marketing Research, *RCS Follow-up Survey,* no. 096-003, prepared for the Southern California Edison Co. (Encino, Calif.: MMR, July 1982), pp. 2-I-23, 2-I-81.

ticipations, they fail to quantify and direct the utility's conservation activities to the maximum target of opportunity. Most utilities do have a variety of repositories of detailed information about their customers, such as appliance saturation surveys, commercial-industrial audit reports, lifeline certificates of eligibility, and major customer load inventories. Collection of such data and analysis by market researchers promise to provide an end-use data base to guide conservation planners in developing programs that better encourage specific customer classes to exercise options in electric buying decisions.

Motivations for Promoting Conservation

What has caused electric utilities to switch from selling electricity to marketing conservation? Why have utilities undertaken difficult, uncertain, and nontraditional programs that differ so significantly from making and selling power and collecting bills for it? There are a number of reasons, which will be detailed below, but several variations from the generalized norm should first be noted: utilities that generate power as well as distribute power at retail have a very different motivation than those who only retail; and utilities in a low-growth area who have excess capacity look at the world quite differently than those in a high-growth, low-margin situation.

Utility motivations to promote conservation can be broadly organized under three headings: internal motivation (short- and long-term), response to federal stimulus, and state law or regulation. Frequently these overlap and reinforce one another. For any organization operating in a complex, semipublic, semiprivate, regulated environment, it is difficult to separate the underlying reasons for conservation action. Public explanations may be completely misleading.

Short-term internal motivation is most likely the genesis of many conservation programs. The TVA in 1976 found itself generating almost 10 percent of its kilowatt-hours with oil, on peak, compared with its "normal" figure of 0.5 to 1 percent. Since generating power for nine cents per kilowatt-hour and selling it for three cents is not a great idea even for a nonprofit utility, the TVA's first conservation program was economically justified by the need to reduce a costly winter heating peak. A rising level of customers' complaints also helped the agency into the conservation era. A real interest in reducing losses is one reason for starting conservation programs in almost every utility, and increasing pressure from customers and regulators is almost always another. An important outgrowth of such customer and regulatory pressure has been the recognition by utilities that consumers do not buy a quart, bushel, or acre of electricity, but rather the comfort, convenience, and other benefits of electricity-using devices. To the extent that such use can be made more efficient, society as a whole will benefit.

Longer-term internal motivations are more complex, but also justify long-term utility conservation investments. Simply stated, new additions to a utility's generating capability cost significantly more than existing capacity. Thus electricity from these new units costs more to make than electricity generated by the existing plant. A conservation program that will save power in a profile comparable to a new plant at less than the capital costs of that new plant is more cost effective than new construction. All other things being equal, this conservation is a better course of action for the utility than building a new generating plant. An increasing number of utilities have come to rely on this argument for justifying conservation programs. And indeed this general premise seems unarguable. However, there still are many unsolved problems, including the proper allocation of program costs among shareholders and participating and nonparticipating customers.

The federal government has played a role in stimulating conservation programs, although the usefulness of this stimulus is being questioned. The energy act passed in 1978 established a residential conservation service program. This law and its implementing regulations require large electric and gas utilities to offer free or nominal-cost audits to all eligible residential customers and to help these customers have the resulting recommendations (energy conservation and solar measures) installed and financed. The program is administered by state agencies, which must formulate a plan acceptable to federal Department of Energy officials. The law itself is fairly restrictive and specific, and the result is a program that some, including the authors, would argue is insufficiently flexible to accommodate utility differences. Nonetheless, as of September 1982 forty states had submitted plans that were approved or were likely to be approved, and at least 350 utilities are now believed to be running residential conservation service programs.[12] Some of this type

12. Fred Boercker, Luisa F. Menendez, and Lois Frogge, *Basic Considerations for Monitoring and Evaluating the Residential Conservation Service*, ORNL/CON-98 (Oak Ridge, Tenn.: Oak Ridge National Laboratory, 1982), p. 9.

of conservation action would never have been undertaken without this federal requirement, because of the high cost and low savings for each individual home audit.

It can be argued that the federal stimulus of residential conservation has in many cases been only additive to a movement that, for other reasons, was already heading in this direction. As with many federal regulatory programs, the laggards have, in fact, been prodded into grudging compliance, while the front-runners have had to expend time and effort to make changes in existing programs that they would rather not have made. In any event, a similar federal mandate for a commercial and apartment conservation service was promulgated in 1983.

State regulatory efforts, in those cases where public utility commissions have taken an interest in conservation, have been more pervasive and more effective than the federal effort. Public utility commissions have frequently acted on their own initiative; in some cases their efforts have been stimulated by the activity of state legislatures. Florida, Wisconsin, New York, North Carolina, Pennsylvania, Arizona, Kansas, and states in the Pacific Northwest have all had strong state efforts in conservation. Nowhere, however, has the public utility commission taken a more aggressive role than in California.

Aided by (and sometimes in competition with) a powerful California Energy Commission with regulatory authority of its own (appliance efficiency, energy facility siting), the California Public Utilities Commission has pushed hard on conservation, load management, small power production, cogeneration, and rate reform. Programs have been proposed or initiated for almost every class of customer and energy-using function: new and existing residential and commercial construction, street lighting, industrial use, irrigation and pumping, and solar water heating.

A number of factors have combined to produce utility conservation programs of remarkable scope and depth in California: the pro-environment sentiments of a sizable element of the population; the continued likelihood of some load growth, coupled with the inordinate difficulty of new power plant siting in or near California (Kaiparowits and Sun Desert are only two memorable examples); the state policy of continuing reliance on high-cost oil and gas for generation; and the sophistication and receptiveness of the major utilities.

The power of a state commission, of course, is based in part on the intellectual respectability of its arguments, and California has been well served by capable commissioners and highly professional staff. With its ultimate control over rates and rate of return, the California Public Utilities Commission has exercised muscle without hesitation. Examples are its 1979 decision to penalize Pacific Gas and Electric's rate of return for what it judged to be an insufficient effort in promoting cogeneration and a similar penalty to Southern California Edison in 1982. Decisions such as these have had a persistent impact on the future behavior of all utilities subject to the commission's jurisdiction.

It should be noted, however, that the California Public Utilities Commission staff, faced with 1982's year-end decline in oil prices, commented in a general rate case:

> The uncertainty about world oil prices makes cost-effectiveness analysis of conservation programs difficult, if not impossible. . . . Conservation programs are one of the best hedges against increasing energy prices, but, on the other hand, they might result in unneeded investments if [oil] prices decline substantially. . . . It is not the time to follow the [California] Energy Commission's recommendation for much accelerated conservation programs, nor is it a time to reject the progress made so far.[13]

Evaluating Programs

We have attempted to demonstrate that utility conservation programs are now widespread, take many forms, and tend to be justified as a less expensive way to provide energy service. The remainder of this chapter will be devoted to trying to answer three evaluative questions:

1. What has been the actual impact of the programs? Have they fulfilled the cost-benefit expectations of the utility planners?
2. What lessons have been learned about their operation and management? Are there special problems and special solutions?
3. What problems or issues have been unsatisfactorily addressed?

Thorough critical evaluation of the impact of a conservation program is, like the assessment of any social program, a difficult task. The uncertainties of both cause and effect have been discussed above. Other practical difficulties abound. Many programs are barely established. The need to collect data for evaluation is now emerging as an important

13. California Public Utilities Commission, "Prepared Testimony and Qualifications of William R. Ahern on Pacific Gas & Electric's Long-Term Planning," Application 82-12-48 (San Francisco: CPUC, March 1983).

program design factor, but it was not always realized when programs were initiated. For example, during the first several years of the TVA's home insulation program, full information on the physical aspects of each home surveyed was collected and stored, but no demographic information on the homeowner or tenant was gathered. Thus one could tell precisely the average number and size of windows in the homes surveyed, but nothing about the race, age, sex, or income of the residents. Questions about differential program impact or even compliance with Equal Employment Opportunity requirements could not easily be answered. In addition, for several years a number of different conservation programs were managed, all using the same accounting code. Determining what each specific program had actually cost at the end of the year was impossible and thus so was any determination of relative cost-benefit ratios for different programs.

Gathering data on consumption is quite expensive, particularly if it is important to know the time profile of the consumption and thus the savings. A kilowatt-hour saved at the time of peak demand is very valuable; one saved during a period of lowest seasonal and daily demand may even cost the utility money. But most residences have meters that record only monthly consumption; to get daily or hourly consumption and demand requires special meters of significantly higher cost both to purchase and to read.

In order to demonstrate change, good baseline data are essential as a reference. However, background or reference data on customer energy use patterns tend to be lacking, for good reason. Until a few years ago, utilities had no apparent need for a detailed understanding of how and when their residential customers used energy. Load forecasting was simple and reliable, derived from a historically consistent data base. Complicated data collection and manipulation would have been a waste of money. This lack of "history" now makes it difficult to construct good elasticity estimates and thus to separate price-induced from program-related actions.

Many questions remain about the persistence of conservation behavior that only longitudinal data will be able to answer satisfactorily. Do people keep using their wood heaters or do they tire of burned hands, cinders, and chopping and hauling wood and go back to their old heating systems? Only data collected over time will tell, and in most cases there has been insufficient time to make any determinations.

Despite the expense and inconvenience of data gathering, planners certainly need to evaluate their conservation programs. It would be irresponsible to build a power plant, fire it up, and then never check to see what its output was or what it cost to run. Similarly, the costs and results of conservation programs must be regularly evaluated.

Eric Hirst and associates at the Oak Ridge National Laboratory have done a substantial amount of work in this area. A review of thirty-five utility audit programs he and his associates conducted in 1980 revealed that half had received little or no evaluation at all; only a few utilities had conducted formal evaluations with published reports; only three studies measured energy consumption with billing histories; and only two used control groups.[14] An EPRI seminar on evaluation held in February 1982 found a good deal of progress in evaluation work, but a summary of the meeting noted, "Data quality and availability seem to be the primary barriers to improving research results. Data acquisition and manipulation require far more resources than do analytical and modelling activities."[15]

So much for the problems. What is known about the programs' impacts? First, the programs "work," in the rudimentary sense of the word. People who receive utility-sponsored information use it to take conservation actions, and they take more actions than people who do not receive the information. Anywhere between 30 and 77 percent of the recommended actions are carried out, with those that are cheaper and have shorter paybacks dominating.[16] Second, these actions do result in overall average savings. Electric heating customers who participated in seven conservation programs in the Pacific Northwest are estimated to have saved from 1,500 to 7,000 kilowatt-hours a year, the equivalent of 10 to 20 percent of average annual consumption.[17]

It is not clear whether the programs are as cost effective as anticipated. Very few analyses have yet tried to answer this question. Whether customers participate, how this participation changes their energy

14. Eric Hirst, Linda Berry, and Jon Sonderstrom, "Review of Evaluations of Utility Home Energy Audit Programs," *Energy,* vol. 6 (July 1981), p. 624.

15. Linda Berry and Eric Hirst, "Evaluating Utility Residential Energy Conservation Programmes: An Overview of an EPRI Workshop," *Energy Policy,* vol. 11 (March 1983), p. 80.

16. Hirst, Berry, and Sonderstrom, "Review of Evaluations of Utility Home Energy Audit Programs," p. 627.

17. Linda Berry and Kim-Elaine Johnson, "Evaluations of Utility Residential Conservation Programs in the Pacific Northwest: A Critical Review" (Oak Ridge, Tenn.: Oak Ridge National Laboratory, 1982), pp. 9-10.

consumption behavior, the persistence of the change, and even how much of this change can be attributed to a utility conservation program (versus price, weather, change in family size or income, or other confounding effects) can all be measured or inferred reasonably well, if not cheaply. Initial and ongoing program costs can also be determined. But then assessing whether these savings, on a net present-value basis, outweigh the costs depends on a fifteen- to thirty-year projection of such factors as load profiles, future construction costs (interest, labor, and material costs and in-service dates). Small changes in assumptions result in large changes in the answers. During one nine-month period at a major utility the estimated value of the same solar water heater program changed five times, ranging from $2,000 a unit to $800 a unit.[18] And each change in this assessment was the result of wholly reasonable and professional modifications in assumptions and estimating models.

Such analyses, inherently difficult as they are, must still be made. At worst they force the specification of assumptions and allow for sensitivity analyses. At best they can determine program cost limitations and help utility managers better order program priorities. And because a half-"completed" conservation program is still of significant usefulness to those who have participated, unlike a half-built power plant, changes in direction or speed should be expected and planned for by program managers. The question of cost effectiveness must be approached very carefully: all assumptions and methodologies must be laid out, and those using the answers need to realize that things may look quite different a year later.

The principal lesson one can draw from program experience to date is that a conservation program undertaking of any scope is a significant management challenge to a utility and should be regarded as such. First and most important, it requires a fundamental adjustment of attitude on the part of management. These programs cannot be viewed as a sop to the public utilities commission or something the company has to do until things get back to normal. Success requires that the utility's internal structure be sold on the program. Otherwise the resources necessary to the success of the program—quality people, dollars, organizational status, access to top management—will be missing. This attitude change may well be more far-reaching than the shift that occurred when a number of utilities changed from a coal to a nuclear supply strategy.

18. TVA staff estimates.

The normal range of management actions are required for these programs: plans, goals, budgets, objectives, control systems, reports, cost accounting. Some existing internal systems may not fit well with these programs, and modifications will be necessary. For example, costs will be hard to estimate because there is no budget history, and accounting systems may require additional codes for the activities to be tracked. Even small things like suitable uniforms, appropriate vehicles, and data collection forms may have to be designed from scratch or significantly modified.

Conservation programs use relatively little utility capital, but they are labor intensive, especially residential programs. To insulate 1,000 attics the utility must make some 1,500 individual surveys of homes and 1,000 postinstallation inspections. That is a large number of man-hours and a lot of direct contact with customers. Auditors must be selected carefully, trained rigorously, and frequently reminded of the large representational role they play. They may well be the only person from the utility that customers have any extensive personal dealings with during their entire life.

These programs are also an enormous marketing and communications challenge, as noted earlier. If a utility pours enough steel and cement and engineers into a power plant, the plant will eventually get built. If it wants to have its customers insulate 100,000 attics, it needs resources under its control *and* 100,000 positive customer decisions. Without the latter, all the unrealized portion of the former becomes a large cost sink. But these programs also offer enormous marketing and communications opportunities as well. At a time when favorable attitudes toward the local utility are deteriorating because of large percentage rate increases, positive conservation contacts with individual customers go a long way toward reestablishing the image of the utility as a caring, helpful service entity.

As to the problems not yet fully appreciated, it must be noted that "soft path" programs are not immune to the physical problems that can beset any undertaking, such as bad design, shoddy fabrication, or sloppy installation. In fact, since many of these programs start with a limited technical base and a utility staff that has no experience with the programs, problems must be expected. In one utility's solar water heater program, for example, the system being installed had not been cleared for code compliance with the county plumbing code inspector, although both program designers and vendors had assured *themselves* that the system met code requirements. The plumbing code inspector did not agree; it was his judgment that the system's heat exchanger was not "double-walled and externally vented," no matter what everyone else thought. The plumbing inspector won, and the utility replaced 300 heat exchangers at a significant cost in dollars and customer inconvenience.[19]

Since most conservation programs must satisfy code inspectors and rely on installers in commercial business to do the actual work, it is important that standards for performance be set, contractors be trained, and installations be inspected by utility personnel. The failure rate in some residential insulation programs approached 20 percent at the initiation of the program. One out of five jobs done by contractors did not meet utility standards for installation. After four years of program experience, the failure rate was still 20 percent.[20]

Because the utility sponsoring a hardware-related conservation program is relying more on the hardware than on consumer behavioral changes for persistent results, it has a legitimate interest in making sure that the hardware works. This is every bit as important as being certain that a newly installed turbine-generator performs according to the specifications under which it was purchased. Moreover, these inspections are a valuable form of customer service and promote the overall levels of program penetration that the utility is seeking.

In summary, a preliminary evaluation indicates that conservation programs are manageable and flexible vehicles for attaining utility goals. They do require utility executives to have a positive attitude and to understand their unique problems. Once these hurdles have been overcome, the results can be very positive, and the good customer relations alone can make the entire undertaking seem worthwhile.

Unresolved Issues

A change of emphasis such as this in a company's business cannot help but raise issues. There are problems that have arisen in the course of developing and implementing conservation programs for which there are as yet no answers or solutions that all involved parties will support.

It appears that utilities may have become the victims of their own

19. Ibid.

20. Robert C. Steffey, Jr., paper presented to American Council for an Energy-Efficient Economy, Santa Cruz, Calif., August 1982, p. 13.

proud record of reliable service. In the light of utility performance over the years, especially during recent hardship times, most people simply cannot imagine a sustained or chronic energy shortage. An entitlement mentality seems to be developing. An adequate power supply is viewed in much the same way as a supply of clean water and air—as a natural "right."

Thus some customers are beginning to resent the repetitive admonitions to conserve and to resist the exhortations not to enjoy their expensive air conditioners on the hottest days. Also, deep in their corporate hearts, dedicated utility managers really want to serve every load the customers demand. The common ground appears in the growing trend to offer a menu of price and service options, ranging from full service at marginal cost pricing to interruptible off-peak service at minimal cost.

The public perceptions of the need for conservation are volatile at best. Again, a sophisticated tracking and analysis system, coupled with imaginative planning and prompt implementation of innovative programs, appears in the success stories of the industry leaders. During the past decade, as conservation evolved as a way of corporate life, utilities found themselves talking to customers in avuncular and tutorial tones about conservation and load management solutions to the utility's supply problems. With the reemergence of marketing skills, the realization has come that conservation indeed offers good answers to customers' concerns about cost, environmental conscience, and quality of life. But role controversy persists.

There are still significant doubts about what role various actors—utilities, government, customers—should be playing in energy use matters. How far can a utility go (or be pushed) in the conservation area? In light of franchise obligations, can utilities refuse service to new homes not built to energy-efficient standards? Strong theoretical economic arguments exist in favor of efficient new construction, but the political power of home builders has generally kept political units from setting and enforcing tough standards. Utility executives generally agree that such standards are needed (and for new appliances as well), yet they are not comfortable serving as the vehicle for a de facto imposition even though such standards would benefit all utility consumers.

Another role question that seems to be less troublesome than originally thought has to do with the anticompetitive potential of a utility, with its monopoly in a service territory, getting into the conservation business.

During the 1976 congressional debate on the residential conservation service, many legislators expressed significant concern about the fate of small businessmen thrown up against giant utilities. They refused to be placated by Carter administration assurances that no one had yet been able to find any such predatory utility just chomping at the bit to get in there and destroy insulation contractors. In fact, if this conservation business were such a lucrative one, there was nothing in 1976 to prevent a utility from already being in it, as several were. Nonetheless, a number of restrictive provisions were inserted into the National Energy Conservation Policy Act to deal with this imaginary threat.[21] To some extent, this same debate was played out again during the debate in 1980 on the California Public Utilities Commission's proposed solar water heater program. In fact, one result of injecting utilities into the conservation business has been a massive upsurge in small contractors' business. But some contractor groups are still wary and complain about unrealistic standards, unreasonable inspectors, and unnecessary rules.

The arguments about who pays for conservation programs are more difficult to deal with adequately. Virtually every survey of program participants shows that they are richer, better educated, and more likely to be Caucasian than the average customer. Even though a program may clearly be cost-justified for all ratepayers, nonparticipation by a whole subset of ratepayers raises nagging questions that are exacerbated as rates go up. The militants' solution seems to be to eliminate any program with such potential, but this means eliminating any program paid for by all ratepayers but affecting only some. It is almost impossible to conceive of a conservation program that wouldn't leave out *some* small set of customers. One counterargument says that perfection isn't attainable: all existing ratepayers now pay disproportionately for all utility costs, and some are paying for costs for which they will never receive equivalent benefits. But the inequity of current cost structures is hardly a strong argument for more inequity.

A more reasonable approach is to make changes in program design so that all eligible ratepayers will be likely to participate, regardless of social or economic distinctions. Southern California Edison and Pacific Gas and Electric, for example, modified their zero-interest loan program proposals after discovering that low-income customers did not really want loans. Now weatherization grants are available to low-income

21. 47 Fed. Reg. 27753 (1982).

customers. The TVA has utilized a number of different approaches to reach lower-income customers, including an aggressive outreach program for public housing. As a result, for fiscal year 1981 the proportion of low-income customers being served by the TVA program approached their share of the overall population for the first time.[22] But reaching this market segment is extremely difficult on any consistent basis.

An additional unresolved problem is one that has an answer that no one much likes. Suppose that these conservation programs work so well that the load begins to decrease and a utility conserves itself into excess capacity. In such a situation can utilities in good conscience resume load building in addition to load shaping? Will the public understand and support such efforts? Can conservation actually make the rates go up? The answer, unfortunately, can be yes, if there is no customer growth. The reason has to do with the nature of utility economics. A utility must pay its fixed costs (depreciation of plant and equipment, operating and maintenance, taxes and debt service) each year no matter how much or how little power it generates. The less power it generates, then the more each kilowatt-hour must carry of these fixed costs. If a utility has high capital-cost base-load plants, such as environmentally approved coal plants or nuclear units, it can reach the point at which a load that declines means that rates must go up. Something along these lines happened to the water utilities in California during the 1976 drought. Water costs are almost entirely fixed costs: water mains, pumping stations, and treatment plants. As Californians heeded appeals to conserve, fewer gallons were used but costs were not reduced proportionately, and thus rates had to go up to cover costs unaffected by conservation.

While such an outcome is theoretically possible for a utility, it is heavily dependent on the utility's balance between fixed and variable costs. Since most utilities have very large fuel bills—all a variable cost—the likelihood of conservation-related rate increases is fairly low. And ultimately the really hard question must be asked: Should customers avoid conservation actions to keep their *rates* low but their *bills* high, or should they take the certainty of lower bills along with the risk of some eventually higher rates? The answer seems clear.

In one attempt to resolve such conflicts, a major segment of the utility industry has embarked on a national marketing program to reestablish former connections and friendships with customers that appear to have

22. Tennessee Valley Authority, "Preliminary Report, Retroactive Participant Survey" (TVA, 1982), p. 5.

deteriorated during the conservation years. Concluding that many of today's customers are alienated from the industry they once perceived as a given good, influential industry figures vow to reestablish positive public perceptions by publicizing the value of the work electricity performs and the strengths of the companies that provide it. The announced objective is to shape load to the ability of individual companies to supply it and to create a feeling of partnership between utilities and customers. Such a program will undoubtedly attract more participating utilities to the idea of conservation professionalism.

Comments by Patrick J. Scullion

There is a general lack of understanding about the effect and benefits of residential energy conservation programs. The individual utility should do a much better job of communicating the benefits to customers in terms that the customer can understand and evaluate. It shouldn't be too difficult to tell customers that if they now pay six cents for each kilowatt-hour of electricity and two and one-half cents of the six cents is for fuel to generate each kilowatt-hour, then the remainder of the six cents, or three and one-half cents in this example, is for all nonfuel costs such as interest on long-term bonds, property taxes, maintenance costs, wages, costs to replace equipment, and profit to stockholders.

So for every kilowatt-hour of electricity that the customer does not use, that customer can save two and one-half cents because the utility will buy less coal to generate less electricity. But interest on loans, wages, maintenance, and other costs just don't go away, so the utility still needs the three and one-half cents to run its business.

We should have an effective communication program to tell customers that conservation provides a net benefit because the monthly bill will go down. And if the customers heard that conservation was driving rates up, we should have had them prepared to understand that rates might go up to recover the three and one-half cents, but the overall bill would go down—which is what the customers are really interested in. We never had an effective communication program to get that point across.

It is even worse within the individual utility. Not only may there be a lack of support for the person running the conservation program, but there is also a lack of understanding of the utility rate structure. So you may have a lot of key people within a particular utility who actually believe that if customers conserve, their bills go up, which is not the case. Thus programs that require customers to make financial decisions are suffering because we are not effectively communicating the financial results of conservation to customers.

I take great exception to one point made by the authors. I see nothing inconsistent with a utility having both a load-addition goal and a conservation goal. One does not exclude the other. Conservation is a good service for utilities to render to consumers. It is a service that every utility ought to render so that customers can try to control their own energy costs. But that doesn't mean you must also forgo new load additions. So I see nothing inconsistent with marketing new energy-consuming devices or adding new customers while providing advice on conservation. Both are good services to consumers.

I am not in favor of requiring homes to meet some kind of a standard before they can obtain utility service. If people want a glass house, let them build it, as long as they are willing to pay for the energy they use. It is still just a financial decision.

Comments by S. David Freeman

This essay supports the basic objective that we set out to achieve at the TVA, namely, to establish that conservation is another source of supply. Most utility executives today do understand that building more power plants hurts them financially, and there is something close to a rush under way to move toward implementing conservation programs as a source of supply.

But conservation has many of the problems, as well as the virtues, of any source of supply. One of the more difficult problems is to have confidence in being able to achieve given amounts of conservation by a given date. There are also other problems. One is estimating the load factor of conservation measures. We are pretty good at estimating what they do in terms of reducing demand. But insulating an all-electric home reduces a kilowatt load that had a much lower load factor than putting a more efficient motor into a refrigerator that runs all the time. So we are now getting into some of the fine points of treating conservation as a source of supply.

On the other hand, I knew that we had achieved success in making conservation a source of supply at the TVA when we were sitting around talking about it at a staff meeting. The person in charge of power production from our central station power plant made the rather apt observation: "Another thing—that insulation doesn't break down on the coldest day of the year like those power plants do." It made me feel that we finally did have our people thinking of conservation as a source of supply and thinking of all its characteristics.

I believe I can report that with five or six years of determined effort it is possible for a utility organization to educate itself down the line to the point where the people who were the greatest promoters of electricity in the land in the 1930s, 1940s, and 1950s now believe that conservation is their best source of supply and are bragging that we will not need to build any more central station power plants in this century. They understand that the longer we put off starting any more units or even finishing any of them that we have had to mothball, the lower our rates are going to be.

It is very important to look at the long-run marginal cost of new power plants and think of conservation as an option that requires a number of years to build a conservation power plant of a certain size. But you are not going to achieve the equivalent of a 1,000-megawatt power plant through conservation with a program that stops and starts on the basis of your short-term marginal situation. You have to think of having the equivalent of interest during construction as a cost to keep the program on a steady course. It just doesn't make sense to stop building a power plant, which is relatively cheap, in midstream. That part of the rationale of treating conservation as a source of supply has to be understood. It is also difficult to build the equivalent of a power plant with a home insulation program and be sophisticated enough to constantly change that program to incorporate all of the new energy conservation measures that are being developed and discovered.

The last point is the failure rate. It is discouraging but true and very important to recognize that when the TVA's conservation program first started, there was a 40 percent failure rate. Having a postconstruction audit is a key feature of our program, but after about a five-year effort we have succeeded in getting the failure rate down only to 20 percent. That is still a very high rate. But it tells you a lot about why people generally are not investing in conservation—because the people out there doing the work just don't do it very well. The workmanship problem is a very formidable obstacle to overcome.

The major reason utilities should be in the conservation business, in addition to their own economic self-interest and their consumers' interest, is the nation's stake in efficiency. The nation has a real interest in not letting utilities, the most capital-intensive industry in the nation, spend extra billions of dollars on central station plants when those same dollars invested in conservation could have three or four times the impact in terms of reduced demand. This result would sharply lower utilities' capital needs. Therefore, it is important that national policy permit, encourage, and if necessary require utilities to become investors in conservation to the extent that they can possibly do so.

HENRY LEE

Local Energy Conservation Programs

"IT IS CLEAR that local government—not Washington—has the greatest capacity to identify local energy needs and problems. The Federal Government . . . cannot match local government in using the ingenuity of our human resources. . . . The best national energy policy is one designed and implemented in the town hall, the city council chamber or the neighborhood."[1] This statement by Senator Paul E. Tsongas, Democrat of Massachusetts, mirrored a belief held by many people during the late 1970s—that the proper loci for the development and delivery of energy conservation programs were local governments.

Local governments' jurisdiction encompasses the regulation of the construction, location, and use of buildings; the traffic flow on local streets; the size and effectiveness of mass transit systems; and, through the power of taxation and subsidies, the growth and development of the nation's communities. Altering the use of any one of these powers can dramatically change the way a society consumes its energy resources. Yet local governments have rarely been motivated to use these powers to focus on energy problems.

The federal government, on the other hand, has been strongly motivated to address the energy dilemma. In the 1970s, reducing energy consumption became a major federal goal, yet the power to realize this goal often lay elsewhere.

To bridge the gap between federal intent and capacity to deliver, Congress decided in the mid-1970s to establish and nourish a relationship between the federal government and the states. This decision may seem

I would like to thank the many individuals who consented to be interviewed for this project. Thanks should also be given to Bill Hogan, Nancy Naismith, Jeff Harris, Robert Stobaugh, Warren Williams, and Mitch Tyson, who reviewed drafts. I am especially grateful for the work of my research assistants Christopher Gates, William Booth, and Susan Baldwin, who did much of the field work, and to Susan Bender, Janice Quinn, and Joan Schnorf, who helped me edit and prepare the manuscript.

1. *Congressional Record,* daily edition (April 7, 1980), p. S3807.

impractical, since the state governments in many cases had neither the motivation of the federal government nor the capabilities of the local governments.[2] The states, though, had worked with federal energy officials to allocate oil during the 1973–74 crisis, and it seemed reasonable to expand upon this established relationship.

In the mid-1970s energy was perceived as a unique issue to be handled in an exclusively energy-related administrative setting. It was only in the latter part of the decade that people perceived energy as a resource constraint to be addressed within the context of other programs such as housing, economic development, and transportation. If energy was to be integrated into this broader context, then it made sense to rely on the level of government responsible for delivering these other programs—local governments. This realization catalyzed the political process and culminated in the introduction of the Community Energy Act (S. 2576) in 1980.

Support for this act was based on a common perception of the nation's energy vulnerability and needs. Overreliance on oil imports demanded a strong government energy program. Such a program should emphasize decentralized, small-scale energy options, such as conservation and renewable resources. As Amory Lovins has stated,

> While soft technologies give everyone the costs and benefits of the energy system he or she chooses, centralized systems inequitably allocate benefits to suburbanites and social costs to politically weaker rural agrarians. Siting big energy systems pits central authority against local autonomy in an increasingly divisive and wasteful form of centrifugal politics. . . .[3]

Any program that relies on decentralized alternatives has to be delivered through a decentralized system; otherwise, Lovins's vision of allocating the cost and benefits would be unworkable.

In the initial stages of debate on the Community Energy Act, there was general agreement on these points both within the executive branch and in Congress. But contention arose over the quantity of resources to commit and whether to rely exclusively on the states as the decentralized delivery arm or to give some responsibilities to local governments.

The act never passed, and the nation never tested the premise that local governments could effectively deliver a menu of energy programs

2. With the exception of utility regulation, most energy-using functions are under the jurisdiction of local or regional (not state) governments. The remaining functions often involve interstate commerce and thus fall within the domain of the federal government.

3. Amory B. Lovins, *Soft Energy Paths: Toward a Durable Peace* (Harper and Row, 1979), p. 55.

that would materially benefit the country. The reasons for the demise of the legislation were multiple, but most revolved around a dramatic reevaluation of the view that a strong government role is essential.

Throughout the energy debate, there has been disagreement as to whether extensive government involvement is beneficial or desirable.[4] During the Carter administration, as well as during the tenure of Presidents Ford and Nixon, there was a strong belief that national security externalities and the equity impacts of the transition from low to high energy prices necessitated a mobilization of government resources. The Reagan administration chose an alternative course, arguing that government intervention exacerbated rather than solved the energy problem and therefore should be kept to a minimum.

It is likely that this debate over the wisdom of government intervention will ebb and flow as long as the specter of another oil disruption remains. The question of which of these two models of government-market interaction predominates is of significance to any analysis of state and local energy efforts. Strong federal interventionism translates into greater availability of federal resources, creating greater incentives for local programs. The absence of aggressive federal leadership forces local programs to depend entirely upon local dollars and reduces the motivation and urgency to pursue these programs.

The federal energy policy during the first half of the 1980s can be characterized as noninterventionist. Energy programs have been reduced or eliminated at all levels of government. Even in the 1970s, when market interventionism was accepted, federal resources were channeled disproportionately to the states.[5] At no time in the last ten years have local governments received sufficient federal resources to establish a track record. This paper, therefore, focuses primarily on local programs and policies that were self-started. Although these programs are limited in scope and number, there is sufficient evidence to draw preliminary conclusions.

This paper addresses two questions: What specific programs devel-

4. Jack N. Barkenbus, "Federal Energy Policy Paradigms and State Energy Roles," *Public Administration Review,* vol. 42 (September–October 1982), pp. 410–18.

5. During 1976–82 states received $1.67 billion in federal monies for energy programs. Approximately 20 percent of this figure was spent to audit and retrofit school and other local government buildings. Control of the funding decisions remained with the states. During this same period the Department of Energy allocated less than $10 million to local governments through the comprehensive community energy management program and the Urban Consortium Project, while less than $250 million of HUD grant monies was used by local governments for energy-related projects.

oped or implemented by local government over the course of the last decade have been successful, and what guidance for the future can be extracted from these experiences? This assignment is straightforward, but it differs markedly from previous efforts. It does not concern itself with unrealized *potential* benefits. The literature is replete with references to programs that would have been enormously successful if it hadn't been for the existence of "unprogressive utility rate structures," "recalcitrant special interest lobbies," or "ineffective or myopic government policy." Institutional barriers protecting the status quo will exist as long as part of society benefits from the status quo. This does not imply that those barriers will never be removed, but rather that their removal is a difficult and long process.

Looking only at the success or failure of programs over a three- to four-year period, one tends to underestimate their long-term effectiveness. In the same way that the adjustment to higher energy prices may take fifteen to twenty years, so too there is a gradual response to institutional change.

A second limitation relates to the dynamic nature of our society. Programs that were developed in the context of a rapid-growth economy will not demonstrate their effectiveness during an economic recession. For example, a point-of-sale ordinance requiring the insulation of homes before their sale may not be judged effective by any statistical evaluation when housing sales are depressed. Where feasible, I will attempt to take these limitations into consideration.

Determinants of Success

In evaluating local programs, one must first determine what constitutes success. The most straightforward measurement would be "energy saved." How many Btus of energy have locally implemented energy programs actually saved, or, more specifically, how many barrels of oil have these programs saved? The problem with this measurement is that almost no local official would use it as the exclusive or primary criterion for determining a program's success. For local officials, energy has been intertwined with four other considerations: economic development, equity concerns, environmental or consumer goals, and political visibility.

Economic Development

Incremental economic activity and job creation have been touted for many years as benefits derived from energy projects. When arguing for a new nuclear power plant, an oil refinery, or the establishment of a wind farm, proponents go to great lengths to spell out the number of likely new jobs and the thousands of dollars to be funneled into a region. In the late 1970s, these arguments were used to support the involvement of city governments in the promotion of energy efficiency and renewable energy investments. If one examines the arguments for St. Paul's involvement in the construction of a district heating system or the justification used by Lawrence, Massachusetts, for subsidizing its complex to convert solid waste to energy, one is struck by their similarity to those offered on behalf of new hotel complexes or convention centers. All of these projects were supposed to catalyze a greater level of economic activity. This argument was most prevalent in communities that imported a disproportionate share of their energy. If dollars for oil or gas were replaced with dollars for fiberglass or storm windows, less money was said to leave the city.

However, after working through the numbers behind these arguments, one finds that the benefits are usually small. The people employed to build a new energy facility often do not reside in the local community and usually are not plucked from the unemployment rolls. The employment multiplier effect that can be significant for an entire region is usually small for an individual city.[6] For these reasons, most mayors have tended to prefer traditional economic development projects.[7]

It does not really matter whether the economic development argument is valid or invalid for *all* cities. The important point is that many of the cities that embarked on aggressive energy programs during the 1970s used economic development as a major rationale, while a careful review of the numbers finds the rhetoric usually far exceeded the projected benefits.

6. Erik J. Stenehjem and James E. Metzger, *A Framework for Projecting Employment and Population Changes Accompanying Energy Development, Phase I,* ANL 76-31 (Argonne, Ill.: Argonne National Laboratory, 1976).

7. One interesting exception is a program undertaken in Fairfield, California. The city is constructing a cogeneration and wind development to supply low-cost power for a proposed industrial park. This program would serve the same function as any other industrial development subsidy; whether it is more or less cost effective than other subsidies remains to be seen.

Equity Concerns

In cities like Hartford, Boston, and Pittsburgh, the effects of energy price increases on the poor have been a major public concern. The response in these cities has been to integrate energy concerns into existing social programs. For example, Boston established the weatherization improvement program, which provided free energy audits and rebates to subsidize energy improvements for owner-occupants of one- to six-unit properties. This program was funded through the community development block grant (CDBG) program and provided rebates ranging from 20 to 40 percent of the cost of weatherizing a home, depending on the income of the applicant and the extent to which tenant units were involved.[8] Pittsburgh also tapped into the CDBG program, while Hartford attempted to obtain funds from the Comprehensive Employment and Training Act of 1973 (CETA) to develop a program to assist low-income residents in weatherizing their homes.[9]

In examining these programs, one reaches three conclusions. First, most were funded through federal grants—either from the Department of Housing and Urban Development (HUD) or the Department of Energy (DOE). Second, the link between housing, energy, and equity is stronger than the link between energy and economic development. Third, despite this linkage, support for energy equity programs at the local level was weak and became appreciably weaker when energy prices stabilized. A low-income tenant plagued with poor electric wiring, ineffective plumbing, and a leak in the roof did not want to hear that the only improvement for which he could get federal funds was to insulate the attic. Further, as John Alschuler, city manager of Santa Monica, California, has pointed out, energy prices affect people in the most marginal economic conditions more significantly than others. The number of people in a city that fit this definition is too small to develop a broad political consensus—a consensus that would be essential if a major portion of the dwindling pot of federal discretionary money were to be allocated toward these programs.[10] The majority of visible local energy efforts have evolved in

8. Office of Technology Assessment, *Energy Efficiency of Buildings in Cities* (GPO, 1982), pp. 273–75.

9. Interview, Ralph Davis, communications director, City of Hartford, Connecticut, January 11, 1983.

10. John Alschuler, "Organizing Local Management Delivery Systems," speech delivered at Community Energy Management Conference on Innovative Strategies, Baltimore, Md., March 24, 1982.

communities in which equity was not a major factor in determining budgetary priorities.

Environmental and Consumer Goals

The environmental and consumer movements grew up in the 1970s, as did most federal environmental and consumer government agencies and the laws these agencies enforce. The strength of the environmental and consumer movements varies by region, but their strongest presence is in the Far West, especially in California, Colorado, Oregon, and Washington. A preponderance of local energy initiatives was also found in these four states. Energy efficiency investments and renewable options were perceived as alternatives to offset the need for new nuclear- or fossil-fueled capacity.[11]

In many communities, the short-term economic effects were considered important but secondary to the longer-term perception that the world has limits, and that this generation has no right to push other generations up against those limits. These arguments were made as vociferously in support of solar and renewable energy programs as they were in support of conservation.

Consumer protection is not generally perceived as the responsibility of local government. It is thought to be the responsibility of the individual, the private sector, or the federal or state government. Thus the consumer movement has greater influence at higher levels of government than at the local level. However, consumerism has also contributed to the shape and substance of local programs, such as local housing codes. For example, the purpose of the point-of-sale ordinance for the city of Davis, California, was to maintain the quality of housing as well as to save energy.[12] In the same way that one would not allow a house to be sold without satisfactory plumbing, one would not allow one to be sold without proper weatherization. Thus, at least in Davis, the justification for one of its most visible energy programs was to protect the consumer from purchasing what the town considered to be a faulty home.

11. In both Portland and Seattle concern over utility proposals to build additional nuclear capacity triggered the debate that resulted in the adoption of their conservation programs. In California the antinuclear movement was especially widespread and was a major force in shaping the energy debate throughout the state.

12. Interview, Warren Williams, planner, City of Davis, California, August 11, 1982.

Political Visibility

Political officials respond to issues in the forefront of public attention. In communities where there are strong interest groups with a stake in the energy issue, public officials will echo the concerns of these groups. In other communities, a local official's record on the energy issue is not an important consideration. In these communities, voters are more concerned with how their officials handle crime, jobs, solid waste, or housing. But in cities like Davis, Boulder, Portland, Seattle, and Santa Clara, candidates' positions on energy issues affected their ability to get elected. In these communities, candidates who took visible positions on energy issues benefited politically.

Summary

There are two major conclusions to be drawn from this discussion. One is that officials in cities that adopted aggressive energy programs during the last decade measured success with these questions: Did energy programs result in incremental economic activity? Did the welfare of the low-income residents improve? Were environmental and consumer goals realized? Were sufficient political benefits derived? To local officials, these measurements of success were more relevant than the amount of energy saved.

The second conclusion is that each of these four considerations is part of a dynamic environment. The priorities of the public are constantly in flux. Diverse issues are constantly competing with each other for a limited resource pie; thus shifts in priorities have a significant effect on the ability of any single issue to garner a piece of that pie. Energy may have been a major concern in 1977, but in 1984 it was secondary to issues such as unemployment and the cost of housing. Environmental concerns that were focused on pollution of lakes and streams became refocused on the danger of seepage from uncontrolled hazardous waste sites. As public perceptions evolve, both fiscal and political resources are reallocated. (Political resources can be defined as the amounts of attention and time elected officials will pay to one issue versus another.) Politicians take a high risk in allocating a disproportionate amount of their attention to issues that are not high on the public's priority list.

Obviously, the importance of energy differs among communities. Energy prices may be stable in one region but rising in another. Further, the size of the pie and the rate at which it is changing affects the allocation of resources. For example, if one compares Portland, Oregon, with Boston, one finds that until the mid-1980s Portland's fiscal situation was healthy, while Boston's was on the decline. Obviously the fiscal pie that was being sliced in Portland was different from the pie being sliced in Boston. In Boston, the mayor was confronted with serious problems of crime, unemployment, deteriorating neighborhoods, and a nearly bankrupt municipal hospital complex, and he had much less fiscal flexibility than the mayor of Portland. If he had allocated the same portion of resources to energy as his Portland counterpart, he would have paid a significant political price.

It is essential to understand these political dynamics. It is also important to understand that the criteria used by cities to measure a program's success are different from those used by the federal government. With this background, one can look at local energy programs both from the narrow perspective of energy savings and in the broader context of the four considerations discussed above.

Types of Local Programs

Over the last decade, local governments have developed a wide array of energy programs, including amended building and zoning codes, mandatory retrofits, tax incentives, information and education programs, subsidies, projects to produce energy from solid or liquid wastes, and management efforts to improve the efficiency of municipal facilities and vehicles. Any attempt to assess whether these programs saved energy runs into a serious problem since in almost every instance no one has ever evaluated them.

This lack of evaluation is not unique. Governments at all levels rarely take the time to evaluate the effectiveness of their programs. When circumstances or governments change, the old programs are discarded and a new generation sprouts up to take their place. Rarely does anyone invest the money to collect data to determine if the old programs really worked. Evaluations can be expensive. Eric Hirst of the Oak Ridge National Laboratory estimates that it would take fifteen months and $250,000 to evaluate the impact of one conservation program in the

Pacific Northwest.[13] Respectable evaluations are sometimes done for less, but they are the exception rather than the rule.

Evaluations of energy programs are fraught with difficulties. How does one determine whether a government program motivated an individual to insulate his home? Did he do it as a response to the price of energy, or because his neighbor invested in insulation, or because he went to a government-sponsored workshop? The answer to this question probably lies more within the expertise of a psychologist than an energy analyst.

Despite the paucity of data and the difficulties inherent in such evaluations, three types of local energy programs seem to have had some success in reducing energy consumption: energy-efficient building codes, joint programs between communities and local electric utilities, and management of energy consumption in city-owned buildings. Six other types of local government programs have had less tangible energy savings: subsidized financing, supply subsidies, mandatory retrofit ordinances, low-cost or no-cost programs, planning, and transportation.

Energy-Efficient Building Codes

During the latter part of the 1970s, several local governments developed energy-sensitive building codes. With the subsequent implementation by states of mandatory thermal standards (a requirement for the receipt of federal grant funds under the Energy Policy and Conservation Act of 1975), these local programs became less unusual. But at the time of their implementation, such codes were pioneer efforts. In some cases, the municipality remained far more advanced in this area than the state.

Davis, California, was one pioneer city. In 1974 Davis received a grant under the HUD innovative grant program to develop an amended building code that would mandate the construction of more-efficient dwellings and maximize the opportunity for the use of active and passive solar systems. On January 1, 1976, after extensive hearings and debate, stringent energy conservation provisions were added to the local building code. The state of California mandated a code approximately as strict as the Davis code several years later. Not to be upstaged, Davis subse-

13. David L. Greene and others, *Estimating the Total Impact on Energy Consumption of Department of Energy Conservation Programs*, ORNL-5925 (Oak Ridge, Tenn.: Oak Ridge National Laboratory, 1982), p. 3.

quently amended its code to make it substantially tougher than the new state requirements.

The California Energy Commission evaluated the Davis building code by comparing per capita energy consumption in Davis with two similar communities, Woodland and Vacaville, over 1973–78.[14] Both towns came under the state's energy building code in 1977, but Davis's more stringent code was grandfathered by the state. Measuring both natural gas and electricity use on a per capita basis, the data show similar reductions in gas consumption in all three communities but much greater reductions in electricity use in Davis (see figure 1). Further, this reduction occurred despite a greater increase in the number of new electricity consumers in Davis than in the other two communities. Another study found that the residential demand for electricity in Davis over 1976–79 was 15 percent less than would have been expected in the absence of the energy building codes.[15]

These figures are reinforced by a study that demonstrates that 46 percent of the energy savings attributable to the federal energy programs come from the Department of Energy's state energy conservation programs. Two-thirds of these estimated savings can be attributed to thermal building efficiency standards, which are implemented primarily at the local level.[16]

Although few communities have evaluated their program as extensively as Davis, others have made an effort in this direction. Seattle and Boulder have demonstrated incremental energy savings as a result of implementing energy-efficient building codes. Further, after extensive study, the Bonneville Power Administration (BPA) has identified the implementation of local energy building codes as one of its major sources of future energy savings. As a result the BPA has developed an extensive program to support local efforts to adopt and enforce such codes.[17]

Thus, using the restrictive criterion of energy saved, it seems that local building codes have saved energy. Whether they save more energy than alternative programs, such as massive education efforts directed at builders, is for others to decide.

14. City of Davis, *Comparative Natural Gas and Kilowatt Hour Use Per Capita: Davis, Vacaville, Woodland* (Davis, Calif.: City of Davis Planning Department, 1982).

15. Thomas Dietz and Edward Vine, "Energy Impacts of a Municipal Conservation Policy," *Energy*, vol. 7 (September 1982), p. 757.

16. Greene and others, *Estimating the Total Impact*, pp. 12, 16.

17. Interview, Kirk Hall, Bonneville Power Administration, April 3, 1984.

Figure 1. *Annual per Capita Energy Use in Davis, Woodland, and Vacaville, California, 1973–78*[a]

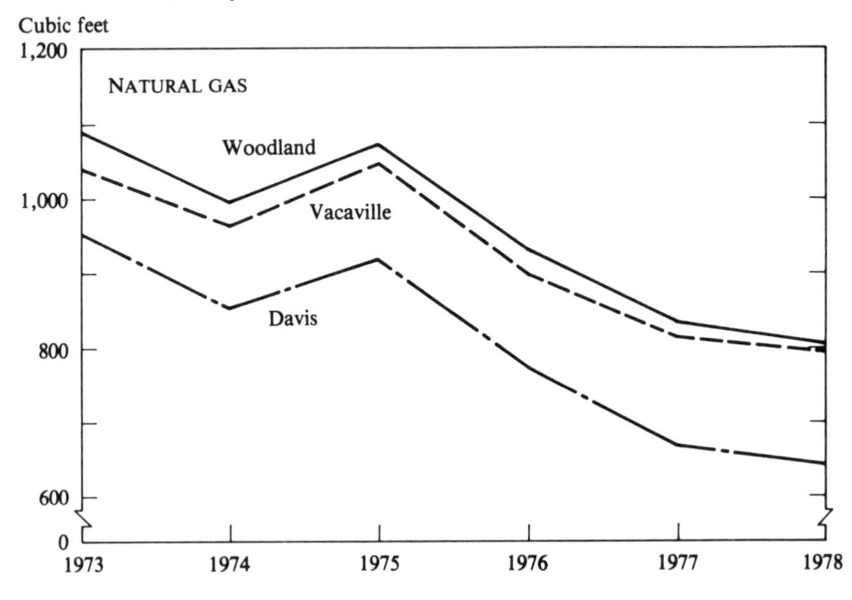

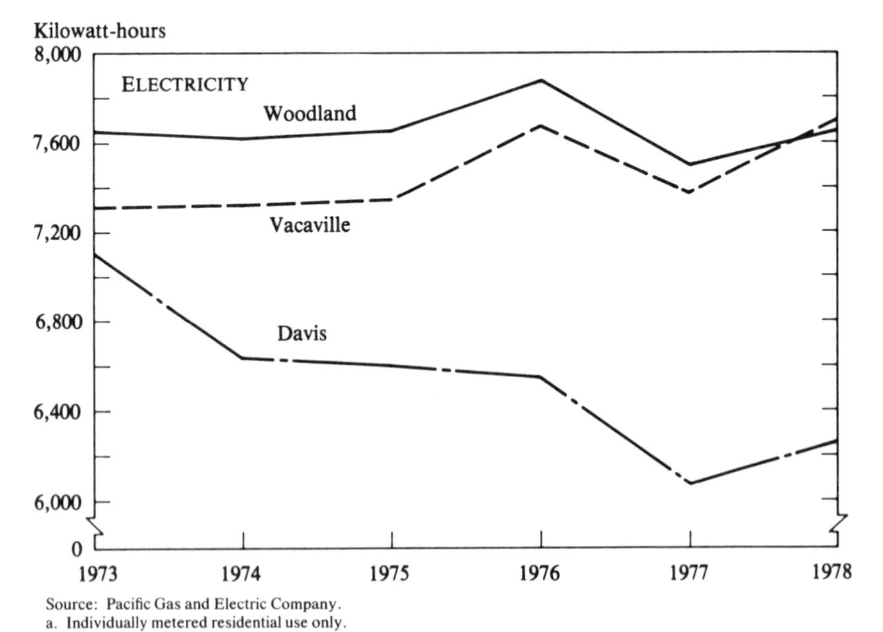

Source: Pacific Gas and Electric Company.
a. Individually metered residential use only.

Joint Programs

Different institutions bring different strengths to bear on issues of public policy. The advantage of combining expertise can be significant. In the energy area, there have been a number of successful projects jointly sponsored and implemented by electric utilities and local governments. Where the local government controls the utility a de facto marriage exists, but even here the relationships between the utility and locally elected officials range from strained to cooperative. Seattle enjoys a good relationship among the mayor, the city council, and the municipal utility, while the relationship between the city of Los Angeles and its municipal utility has historically been more strained.[18]

Where the utility is not part of the local government the linkage between the interest of public officials and that of a private utility company is more tenuous. Local officials are wary about appearing to be too friendly with an electric utility that often is a lightning rod for public discontent. Many electric utility officials would prefer to stay away from the vicissitudes of local politics. Yet in communities where a bridge can be built between complementary interests of the two parties, effective projects have emerged.

For example, Pacific Power and Light Company was a major catalyst behind and a vigorous supporter of the Portland energy program. Ted Davenport, former vice-president of the company, summarizing the company's relationship with the city, stated, "A lot of people who do not trust us trust the city—we needed to buy credibility. On the other hand, a municipality marketing conservation is doomed to failure without the support of the utility."[19] Pacific Power and Light perceived the Portland energy program to be in the long-term interest of the company, while the city recognized the value of having its major utility commit fiscal and staff resources in support of the program. The company's zero-interest loans for electric heat users became a major complement to Portland's loan programs, which serve primarily oil and gas users.

Pacific Gas and Electric Company, serving central and northern

18. Los Angeles developed a comprehensive energy plan but as of spring 1984 many of its provisions had not been implemented. One of the reasons for this lack of approval was a disagreement between the Los Angeles Department of Water and Power and the executive offices, such as the Energy Office, over several of the key provisions. A process was under way to resolve these differences.

19. Interview, Ted Davenport, vice-president, Pacific Power and Light, August 12, 1982.

California, has been worried about its inability to control the growth in peak electricity consumption. To meet this concern, it adopted several programs—two of which directly involved local governments. The first, entitled the cooperative electricity management program, was a competition held over two summers (1980 and 1981) in three California communities: Davis, Chico, and Merced. Pacific Gas and Electric offered each of these communities $10,000 for every 1 percent reduction in electricity use compared with consumption in the summer of 1979. (Figures were adjusted for growth, but not climate.) There was a maximum award of $100,000 per community per year, and Pacific Gas and Electric helped meet some of the program's marketing and operating expenses.[20]

All three communities "won" the full $100,000. In fact, Davis cut its peak consumption 22 percent in the first year.[21] A later study by a group of California analysts determined that 7.5 percent of these savings was directly attributable to the program, with the remaining 14.5 percent attributable to price, weather, and other factors.[22] Spurred by this success, the company initiated this program in other communities.

Pacific Gas and Electric also entered into an arrangement with Contra Costa County (north of San Francisco) to install meters for time-of-day pricing in 100,000 homes.[23] The initiative for the program came from the county, which petitioned both the utility and the California Public Utility Commission to support the program. In the program's first year 1,000 families signed up and experienced savings averaging $20 a month.[24]

Three other impressive examples of local government-utility interaction are programs in Santa Monica, Austin, and the Bonneville Power Administration region. The city of Santa Monica proposed to deliver the federally mandated residential conservation service program as the agent for Southern California Edison. Under this program, local officials would offer an energy audit and simultaneous installation of several low-cost energy efficiency improvements to each household. As with the other examples, this program demonstrated an effort on the part of the utility to use the credibility and knowledge of local government and an

20. City of Davis, *The Davis Energy Book* (Davis, Calif.: March 1982), p. 40.

21. Interview, Warren Williams.

22. Dan Kowalczyk and others, "Evaluation of a Community-Based Electricity Load Management Program," *Energy*, vol. 8 (August 1983), p. 242.

23. Interview, Robert Weisenmiller, Kent Smith, and Roger Ganse, California Energy Commission, August 10, 1982.

24. "Use Time Determines Rates," *County News*, no. 19 (September 5, 1983).

interest by the government to tap into the financial and staff resources of the utility.

In Austin, the city's Energy Management Department is the major implementing agent for the municipal utility's energy conservation program. The utility sought to save 553 megawatts by 1996, and provided funds to the Energy Management Department to implement programs for audits, low-interest loans, dissemination of information on energy efficiency investments, and rebates to purchasers of energy-efficient appliances.[25]

The Bonneville Power Administration, in response to the Pacific Northwest Electric Planning and Conservation Act of 1980, has adopted a policy to treat energy conservation as a power resource: kilowatt-hours of energy savings are credited to utilities on the same cost-effective basis as kilowatt-hours produced by a generating plant.[26] One strategy for acquiring these savings is to seek proposals from potential contractors. Local communities are eligible to bid on all requests for proposals and are actively encouraged to bid on proposals to disseminate information and adopt and enforce building codes.

In a world in which uncertainties reign supreme, the ability of governments to share risk with private-sector concerns becomes increasingly attractive. Cities have always realized that to attract major developments such as hotel complexes they must share some of the financial and political risks with the developer. Both sides recognize their interdependence. As electric utilities make the transition from simple generators of electricity to a broader role as energy service companies, they will need support from local governments, which have decades of experience in providing local services. Community energy programs are by nature decentralized and fragmented, and thus electric utilities will be increasingly interested in local government assistance in delivering and marketing a subset of their programs in much the same way that the federal government purchased such services from the states under the old DOE conservation programs.

Energy Management

As a private company responds to higher input prices by seeking ways to either reduce use of the input or find substitutes for it, so too

25. Interviews, Adolph Stickelbault, director, Energy Management Department, City of Austin, Texas, December 1983 and December 1984.

26. Bonneville Power Administration, *Conservation Source Book*, DOE/B (Department of Energy, January 1983), p. i.

will a local government respond to price signals. Local governments administer buildings, illuminate streets, maintain public safety vehicles, and provide transportation for their employees and in some instances the public at large. All of these functions demand energy as an input. By the mid-1980s energy represented anywhere from 3 to 8 percent of a typical city's total budget.[27] As energy prices rise, local governments are under increasing pressure to find ways to reduce consumption or substitute low-priced energy sources.

The vast majority of local governments have already implemented some form of energy management program aimed at reducing energy consumption in city buildings. Although aggregate statistics on the total amount of energy saved from these programs do not exist, data on the effectiveness of these programs in individual communities indicate that a measurable amount of energy savings is occurring. The success of the one federal program directed at local buildings, the institutional conservation program, reinforces this conclusion. This program provides federal funds to audit and in some instances install energy-conserving equipment and materials. Although the program is delivered by state governments, the primary direct beneficiaries are local communities and school districts. A DOE evaluation of this program estimated that the audit and technical assistance portions of the program saved approximately 10 million barrels of oil annually, and the projected savings from the actual installation of energy efficiency improvements show an average payback period of 4.2 years.[28]

Given the increases in oil prices and more recently in electricity and natural gas prices, the dollar savings achieved by municipal programs are probably less than initially expected. Numerous institutional barriers have limited the ability to realize these savings. First, energy savings demand up-front capital to purchase equipment. Storm windows, insulation, better air conditioning and heating systems, and more effective control equipment all cost money. In most localities, these purchases would fall under the category of "capital improvements" and must compete against other possible investments. Often these other possible uses of capital are more visible and thus more politically rewarding. For example, most mayors would rather spend their two years in office

27. There is no single agreed-upon figure. The 3 to 8 percent range is based on figures used by the Office of Technology Assessment and on figures cited by the local officials interviewed.

28. EG&G Idaho, "Title X Sunset Provisions: Institutional Conservation Programs Division," prepared for the Department of Energy (Idaho Falls: EG&G, 1981), p. 6-6.

building a new park that they will be able to dedicate two weeks before the next election than putting storm windows on all the city buildings. Further, as many cities confront the dilemma of declining revenues and escalating costs, a bond issue could cost a city several times its face value in interest payments over the life of the bond. Many cities are reluctant to seek large amounts of capital for improvement until their credit situation improves. In Buffalo, voters on two occasions rejected bond issues to raise money to retrofit city buildings.[29]

This competition for funds initially takes place within a city agency equivalent to the federal General Services Administration. These agencies were traditionally not preoccupied with energy matters. Moreover, they had developed large constituencies that supported conventional construction programs. Thus energy programs tended to be more vigorously supported when they were placed under the auspices of another agency. Although there were exceptions, the cities with the most effective energy conservation programs established separate capital improvement funds earmarked for energy, to be dispersed by an agency or board other than the local general services agency. For example, in San Francisco and Portland, funds in the capital budget are earmarked for energy investments, and the agency that decides on their allocation is not the same one that decides on other capital improvements.

Most cities that have effectively reduced their energy consumption point to their transportation fleet as a primary success story. Usually the purchase and maintenance of public vehicles is not the responsibility of the same agency that maintains buildings, but rather is handled by a purchasing or administration department traditionally more responsive to the mayor. Further, cars are replaced more frequently than buildings. It is much easier to monitor usage. Therefore, there are far fewer institutional or technical obstacles to establishing an energy efficiency program for fleet vehicles than for buildings.

Most cities now recognize that there is a relationship between energy consumption and budgetary health. As mentioned earlier, some cities have already achieved significant energy savings and this list is growing rapidly. Others are now developing innovative programs, such as using third-party energy service companies to install and operate energy-efficient equipment or providing incentives to their agencies to reduce consumption by allowing them to retain a portion of the money saved.

As cities continue to be confronted with serious financial problems

29. Office of Technology Assessment, *Energy Efficiency,* pp. 265–66.

and increasing energy prices, their focus on internal energy consumption will increase.[30] In 1982 and 1983 the emphasis at the city level visibly shifted from externally oriented energy programs toward internally oriented programs. If the political and fiscal environment prevalent in 1983–84 continues, this trend should accelerate. The rate of acceleration will depend on the outlook for municipal bonds and the cities' willingness to adopt innovative institutional programs.

Subsidized Financing

Several cities, including Baltimore, Boulder, Minneapolis, St. Paul, and Portland, have established subsidized loan programs to finance residential energy retrofits. (Other cities have adopted similar programs through their municipal utility.) The Portland program has a sufficient track record to merit some conclusions, and its effectiveness serves as a barometer for similar programs.

In 1979 Portland passed an ordinance mandating the retrofit of existing buildings by 1984. In order to ensure that this requirement did not cause homeowners financial hardship, the city committed itself to establishing a low-interest loan program to provide funds for retrofits. The loan mechanism eventually agreed upon was a nonprofit corporation that was able to borrow $12 million from local banks to supplement a $3 million urban development action grant from HUD. The corporation offered four categories of loans: 8 percent loans for single-family homeowners, 8 percent loans for multifamily building owners, 4¾ percent loans for low- and moderate-income families (110 percent of median income), and zero-percent loans for one year to fund energy audits for commercial and industrial users. In the first eighteen months of the program, the corporation made 476 loans to single-family homeowners and 15 loans to multifamily dwelling owners. In the six-month period ending June 1982 it had made 120 loans to low- and moderate-income families and approved 277 loans for commercial and industrial audits.[31] With the

30. The Joint Economic Committee of the U.S. Congress reported that in 1982 city revenues were expected to increase by only 1.3 percent—a reduction of 6 percent in real terms from 1981 levels, while expenditures were expected to rise by an average of 7.8 percent. See *Trends in the Fiscal Condition of Cities,* Joint Committee Print, prepared for the Joint Economic Committee, 97 Cong. 2 sess. (GPO, 1982), p. vi.

31. Figures on the loan program are from an interview with Steve Chadima, director, Portland Conservation Corporation, August 12, 1982. In February 1983 the Portland Energy Office reported that 1,175 homes and apartment units had received loans, as had 361 commercial establishments.

exception of the commercial audit loans, these figures are not impressive. Portland has approximately 165,000 residential units and its populace is well informed on energy issues, yet over a two-year period less than 1 percent of the city's homeowners took advantage of this program. In fact, a vast majority of the Portland homeowners financed their weatherization out of personal funds and did not seek financial assistance.[32]

However, before this program is categorized as unsuccessful, one should examine why these figures are low. After the development of the program, three events substantially affected the market for loan programs. First, the mandatory retrofit program was put on standby, awaiting future approval by the voters. Second, the local utilities, both on their own and through the federally mandated residential conservation service program, elected to provide loans at rates lower than those of the Portland Conservation Corporation. Finally, the state of Oregon decided to provide 6.5 percent loans for energy efficiency improvements, 1.5 percent lower than those provided by the corporation.

One can debate the extent to which Portland's initiatives pushed the electric utilities and the state into adopting loan programs, but one cannot deny that Portland's example had some effect upon the decisions of others. In conversations with officials in Seattle, the Portland experience was cited as a factor in Seattle's decision to adopt an aggressive energy conservation program.[33] Further, the three-year planning and decision process, which involved thousands of citizens, increased the energy awareness of the city's citizens. By 1983, over 90 percent of Portland's homeowners had either weatherized or begun to weatherize their homes.[34] Although it is difficult to isolate the cause of the resulting energy savings, some must be attributable to improved awareness. Finally, the one program that has no competition, the loans for commercial and industrial audits, has met with relative success, as measured by the number of loan applications.

Minneapolis supplemented its loan program with an imaginative outreach effort designed to assist the city in reaching a goal of reducing residential energy use by 30 percent by 1990. Through the use of revenue bonds, Minneapolis established a tax-exempt line of credit with a consortium of seventeen banks that provided loans at a rate of 11 percent

32. Portland Energy Office, *Residential Energy Conservation Survey* (Portland, Ore.: City of Portland, Fall 1982), p. 10.

33. Interview, Charles Royer, deputy mayor, Seattle, August 13, 1982.

34. Portland Energy Office, *Residential Energy Conservation Survey,* p. 8.

for ten years.[35] To build momentum for the loan program and supplement its benefits, the city set up a neighborhood energy workshop program. Under this program, the city held energy workshops every Saturday for a specific block within one of the city's neighborhoods. All participants were required to come to this session equipped with a completed audit form describing the characteristics of their homes and their rate of energy consumption. After a presentation on energy-saving techniques, participants were given materials and tools to begin weatherizing their houses. They also became automatically eligible for the 11 percent loans. During the afternoon, trained energy auditors visited each home to provide individualized technical assistance.

Although the level of participation in the workshop program has been impressive (1,800 houses during 1982), city officials admit that demand for the loans lagged behind expectations and the applications came predominantly from upper-middle-income families who could have easily financed the improvements through conventional vehicles.[36] Further, there has been no evaluation of actual savings, although there is a consensus among Minneapolis energy officials that consumption was reduced.

Finally, several cities encouraged the use of federal community development block grants for energy conservation. Boston and Pittsburgh both set up programs that provided either grants or rebates for conservation improvements.[37] As mentioned earlier, these programs were perceived as community development or equity programs. Officials in Boston and Pittsburgh considered increasing energy costs to be one of the critical *housing* problems confronting their city.

In summary, there were only a few cities that attempted to administer energy loan programs. Financial subsidy programs such as these are usually more effectively handled by an institution with greater access to monies and a larger geographic jurisdiction than that of an individual city or community. Economies of scale and the need to strive for geographic and fiscal equality indicate that loan programs should probably be handled either by existing lending institutions or the utilities. If government needs to be involved, federal or state agencies are in a better position to undertake this responsibility than local governments. In some

35. Office of Technology Assessment, *Energy Efficiency*, pp. 272–73.

36. Interview, Robert Henderson and Sheldon Strom, Minneapolis Energy Office, August 10, 1982.

37. Office of Technology Assessment, *Energy Efficiency*, pp. 274–75.

circumstances, a partnership between a local government and a utility or federal agency whereby the locals spearhead the marketing of the loans might also work well.

Supply Subsidies

If the geographic distribution of resources is varied and uneven, so is the interest and willingness of local communities to invest in energy supply alternatives. Communities with municipal utilities have been investing in energy production options (primarily hydroelectric) for over thirty-five years. For these communities, local initiatives are nothing new. As energy prices have increased, the attractiveness of energy production investments has grown appreciably for other communities as well. In the same way that higher prices will induce a private company to reevaluate investments previously found to be unattractive, so too will local communities consider promoting energy production options if the financial, social, and political payback is sufficiently seductive. Communities such as Trinidad, Colorado, and Youngstown, Ohio, have drilled for natural gas on town land. Others, such as Shreveport, Louisiana, and Pompano Beach, Florida, have recovered methane from their solid waste landfills and used the gas both for supplying their own buildings and for sale to local distributors.[38] Many cities and towns have either invested directly or cooperated closely with private developers to construct small-scale hydroelectric facilities. Others have supported the construction of facilities that convert solid waste to energy, although some of these have gone aground because of either a lack of available capital or technical problems. Finally, several cities examined the prospect of establishing district heating systems similar to those built in Scandinavian countries.[39]

It is impossible in this short space to thoroughly evaluate each and every type of local energy investment. Two key elements seem to be present in successful programs: the economic soundness of the project and the availability of subsidies from either the state or federal government.

38. David J. Morris, *Self-Reliant Cities: Energy and the Transformation of Urban America* (San Francisco: Sierra Club, 1982), pp. 153, 154.

39. St. Paul, Minnesota, is building a 165-megawatt district heating facility. HUD, DOE, and the Electric Power Research Institute have sponsored many studies examining the feasibility of district heating either generically or for specific sites.

Perhaps the best example of the latter is the California solar effort. In the early 1980s the state of California adopted the most aggressive solar program in the country. A primary delivery mechanism for this program was local governments. Although the statistics are somewhat unreliable, by mid-1982 approximately seventy-four communities in California had adopted ordinances to protect a building owner's access to sunlight. Twenty communities had either passed or were considering ordinances requiring the mandatory use of solar heat on all new swimming pools, and twelve cities had adopted regulations requiring solar hot water heating for all new buildings.[40]

The city of Oceanside, California, adopted a third-party investment financing scheme for solar leasing. This program, the Oceanside municipal solar utility plan, called for the sale of solar equipment to investors who subsequently claimed the tax depreciation and investment tax credits. The solar equipment was then leased by the municipal solar utilities, acting as the agent for the investors, to homeowners, who could deduct 55 percent of the lease payment from their California state income taxes as part of the state's solar tax credit program.

The key to these programs was the 55 percent solar tax credit. Without this credit, many of the California solar programs would not have been cost effective. In September 1982 the California legislature made municipal solar utilities eligible for the tax credit, but only for solar utilities in existence as of December 31, 1982. As a result, twenty-six cities established programs similar to that adopted by Oceanside within a three-month period.[41]

There are questions about the wisdom of requiring or promoting the installation of a specific piece of energy equipment. What is economical today may not be economical tomorrow. For example, heat pumps and shower flow restrictors might be more economical investments than solar collectors. Is it wise public policy to force consumers to purchase equipment for which there are more economical alternatives? If the externalities that might justify such investments are blurred or reduced in scope by exogenous forces, then one must question the long-run viability of such programs. With electricity prices rising and with the continuation of the 55 percent tax credit, solar may be more cost effective

40. California Office of Appropriate Technology, *Local Governments Requiring Solar Access for New Construction* (Sacramento: Office of Appropriate Technology, 1982), p. 26.

41. Interview, Jennifer Sansone, Oceanside energy coordinator, December 1982.

in California than elsewhere. But the key is the tax credit. If that credit is eliminated or amended either because it is perceived as regressive or because there are more pressing demands on California's fiscal resources, it is likely that many of that state's solar programs would be in jeopardy.

In summary, local initiatives aimed at inducing investments in supply-oriented energy projects have been responses to either market opportunities or government subsidies. During 1975–84 the latter played a more significant role than the former.

Mandatory Retrofit Programs

The ordinance passed in Portland in 1979 mandating the retrofit of all existing commercial and residential buildings was one of the most controversial and visible energy initiatives undertaken anywhere in the country. Mandating individuals to make specific investments in their homes is a measure politicians have difficulty supporting. To many people, such requirements represent an excessive intrusion of government upon the rights of individuals. Yet a number of cities, especially on the West Coast, adopted regulations that require citizens to retrofit their homes either by a certain date or at the point of sale.

As with several of the other programs discussed here, it is almost impossible to determine quantitatively whether such programs succeeded. Since Portland has delayed implementation of its ordinance, only Davis has data on the effectiveness of a mandatory point-of-sale program. These data were collected during a two-year period in which housing turnover in the city was low. Even so, the number of homes that failed the initial inspection was large. For example, of the 413 single-family units inspected in 1980, 58 percent had insufficient attic insulation, 50 percent had not weather-stripped their doors, and 61 percent had not wrapped their water heater.[42] Assuming that those homeowners passed a subsequent inspection and were eventually able to sell their homes, one can conclude that some energy investments were made that would otherwise not have occurred.

By the fall of 1982 twelve other California communities had adopted point-of-sale ordinances. Because of problems of enforcement and

42. City of Davis, "Housing Resale/Retrofit Program Monthly Report," December 1980, p. 2.

political acceptability it is uncertain whether these laws will have a measurable effect on residential energy consumption.

Consumer protection and social welfare concerns have been major factors in the decision by some cities to adopt these ordinances. For example, in San Francisco the major purpose was to provide relief to tenants from ever-escalating energy costs.[43] Officials in that city argued that historically landlords tended to turn over their buildings rapidly in order to take advantage of tax depreciation schedules. If they were required to install a number of low-cost energy efficiency investments at the time of turnover, tenant energy bills could be lowered. Obviously the amount of energy saved would be related to the rate at which landlords turned over their dwellings. If building sales were slow, the potential impact of the program would be less. On the other hand, a rapid turnover rate might galvanize political resistance and put the program in greater jeopardy.

A second reason for the adoption of these programs was political visibility. Many public officials in California wanted to be perceived as aggressive. If neighboring cities adopted a visible program that caught the media's attention, pressures arose to adopt a similar program for their city. For example, in promulgating its mandatory retrofit ordinance, Sacramento was influenced by the city of Davis, ten miles to the west.

In summary, mandatory retrofit ordinances, if properly enforced, will probably save energy. The key question is, are the energy savings worth the political fallout arising from the perception that government may be exceeding its bounds? Further, can these programs survive if government subsidies for energy retrofits are reduced? During 1980–82 the cost of these ordinances was minimized by the availability of government subsidies such as low-interest loans and tax credits and by the rapid inflation in housing prices, which reduced the pinch of paying out-of-pocket for energy improvements. If this situation changes, political support for such programs will also change.

Low-Cost or No-Cost Programs

In 1979 the residents of Fitchburg, Massachusetts, installed caulking, weather stripping, and insulation in more than half the homes in the city, reducing their space-heating needs by 14 percent. This program received

43. Interview, Donald Bules, planner, City of San Francisco, August 9, 1982.

national attention and today is extolled as an example of what local initiative with limited government dollars can accomplish.

In addition to Fitchburg, several other cities either adopted or considered adopting similar programs. For example, Buffalo administered such a program in 1981–82. Are these programs successful? To even begin to respond, one must know the answers to three questions. First, how many of the participants actually were persuaded to act because of the program? In almost every instance, there has been very little follow-up to determine whether the participants took action because of encouragement by the program or because of other factors. Most city officials believe, though, that the percentage of individuals falling in the former category is high. Thus a subjective evaluation would conclude that these programs have been relatively successful, but no objective data support these preliminary assessments. Second, how permanent are the improvements? For example, in Fitchburg one of the major ingredients was putting a plastic cover over windows. Over a span of years, this plastic wears away; there is no available information on whether people subsequently replace it. Third, has the program diverted attention away from the need for permanent energy efficiency improvements and thereby indirectly decreased the incentive for greater long-term reductions in energy consumption?

Documenting the motivation and actions of homeowners is a difficult science. In 1979 the federal government mailed out millions of shower flow restrictors to homeowners. How many of these were actually installed? If the answer is few, then the program was a waste of taxpayers' dollars. Skeptics would argue that too often no-cost or low-cost programs do not deliver significant energy savings, but rather rely entirely on measurements of participation as determinants of their success. Supporters, on the other hand, will argue that these programs are significantly more successful from an educational and investment perspective than most of the federal and state conservation programs. The Fitchburg model depended on extensive use of volunteer labor, combined with a highly motivated clientele. In 1979 the energy issue was sufficiently prominent to garner the enthusiasm needed to make that program a success. By 1981 and 1982 these conditions had disappeared. Local officials had become less interested in investing their political capital in a campaign to meet what had become a lower-priority concern. Without this political investment, it is almost impossible to obtain the media coverage and neighborhood support needed for these types of programs.

Planning

The issue of planning, whether it be for energy or any other topic, sparks a wide spectrum of responses. To some, planning evokes images of unnecessary government intervention. To others, planning is seen as an excuse to avoid making decisions. From a more positive perspective, planning is viewed as an essential part of making public policy decisions. The more complex the problems confronting society, the greater the need for an effective planning process.

During the 1960s and 1970s, planning became a prerequisite for the receipt of federal funding for programs such as housing, air and water pollution control, and law enforcement. Hundreds of new local and regional planning agencies were created to meet federal requirements. With this planning capability in place, many communities decided to use it to assess and resolve their energy problems. In some cases energy plans were incorporated as an element of the city's general long-range development plan, the preparation of which is a state requirement in California. In cities such as Portland and St. Paul the development of energy plans involved an extensive public participation process that developed broad constituencies for a wide range of recommendations. Some of the plans were more imaginative than those contained in any federal or state program.

Obviously, a plan in and of itself does not save energy. It must be implemented to be effective. Yet the process by which the plan was developed can be a key ingredient in determining whether or not the plan will be implemented.

There are two schools of thought on this subject. The first argues that the development and approval process for a plan actually impedes its implementation. It is much easier to obtain approval for two or three select energy programs than to gain support for a comprehensive energy plan containing fifty or sixty provisions, each of which has its supporters and opponents. There is a fear that opposition to certain provisions will undercut the momentum for other less controversial programs. To avoid this situation, it would be strategically better to submit the programs assured of passage, implement them, and move on to new projects when and if the opportunity presents itself. In Portland, where public debate over the energy plan was extensive, the subsequent battle over the mandatory requirement to retrofit existing homes affected the success of the other components of the plan. Interestingly, until 1984 Davis had never adopted an energy component to its city plan. Warren Williams, the Davis city planner, argued articulately that such a plan would only create paralysis.[44]

The second view of the planning process believes that planning creates the constituency necessary to support and implement an energy program. Planning can be a catalyst spurring the adoption of a large body of programs that are not necessarily perceived as the traditional responsibility of local government. There is general agreement that local officials are responsible for law enforcement, fire protection, and economic development. There is not a general perception that they are responsible for energy. If a mayor believes that it is important for a city to embark on an energy program, it is essential that he or she first create a constituency for the city's involvement with the issue. Grassroots planning processes are an effective tool for doing this. In Portland over 2,000 people participated in the process and Seattle reported similar participation. In Wichita, Kansas, six task forces of eight individuals were set up to produce a comprehensive plan for the city, and in St. Paul the mayor established a "Committee of 100." Each of these cities considered it essential to develop an informed, involved, and committed public in order for the subsequent policy to be implementable.

It is important to differentiate these grassroots planning processes from the more technical planning exercises usually associated with federal grant applications. The former build constituencies, while the latter assume that the constituency already exists or will be automatically created. Technical comprehensive planning processes focused toward local energy problems have been uniformly unsuccessful unless coupled with a grassroots participatory process.

It is difficult to determine whether one of these views is closer to the truth than the other, especially since both focus on how best to integrate the products of the planning process into the local political decisionmaking process. The effectiveness of each approach depends on a city's political environment. In Portland, where the planning process brought out opposition as well as support, it is generally conceded that the city benefited from the incremental energy awareness created by the lengthy and broad participatory planning process. On the other hand, it would be difficult to challenge Williams's contention that Davis would not have been able to implement some of its major projects if it had spent an

44. Interview, Warren Williams.

inordinate amount of time trying to agree on an energy plan. Many cities have developed imaginative plans that were only partially implemented. For example, Los Angeles's energy plan was only beginning to be implemented in 1983, five years after it was first submitted to the city government.

Both the Davis and Portland approaches emphasize grassroots participation. In Portland the participation process focused on policy, while in Davis it focused on implementation. One of the key results of this emphasis on citizen participation is that a significant proportion of the population in those cities became "energy literate." Not only did they understand the basic fundamentals of energy economics and the ways in which they could reduce energy consumption, but they became more receptive to energy initiatives. People who are energy literate may not necessarily save a lot of energy, but they are more likely to respond to both market forces and government programs than people who are not as well versed.

In 1982 the Urban Consortium, a coalition of thirty-seven major urban governments, developed a program that attempted to consolidate the advantages of both the Davis and Portland approaches. The consortium program provided research and planning funds to develop and implement specific projects and to transfer the results to other consortium members. This effort was much more focused than the broad comprehensive planning efforts supported in the 1970s, but retained the emphasis on public participation.[45]

Transportation

The transportation of people and goods accounts for approximately 25 percent of the nation's energy and 50 percent of its oil consumption. If the crux of the energy problem is the nation's vulnerability to oil disruptions, then conservation of transportation fuels is essential. There are three ways to achieve this goal: build more efficient vehicles, develop vehicles that use alternative fuels such as methanol or electricity, or adopt measures to reduce vehicle use.

The first option has enjoyed widespread support not only in the United

45. The Department of Energy's comprehensive community energy management program provides local communities with monies to undertake comprehensive energy plans. This program can point to few, if any, success stories. DOE sponsored the Urban Consortium, which seemed more successful.

States but throughout the industrialized world. It is easy to implement, both politically and administratively, and it does not impinge on the public's existing driving habits. It is, however, an option that does not lend itself to local community involvement. The second is primarily a long-run research and development strategy and at present has little relevance to local governments.

The third alternative emphasizes the changing of use habits and is fraught with implementation difficulties. Local governments are capable of administering a wide variety of transportation programs to save energy, including marketing vanpools or carpools, reforming taxicab regulations, amending traffic patterns, promoting mass transit, and regulating downtown parking. Although some cities have implemented such programs, most localities have chosen to place their money, and their interest, elsewhere.

One of the reasons for this lack of enthusiasm is that energy is only one of a municipality's many considerations when designing transportation policy. In fact, energy concerns may directly conflict with other local priorities. Synchronizing traffic lights may decrease gasoline consumption, but at the same time it may increase accidents. Vanpools and carpools may be less energy intensive than buses and subways, but they do not provide a suitable transportation alternative for the low-income community nor do they have the same potential for encouraging community development. Banning cars in downtown areas would reduce air pollution and energy use, but might also induce shoppers to abandon local merchants for more accessible suburban shopping centers.

Local governments are also concerned about the cost of marketing these programs. There is no question that carpools and vanpools are a more energy-efficient alternative than most of the existing modes of commuting. Yet the crux of the dilemma is how to get the average commuter to join a carpool. Efforts to match riders can be expensive, since for every new carpooler many others have probably been approached. In the early 1980s the Urban Mass Transit Administration funded an "Easyride" program in several cities, including Newport News and Hampton, Virginia. The estimated total program cost in these two communities was $505 for each new ridesharer. Costs included the purchase of vans as well as marketing, information, and maintenance efforts. A subsequent survey indicated that the number of work trips using either mass transit or carpools and vanpools increased from 25.1 percent to 32.8 percent between June 1979 and March 1982, but the high costs cast doubt on the cost effectiveness of these programs, at least as implemented at the local level.[46]

Portland set aside on-street downtown parking for carpools and sold approximately 600 permits for the use of these spaces. But energy is a higher public priority in Portland than elsewhere. Without public support, transportation officials in that city might have found themselves in the same political hot seat as their colleagues in Boston who promoted downtown parking bans and the idea of reserving one of the lanes of their major arteries for carpools. The political costs simply offset the energy and environmental benefits, and the projects were either abandoned or amended.

One of the characteristics of programs that work is that they fit in with existing priorities. For example, measures like taxicab ridesharing and allowing cabs to pick up riders in other jurisdictions are not only profitable for taxi companies and convenient for consumers, but they measurably increase the energy-efficient operation of the cabs. San Diego, Seattle, and Dade County, Florida, have adopted regulations to promote one or more of these provisions.

In summary, reducing energy consumption through policies and programs aimed at altering vehicle use has been a low priority for local officials, and this situation is not likely to change. There will, however, be isolated success stories similar to Portland's, as well as cases in which programs adopted to meet other local priorities also provide energy benefits.

The Local Experience: A Summary

Between 1978 and 1982 the United States was able to reduce its energy consumption by 7.2 quadrillion Btus (quads) and its consumption of imported oil by 3.7 million barrels a day.[47] Locally implemented energy conservation programs account for a very small share of those savings. In fact, an Oak Ridge study, using optimistic estimates, claims that between fiscal years 1974 and 1979 all federally funded conservation

46. Peat, Marwick, Mitchell and Co., *Evaluation of the Easyride Transportation Brokerage Demonstration,* prepared for Urban Mass Transit Administration (Department of Transportation, 1982), pp. xix, xx, 134.

47. U.S. Department of Energy, Energy Information Administration, *Monthly Energy Review* (February 1984), pp. 3, 15.

programs combined saved only 0.55 quads, or about 11 percent of the energy saved.[48] William Hogan, in a more recent study, argues that the Oak Ridge figures are too high and that almost all of the energy saved during this period can be attributed to changes in prices or economic activity.[49]

Except for internal management efforts, few cities adopted energy programs. Those that did were exceptions in which several factors came together to produce a unique political environment. These factors included the presence of vigorous leadership by senior elected officials who were willing to take political risks to alter the traditional agenda; a tradition of open government and local resource management; a pervasive belief that greater energy efficiency would improve the city's long-run economic health; and an extensive participatory process that served to legitimize the issue of energy conservation in the eyes of the electorate.[50] In addition, most of these cities enjoyed relatively good fiscal health, and many had their own municipal electric utility.

Most cities, especially in the fiscal climate that characterized the beginning of the 1980s, have not rated energy high on their priority list. How many city mayors have the luxury of placing energy on a par with problems such as crime, a declining tax base, unemployment, and the provision of traditional municipal services? How many mayors can obtain significant political benefits by embarking on aggressive energy-related programs? Many cities—even Seattle, which has placed energy higher on its political agenda than most—have eliminated their energy offices. In fact, most of the more publicized local energy initiatives have been funded not by local revenues, but by either federal or state grants. San Francisco's program is funded by the Department of Energy through the Urban Consortium. Other local initiatives have been funded through the federally initiated comprehensive community energy management program or through allocations from HUD's community development block grants or urban development action grants (UDAGs). Even at the height of the energy crisis few cities were willing to put their own monies into energy-related programs.

Therefore, in terms of direct energy savings, it is probably fair to say

48. Greene and others, *Estimating the Total Impact,* p. 16.

49. William W. Hogan, *Patterns of Energy Use* (Cambridge, Mass.: J. F. Kennedy School of Government, Energy and Environmental Policy Center, May 1984), pp. 29–30.

50. Henry Lee, "The Role of Local Government in Promoting Energy Efficiency," *Annual Review of Energy,* vol. 6 (1981), p. 322.

that local programs, with the exception of building codes and perhaps internal energy management programs, have not yet made a measurable contribution to reducing the nation's consumption of energy. Cities that adopt aggressive programs in the future will be the exception rather than the rule.

It would be a serious mistake, though, to measure only the direct benefits of local conservation efforts. The indirect benefits from these programs have been of significant value. These benefits include the role played by local governments as pathfinders or laboratories for new ideas and as energy educators. Again, the measurement of these indirect benefits must be qualitative rather than quantitative, but this analytic limitation in no way denigrates their importance.

Local Governments as Pathfinders

David Knapp, assistant city manager of Boulder, related that any time there was a newspaper article describing energy initiatives in another city, City Council members would send it to him with a note asking why he had not been doing the same things in Boulder.[51] Deputy Mayor Charles Royer in Seattle argued that the visibility of the Portland program put tremendous pressure on city politicians in Seattle to be as progressive as their sister city to the south.[52] Oregon has adopted one of the most progressive energy efficiency loan programs in the country, while California has adopted stringent energy conservation building codes and is considering a statewide point-of-sale law for residential buildings. In discussions with officials in both states, it was evident that the pioneering efforts of Portland and Davis had a significant effect on the willingness of state officials to replicate their own versions of these programs. Energy-efficient building codes, point-of-sale ordinances, residential energy loans, the use of solid waste as an energy fuel, extraction of methane from landfills, solar municipal utilities, and the promotion of district heating units were all originally initiated at the local level and later embraced by state and federal officials.

The use of local government as a laboratory to foster the development of new institutional vehicles to meet public policy problems benefits the nation as a whole. The federal government, sensitive to this potential,

51. Interview, David Knapp, assistant city manager, Boulder, July 30, 1982.
52. Interview, Charles Royer.

has historically been willing to provide seed monies for the development of experimental programs. Davis and Portland were both recipients of federal grants without which their programs would not have been possible. The benefits of these pioneering efforts far exceeded their cost. Independent of failure or success, these programs generate hands-on knowledge that is instrumental in designing innovative and workable programs to address public needs.

Local Governments as Energy Educators

An educated consumer is essential to almost any energy conservation strategy. Without knowledge people are reluctant to act. Information barriers have been cited as a major obstacle to reducing energy consumption. Thus efforts to reduce those barriers would seem to be an important contribution to energy conservation. Even if the people attending the neighborhood energy workshops in Minneapolis went home in the afternoon and watched football rather than insulate their attic, three or four weeks later they may have found a spare hour or two to finally roll the fiberglass in between the rafters. Maybe they did not do it until the next spring, but after spending a few hours listening to a technical presentation on energy conservation and taking the time to fill out the audit forms, they were more aware of the potential for energy savings than they were before they attended the meetings. Similarly, the public processes used to develop energy programs in Portland and Seattle could not help but have a significant effect on the awareness of the citizenry. Energy became a major topic of conversation in those cities. It is highly likely that more people acted to retrofit their homes in Portland because of the increased awareness generated by this process than because of any specific program.

Educational programs are anathema to analysts. They are impossible to quantify. They deal more with human psychology than they do with public policy. Yet cities that have adopted aggressive grassroots programs have heightened awareness not only for their own residents, but also within their state and region—an awareness that has reduced energy consumption.

The Future

What guidance for the future can be extracted from the experience of the last decade? What can local governments do well and what can be expected of them? The answers to these questions depend on the extent of government involvement in addressing energy issues.

A Policy of Nonintervention

If the federal and state governments take the position that government programs usually exacerbate rather than ameliorate the energy problem, it is unlikely that local governments will stampede to fill the vacuum. A few cities, because of a convergence of factors, will develop or maintain energy programs; but they will be the exception rather than the rule.

As energy prices decline, the perception of energy as a high-priority public problem also declines. Further, if there is a continuing environment of low economic growth and fiscal austerity, the political competitiveness of energy programs will weaken relative to other programs. Local politicians simply cannot invest their time and their city's money in issues for which there is negligible public concern. Even in the late 1970s energy programs had difficulty competing with more traditional priorities. In the environment of the 1980s, energy's competitive position is weak. This erosion of support has resulted in the phasing out of existing programs and the elimination of energy bureaucracies. Yet even under these circumstances, there are two areas where city governments will continue to increase their involvement: managing their own energy use and interacting with energy programs initiated by private interests, primarily electric and gas utilities.

Most cities have adopted some form of energy management for their buildings and vehicles. But the vast majority have not realized their full potential. As the revenue pie shrinks, the significance of reducing energy expenditures will grow. If a city can reduce its energy bill, it can increase its expenditures for other programs. For example, if a city spending 5 percent of a $20 million budget on energy manages to reduce its energy expenditures by 20 percent, it saves $200,000. This figure is sufficient to purchase twenty new police cars, hire eight additional firemen, or maintain an athletic program at the local high school.

The incentive for a city to reduce its energy use depends on the ratio of energy expenditures to total city revenues. As this ratio increases, cities will place a greater emphasis on energy efficiency investments and will be more willing to tackle the institutional problems that might impede those investments.

As electric utility companies confront skyrocketing capital costs and diminishing economies of scale, small-scale investments, including conservation, look increasingly attractive. Many utilities have already altered their investment strategies and others are being pushed by state regulatory commissions to do the same. To the extent that these investments are decentralized, small utilities will interact more with local governments than they have been accustomed. Furthermore, even if oil and gas prices decline, electricity prices in most regions will continue to increase throughout the 1980s. As prices increase, so too will the receptivity to efforts to reduce consumption. Thus efforts by private utilities to enlist the support of local governments are likely to become more frequent.

Further, if adopting these small-scale technologies involves persuading individuals to make investments—as is the case with conservation and most direct and passive solar systems—new marketing strategies will have to be developed. In some cases, utilities will contract out to third parties or form subsidiaries, but in some cases they will adopt programs similar to those adopted by Pacific Power and Light in Portland, Pacific Gas and Electric in Contra Costa County in California, Southern California Edison in Santa Monica, and the Bonneville Power Administration in the Northwest. These programs all involve some form of partnership with local governments for the purpose of delivering and marketing certain services. The difference between these programs and those that preceded them is that the utilities will be more insistent on saving Btus and less on achieving broad social goals. This attitude will be the source of continuing friction between the two parties and may limit the number of local communities participating in these programs.

A Policy of Intervention

Barring a disruption, it is unlikely that the federal government will soon reembrace a program of extensive intervention into energy markets. However, there is a probability of a disruption sometime in the future. Regardless of whether one believes intervention is good public policy, there remains a distinct possibility that under certain circumstances, Congress will once again establish a strong federal energy presence. If this situation comes about, it is important that the conservation programs adopted avoid the mistakes of the past.

Assuming that an interventionist policy includes a major commitment of resources over several years to encourage investments in energy conservation, the federal government would again have to decide how to deliver such a program. There will be four possible choices: assume total responsibility at the federal level, renew the partnership with the states, expand the existing residential utility service program, or develop a new relationship with local governments. These options are not mutually exclusive.

In making this decision, Congress and the executive will have to answer the question, what do each of these institutions do well? For the purposes of this discussion, the question can be limited to, what can local governments do well?

Energy planners are confronted with a paradox. Local governments possess extensive authority to alter the way society consumes its energy resources, but have rarely been motivated to use this authority. Throwing money at nonmotivated institutions is probably not a prescription for success. Thus it is essential to focus on those areas where the interests of local governments may coincide with those of the federal government.

In making this determination, three factors should be considered: Do localities possess an existing capacity to implement and deliver a specific type of program? Will a given program utilize that capacity without any major alterations in the local bureaucracy? Would this program merge with existing local priorities, such as economic development, equity concerns, and environmental or consumer goals?

Programs that force local governments to compromise existing or traditional priorities will not be effective. For example, a program that is perceived as stifling economic growth is not going to be implemented by a city confronting a declining tax base and a shrinking revenue pie.

Asking cities to implement programs that traditionally have been delivered by other levels of governments may receive some rhetorical support, but in the long run city governments are not going to develop new delivery vehicles when state, county, or federal vehicles already exist.

Two areas that do meet the three criteria are housing programs that encourage energy efficiency investments and economic or community development programs that have a strong energy component. Under the aegis of HUD, authority for such programs already exists. In the case of housing, community development block grants have been used in several cities to weatherize homes. The urban development grant program has been a major source of funds for the Portland loan program, Trenton's study of district heating, and Lawrence, Massachusetts's, plant for converting solid waste to energy.

In each area there exists a federal agency with an ongoing working relationship with local governments, local agencies with a proven ability to deliver these types of programs, and the potential to integrate energy concerns with other more traditional concerns.

If all of these statements are true, why aren't local governments using more of their community development block grants for energy-related projects? The answer is that cities are not willing to fund energy projects by forgoing other concerns. As long as CDBG and UDAG funds are declining, most cities will not rechannel these funds away from existing priorities. On the other hand, if there were a renewed federal commitment to energy conservation and incremental funds were made available, cities would be willing and able to deliver programs in these two areas.

This agenda for a possible federal-local partnership is limited. Further, it depends on a major shift in federal energy policy, which is not likely short of an oil supply disruption. If the pendulum swings back, interest in utilizing the capabilities of local governments to augment existing federal-local housing and community development programs represents a viable option.

Conclusion

This paper began with two simple questions: What programs developed or implemented by local governments have been successful, and what guidance for the future can be extracted from the experiences of the last decade?

Answers to these questions can be summarized as follows:

—Although data on energy saving in response to local programs is almost nonexistent, energy-conserving building codes, joint utility-municipal programs, and internal energy management efforts have resulted in some reductions in direct energy use in a number of localities.

—There are many other local programs in areas such as subsidized financing, supply subsidies, mandatory retrofit ordinances, low-cost or no-cost efforts, energy planning, and transportation projects that were established to save energy. In most instances, the benefits of these programs have been evaluated in light of their indirect benefits, such as educating consumers and providing a laboratory for new ideas. However, where there is some documentation, in most instances the aggregate energy reductions resulting from these programs have been small and the programs themselves have not been widely replicated.

—The future role of local governments in energy is closely tied to that of the federal government. If the federal government continues a hands-off policy, local government efforts will decline and in some cases disappear. Two programmatic exceptions to this trend will be internal energy management and joint partnerships with private enterprises, most probably electric and gas utilities.

—If events force the federal government to return to a more interventionist energy policy, local governments have the capability and the motivation to deliver a limited agenda of federally funded energy programs. The areas of greatest potential are housing and community development. Although localities possess the statutory authority to assume a greater role, they lack the motivation to transfer resources away from traditional priorities to meet the requirements of that role.

Comments by John H. Alschuler, Jr.

I agree there is a theoretical capacity for local government to play an important role in promoting energy conservation. There probably is sufficient regulatory and institutional capacity for local government to play that role. But to assume that there is a practical or political possibility is a very wide leap and one we should take with a great degree of caution. Local government will probably only follow federal leadership and at some great and cautious distance.

Local government can be effective, particularly in mass marketing. We can actually deliver service to large numbers of people. We can put out fires; we can arrest people who are doing things they shouldn't be doing; we can pick up trash; we can affect large numbers of people in their homes and in their businesses. That is not something states do, and that is not something the federal government does. It is distinctly local in the intergovernmental delivery system.

We can market and deliver services, but only when there is a powerful political will for us to do so. We have no trouble marketing and inspecting fire codes. Every year I send a fire inspector to every single home and business in Santa Monica. Nobody asks, "What is the cost effectiveness of this program?" Nobody asks that question when the health inspector goes out. But at present there simply is not the political will to have local government address energy issues. Without that political will, the theoretical capacity of local government will not be utilized.

Local government also needs an economic motivation, a way for local government to make some money out of a new activity. Santa Monica sought out additional program responsibilities in energy conservation at least in part because we would make a fair amount of money.

One point about regulation: local government primarily regulates the real estate industry and the use of land. Developers do not believe that rational transit policy based on energy considerations has the slightest bit to do with their investment decisions. Their time frame is short. They want to be in and out of a development project in three or four years. The political and economic pressure on us is overwhelmingly to make energy-inefficient decisions. Where we really could have a major impact on energy use over time in California would be through zoning power. But we are always running contrary to the immediate balance sheet of the investment community that we are dealing with. Developers will not build buildings away from the freeways as part of a public planning effort to zone in support of a future subway system. It is a political impossibility to take vague public ideals and play them against the private balance sheet.

We are examining programs that were initiated four or five years ago. I will be surprised if we see one-tenth of the rate of activity that we saw in the last five years, without major federal intervention. The rate of local government activity is shrinking quite dramatically.

Energy is by and large not the concern of mayors anymore. Mayors today are a lot more concerned about crime, fiscal constraints, and basic services to property. Energy is fundamentally irrelevant to any of those things. Until that agenda shifts, we will continue to encounter very severe political problems in getting the significant theoretical capacity of local government to effectuate energy programs translated through political will into an actual and practical capacity.

Comments by Angus Duncan

There is unquestionably an absence of hard evidence that local governments have made a substantial contribution to saving energy. Most local government energy programs have been relatively poorly funded; the funds were of uncertain duration. Inevitably evaluation programs had the lowest possible priority when the programs came before city councils, and little or no evaluation was done by the local governments themselves.

The federal government had a studied lack of interest in local governments. Its liaison was with fifty-odd state governments and not with several tens of thousands of local governments. Most local government programs, usually by creative use of funding sources, were pretty much self-starters. That by itself accounts in part for the relative sparsity of local government programs. But the result is that there is little hard, documented evidence of energy conservation savings that can be attributed to local governments.

Lee's conclusion that these programs must run true to traditional local priorities, while not startling, is certainly a useful dose of cold water for many of us who were strong and sometimes naive advocates of activity at the local level in the late 1970s. His point derives further support from the fact that those energy activities that local governments still are pursuing are those that tie most closely to traditional priorities. For example, the internal management of energy use in city buildings and vehicles contributes to municipal belt-tightening in a period of tight budgetary constraints.

One important exception to Lee's contention that municipal energy programs must follow traditional priorities may be seen in cooperative programs between utilities and municipalities. Some utilities seek cooperative arrangements to acquire the credibility or the delivery capability of local governments for utility programs. These linkups have some promise for the future in situations where both the utility and the local government see advantages to their institutional interests. Those joint programs are particularly promising because they allow the community and the utility to deal with energy management in the community on the basis of the incremental cost of new capacity that the utility faces rather than the averaged costs of old and new resources that the individual consumer sees in his monthly bill. In certain instances these joint utility-municipal programs have shown considerable promise and have resulted in the expenditure of very respectable sums of money to achieve greater energy efficiencies in commercial and industrial plants and processes. But in many cases these programs materialized only because the local government saw a specific financial benefit—a budgetary benefit to the municipality as well as a community benefit.

Finally, it is important to note that there are local governments that have the ability to take a longer view. These municipalities have tended to see energy as one of those currencies of community development—like land or capital—that they can manage to their own benefit over the long term. They have sought to take energy management out of the realm of polemics and advocacy and integrate it into traditional urban management concerns.

In the Pacific Northwest, a recent federal statute may test municipal capabilities in energy conservation in a serious way. The Regional Power Planning Act puts the Bonneville Power Administration in the unusual and fairly nontraditional role of being an energy manager rather than an energy marketer. The statute gives priority to energy conservation activities and specifically provides that different entities within the region—utilities are at the top of the list, but local governments are not far behind—should play important roles in the delivery of those energy conservation services. Thus the region generally and local governments in particular should become experimental laboratories in energy management. Bonneville is also obligated, again by statute and also by policy in the region, to try to evaluate and disaggregate the effects of the different programs and the influence of the different entities on energy savings over the next ten years. Bonneville, and the Northwest, may generate the evaluative data on energy conservation programs that appears to be missing from the record of these programs to date.

KAREN GRIFFIN

State Government Conservation Programs

ALTHOUGH much of the funding and program design emanates from Washington, America's energy conservation programs rely heavily on the states. The states are expected to provide consumer information and analytic data, plan and manage grant and loan programs, and regulate public and private activities. Most federal programs, recognizing the tremendous diversity of regional needs and interests, are carried out by delegation of authority and funding to the states.[1] Local governments have found it almost impossible to support comprehensive energy programs. With broader basic missions, sustained interest, capacity to build a critical mass of staff, and less vulnerable revenue sources, the states have outperformed most local governments in the development and implementation of conservation programs.

After several years of rapid growth, state energy programs went through a period of reduction and redirection in 1982–84. A new political climate, a recession-related budget squeeze, and a leveling off of energy prices combined to lessen government support for conservation programs. State energy programs still dominate conservation policy, however. There are three reasons that they will continue to do so: a core of effective programs, a new source of state-controlled funding, and the development of off-budget expenditures. Lessons learned since 1973 will have ample opportunity to be applied in the late 1980s. Programs have been winnowed to those that emphasize energy savings as a measure of success. These can be translated into economic development and a decreased call on the state treasury to fund its own energy bills, bail out local governments, or redress the grievances of citizens.

1. State programs are defined broadly as those that use a high percentage of state personnel or dollars, including those that use the state as an administrative vehicle for federal directives, block grants, state-funded programs, and state regulation.

Since 1983 the focus has changed away from simply managing oil use, and states have found new roles in energy conservation. State conservation programs can expedite consumer response to supply and demand pressures, ensure that market-clearing prices do not exact unacceptable penalties on the disadvantaged, and support long-term energy market decentralization.

So long as states have power plant-siting and rate-making authority, they will also be interested in the development of lower-cost alternatives to central station power plants. Independently, the market may not make conservation adjustments in a timely enough manner to accommodate the long lead times of power planning. States learned this lesson in the early 1980s, when conservation gains occurred faster than had been anticipated, and many states were left with overcapacity. For those parts of the country, conservation as a utility planning tool is a missed opportunity and will not become important again until the 1990s. At the same time, conservation may still be cost effective for consumers, and state policymakers will need to weigh the competing claims of producers and consumers.

The question of whether state energy programs reduce barriers to energy conservation must be answered in two parts. First is consideration of the organizational and institutional issues that influence service delivery. Was the choice of states as the primary administrator an effective one? Did states supplement and then replace federal funding with their own dollars? How have states worked with local governments and businesses? Are organizational relationships changing?

The second part of the answer is consideration of the programs themselves. What goals were addressed and how were they chosen? Who were the target audiences? Was the approach appropriate for the barrier? Was the most cost-effective option selected? Were the same errors repeated in other states or in the design of follow-on programs? How innovative have states been?

Historical Perspective

State energy programs started in the mid-1970s and built to a crescendo of federal funding in 1981–82. The two years after that saw an abruptly reduced government policy emphasis on energy. In reaction, a variety of solutions emerged to deal with the questions of how to integrate an energy function into line agencies and which activities would be supported.

State Programs before 1982

Most state energy offices were established in response to federal initiatives arising out of the oil embargo in 1973 and were enlarged after the 1975 passage of the federal Energy Policy and Conservation Act. This act created the state energy conservation program (SECP), through which states were to plan a statewide program; fund outreach, education, and technical assistance; and strive to reduce statewide energy use by 5 percent through voluntary and mandatory programs.

Additional federal legislation in 1976, 1977, 1978, and 1980 enacted the core of state-implemented programs: the residential conservation service (audits of home utility use), low-income energy assistance program (partial payments of fuel bills for the poor, emergency energy assistance, and weatherization), weatherization assistance program (direct weatherization of low-income homes through contracts with community-based organizations), energy extension service (small grants and technical information to community-based projects), institutional conservation program (50 percent matching grants to schools and hospitals for audits and installation of energy-efficient equipment), Solar Energy and Energy Conservation Bank (loan subsidies and partial grants for residential measures), and commercial and apartment conservation service (utility commercial and apartment audits).[2]

While states were to carry out most federal conservation efforts, the federal government did reserve for itself key conservation programs, including national building energy performance standards, appliance standards, industrial research, and transportation conservation. When the federal government chose later not to adopt either building or appliance standards, it opened the option for states to play an even larger role by setting their own energy conservation standards. In addition to

2. The Reagan administration opposed the latter two programs, and they were not actually implemented until 1982 and 1983, respectively. The Department of Energy was assigned responsibility for the state energy conservation program, residential conservation service, weatherization assistance program, energy extension service, institutional conservation program, and commercial and apartment conservation service. The low-income assistance program is administered by the Department of Health and Human Services, and the Solar Energy and Energy Conservation Bank by the Department of Housing and Urban Development.

Table 1. *Conservation Expenditures in California, 1982*[a]
Millions of dollars

Expenditure category	*Federal payments to state*[b]	*State expenditures*	*Utilities' expenditures*
Residential			
Tax credits	24.3	52.8	. . .
Programs	11.3	. . .	91.9
Business and public			
Tax credits	. . .	3.5	. . .
Programs	5.5	7.3	38.8
Program support	2.0	3.6	50.2
Total	43.1	67.2	180.9

Sources: Tax credits are from *Energy Conservation Bulletin*, vol. 6 (May–June 1983), p. 5 (federal), and California Franchise Tax Board files (state). Utility expenditures are summarized from annual reports. Program expenditures are from data provided by various state agencies.

a. Tax credit expenditures are for tax year 1981, taken in calendar year 1982. Utility expenditures are for calendar year 1982. All other costs are for fiscal year 1983 (July 1, 1982, to June 30, 1983).

b. Does not include the federal costs of administering programs in the state.

these core programs, most states have a host of their own initiatives, including state tax credits, renewable energy demonstrations and outreach, state grant or loan programs, and building and appliance standards.

The relative funding of state-administered conservation programs can be illustrated by looking at California, the state considered to have the largest conservation program. In 1982 California spent $67.2 million in state funds for its conservation programs. The residential tax credit and federal funds passed through the state added $43 million (see table 1). But the big spenders were California's utilities, which overshadowed direct government expenditures of $110 million with their $180 million outlay. On a per capita basis, this represents $1.78 from Washington, $2.78 from Sacramento, and $7.48 from the electric and gas industry.

While detailed program evaluations will be discussed later, it is helpful at this point to note the baseline status of state performance in 1980. By 1980 most of the required SECP program measures had been achieved. All states were in compliance with requirements for energy audits, public education, and intergovernmental coordination; fifty-six states and territories had carpool, vanpool, and public transportation programs; fifty-four states and territories had energy-efficient procurement practices; and fifty-two had right turn on red.[3] Only thirty-seven states had

3. U.S. Department of Energy, *Annual Report to the President and the Congress on the State Energy Conservation Program for Calendar Year 1980*, DOE/CE-0016 (DOE, 1981), pp. 6, 7.

Table 2. *Appropriations for Department of Energy State and Local Assistance Programs, Fiscal Years 1979–84*
Millions of dollars

Year	*State energy conservation program*	*Schools and hospitals*	*Energy extension service*	*Weatherization assistance program*	*Low-income energy assistance*[a]
1979	57.8	107.4	15.0	198.9	...
1980	47.8	161.4	25.0	198.9	...
1981	47.8	150.2	20.0	175.0	1,850.0
1982	24.0	48.0	9.6	144.0	1,875.0
1983[b]	24.0	48.0	10.0	145.0	1,975.0
1983[c]	...	50.0	...	100.0	...
1984[b]	24.0	48.0	10.0	190.0	1,300.0
Total	225.4	613.0	89.6	1,151.8	7,011.0

Source: *Energy Conservation Digest*, vol. 6 (October 24, 1983), p. 5; and previous issues.
a. Administered by the Department of Health and Human Services. At the discretion of each state, a maximum of 15 percent may be used for direct weatherization.
b. Estimated.
c. Enacted as part of an emergency supplemental appropriations bill (P.L. 98-8) to provide unemployment relief.

implemented the residential conservation service, but all were active in the direct grant programs. The energy extension service had passed a ten-state pilot test and had been expanded to all states.

State Programs: 1982 and Beyond

The high-water mark of state energy programs was probably in 1980–82. Momentum had been established, federal funding was at record levels (as shown in table 2), and consumers were concerned over high energy prices, which kept the political pressure on for energy conservation. After that time, however, as energy prices stabilized and the recession ground on, governments retrenched and public opinion no longer saw energy as the number one problem.

Between 1975 and 1983, public support for major government efforts to develop new energy sources and to find better ways to conserve fuel dropped from 81 percent to 66 percent.[4] In a state-level survey in California, public concern about the energy supply ranked fourteenth out of sixteen possible issues in 1984, compared with second position in 1979.[5] (Interestingly enough, there is virtually no relationship between

4. Roper surveys, reported in "Government Priorities," *Washington Post National Weekly Edition,* May 21, 1984, p. 38.
5. Field Institute, *California Opinion Index: Energy,* vol. 4 (May 1984), p. 1.

people's perception of the seriousness of the energy crisis and their self-reported conservation behavior.[6] So, while government officials might feel less pressured to take action on this issue, they cannot interpret the effect of lessened concern on individuals' behavior.)

When federal funding was cut in many programs in 1982–83, states responded by trimming the federally assisted programs accordingly, instead of substituting state dollars.[7] Energy conservation programs were no exception; most states sharply reduced conservation funding for schools and hospitals and for low-income weatherization. The 50 percent cuts in funding for the energy extension service and the SECP had a more adverse influence on state and local innovation, because these programs were the sources of baseline funding and offered the most flexibility. States had also built heavily on a network of nonprofit social service organizations as a low-cost delivery mechanism. When even small amounts of funding were lost, these organizations had no capital reserves, and the entire network collapsed. With the loss of discretionary funding, eight states abolished their separate energy offices, a visible demonstration of the decline of conservation as a crisis issue.[8] In telephone interviews, state energy officials and energy observers mentioned three frequent themes supporting the dissolution of energy offices: a new political belief that private business and consumers could now carry on conservation without government intervention, a loss of federal dollars with no surplus state funds to take up the slack, and a consensus that the "energy crisis is over."

States typically reduced their policy and planning functions, research and development, and outreach for renewable resources. According to interviewed officials, the primary products of policy and planning units were analyses that recommended expanding conservation and renewable investments. Since expansion was politically infeasible, limited staff resources were better directed to operating programs with an immediate community impact. Outreach and constituency building for renewable

6. Larry Condelli and others, "Improving Utility Conservation Programs: Outcomes, Interventions, and Evaluations," in the American Council for an Energy-Efficient Economy, *Doing Better: Setting an Agenda for the Second Decade,* vol. J (Washington, D.C.: ACEEE, 1984), pp. 173–88.

7. Rochelle L. Stanfield, "State Taxes Are Up, But Don't Worry—Federal Taxes Are Down by Much More," *National Journal,* vol. 15 (June 25, 1983), p. 1327.

8. The states were Nevada, Tennessee, Texas, Vermont, Alabama, Alaska, Kansas, and Ohio.

energy carried an aura of soft path futurism ("woodchips and windmills"), which meant they could not be supported as baseline activities. Research was considered expensive and was regarded as a federal responsibility. Two programs, which were rated by state energy program managers as relatively ineffective,[9] were saved and transferred to line agencies: ridesharing and vanpools went to the transportation departments, and conservation by state-owned facilities was assigned to the departments of general services.

The impact of the 1982 federal budget reductions on state activities depended on the states' relative reliance on federal spending. A review of six New England state offices found an average state contribution of 17 percent in 1981, with a range from 30 percent for Connecticut to zero for New Hampshire.[10] In fiscal year 1982 the six offices collectively took a 41 percent cut, even though the states increased their own support slightly. The states funded 32 percent of operations that year. Fewer schools, hospitals, and weatherization grants were awarded. Among programs curtailed were planning, data gathering, staff support for renewable resource efforts, coordinated hydroelectric planning, and information on public utility rates for independent generation, which was needed by developers and financiers.[11]

In contrast with the wealth of legislation in the preceding years, most new state initiatives in this period were limited to utility reforms, such as citizen advocates for rate cases (Iowa, Texas, and Illinois) and limitations on construction work in progress as a means of keeping rates lower (Texas, Connecticut, and Illinois). The one area of innovation was new conservation financing programs established by Florida, Maryland, Massachusetts, New Jersey, Oregon, Pennsylvania, and Rhode Island.[12]

In February 1983 the states were given a unique opportunity to set conservation priorities. As part of a settlement of cases involving allegations of petroleum misallocation and price control violations,

9. Stephen W. Sawyer, "Improving Federal-State Energy Conservation Programs: The States' Perspective," in the American Council for an Energy-Efficient Economy, *Doing Better,* vol. G, pp. 84–95.

10. "Budget Cuts Hit Regional Energy Offices," *Energy Forum in New England,* vol. 2 (Winter 1982), p. 6.

11. Neal R. Peirce and Jerry Hagstrom, "The Resilient Society," *National Journal,* vol. 15 (May 21, 1983), pp. 1047–52.

12. *Energy User News,* June 28, 1982; August 30, 1982; December 20, 1982; May 30, 1983; October 3, 1983; and November 28, 1983.

Congress gave the states "oil overcharge" funds for energy conservation programs to serve parties injured by such violations. The states received $200 million; the only conditions were that the money had to be spent among five categorical conservation programs and that it couldn't be used for administration.[13] The five eligible programs were: the state energy conservation program, energy extension service, schools and hospitals, low-income energy assistance program, and weatherization assistance program.

The oil overcharge money was an unexpected windfall, but within four months most governors had made their allocations and begun expenditures. For some states it was directed to emergency uses; Kentucky's abnormally cold winter had caused multiple deaths from hypothermia, and the oil overcharge money was immediately dispensed for low-income assistance payments for heating bills. Despite the fact that governors had been given responsibility for allocating the money, several state legislatures immediately stepped in. In Texas, Pennsylvania, and California, the legislature altered spending priorities. These states also took a longer time to decide how to spend their money.

Forty-five states, which collectively received 90 percent of the funds, responded to a National Governors' Association survey on their allocation of oil overcharge funds.[14] Expenditure choices diverged both from state to state and from the federal level of base program support, as the following table shows. No eligible program was chosen by every state. Low-income energy assistance was picked most often, and Georgia, Indiana, Kentucky, Michigan, and North Dakota gave it all their money. Even so, low-income assistance received only 2 percent of its annual federal support level. Compared with their annual federal allocations, the state energy conservation program, energy extension service, and schools and hospital program received a much higher percentage of funds. As observers of one state legislature explained, putting more money into low-income energy assistance was a drop in the bucket compared with the relative impact that could be made by funding the schools and hospitals program.

13. A previous fund of $86 million settled in consent orders had been deposited in the U.S. Treasury as miscellaneous receipts, delivered to the Strategic Petroleum Reserve in the form of crude oil or distributed to the states with no restrictions.

14. Memorandum, Jeff Genzer, National Governors' Association, Committee on Energy and Environment, to state energy directors, August 29, 1983.

Program	Percent of funds allocated	Number of states that put money into program		State allocation as a percent of federal funding
		Some money	All money	
State energy conservation program	18	27	1	133
Energy extension service	7	22	. . .	123
Schools and hospitals	25	24	2	93
Low-income energy assistance	24	25	5	2
Weatherization assistance	26	27	2	33

Oil overcharge settlements are certainly the major new funding opportunity for conservation programs in the 1980s. They materially changed the states' role in conservation program design. The states have new discretion in allocating funds and have ultimate control, since the money cannot be recovered by the federal government. In 1983 and 1984 small amounts from additional cases were dribbled out to the states, while in Washington debate raged over possible alternative uses. With so much money at stake, political struggles over control were inevitable. One case alone contained $1.6 billion to be remanded to the states, and another contains an additional billion dollars. In all approximately $3 billion will be shared among contending parties.

Preconditions for a Strong or Weak Role

Any assessment of state roles must take into account the tremendous regional variation in energy uses, costs, and impacts, as well as local expectations about the role of government. Table 3 shows the top and bottom quintiles among the states' 1981 per capita energy use for major end-use sectors. Contrary to expectations, high per capita energy use is only partially correlated with strong state conservation programs. For example, California, Florida, and New York were among the lowest residential users in 1981, yet they continued to develop three of the largest and most effective state programs.

The first condition for determining how strong a role states have played in conservation is to discover what they wanted to do. As was

Table 3. *Highest and Lowest Quintiles of States' per Capita Energy Use, by Sector, 1981*

Ten highest			*Ten lowest*		
Residential	*Commercial*	*Transportation*	*Residential*	*Commercial*	*Transportation*
1. Washington	Alaska	Alaska	41. South Carolina	South Dakota	Illinois
2. Alaska	Louisiana	Colorado	42. Mississippi	Minnesota	Michigan
3. Indiana	Idaho	Louisiana	43. Florida	Maryland	Vermont
4. Iowa	Nebraska	New Mexico	44. Delaware	Alabama	Pennsylvania
5. North Dakota	Delaware	Nevada	45. Rhode Island	Rhode Island	Wisconsin
6. Ohio	Washington	Hawaii	46. New York	Maine	Massachusetts
7. Oklahoma	Kansas	Texas	47. Arizona	Vermont	New Hampshire
8. Nebraska	Illinois	Nebraska	48. California	New Hampshire	Connecticut
9. Wisconsin	Wyoming	North Dakota	49. New Mexico	Nevada	Rhode Island
10. Idaho	Oklahoma	Oklahoma	50. Hawaii	Hawaii	New York

Source: U.S. Department of Energy, Energy Information Administration, *State Energy Overview*, DOE/EIA-0354 (83) (DOE, 1983).

pointed out in a 1978 Department of Energy (DOE) study, state governments did not all agree that the responsibilities assigned to them by the federal government were appropriate. They also did not all agree that responding to federal actions was in their self-interest, or that the roles assigned to them were cost effective.[15] For example, Alabama officials were concerned over the "big government" potential associated with a public-sector role, while other states opted for an aggressive posture.

Of major importance in motivating states were two variables: whether the state was a net energy producer, and whether the state was highly dependent on oil and hence most affected by the 1970s price increases.[16] Highly oil-dependent states had the highest probability of establishing their own conservation programs.[17] Over half of these states have maintained strong programs. In fact, oil was conserved more in the oil-dependent states. During the first five years of state program operation (1976–81), overall U.S. petroleum consumption decreased 4 percent. None of the oil-dependent states increased their petroleum use (seven states did), and, on average, their dependency dropped from 73 percent of all energy consumption to 64 percent, over twice the U.S. average decline.[18]

When electricity and natural gas prices overtook oil prices as a fuel concern, states with economies highly dependent on electricity and gas became aware of the economic fragility of being an energy importer. Wisconsin justified its conservation programs on the basis that 96 percent of its 1980 energy was imported, with seventy-eight cents of every energy dollar leaving the state's economy.[19] Iowa, which ranks forty-seventh nationally in the amount of energy it consumes as a percentage of its energy production, saw $5 billion leaving its borders every year. Its

15. U.S. Department of Energy, *The Role of the States in Energy* (Government Printing Office, 1978), p. 9.

16. See Henry Lee, "Energy at the State and Local Levels: An Evolving Perspective," *Discussion Paper Series,* E-82-06 (Cambridge, Mass.: J. F. Kennedy School of Government, Energy and Environmental Policy Center, June 1982); and Nancy Ginn and Heidi Zukoski, *Profiles in State Energy Management: Strength in Diversity* (Washington, D.C.: National Governors' Association, 1981).

17. States with 1976 petroleum consumption greater than 50 percent of total consumption were Alaska, Arkansas, California, Connecticut, Delaware, Florida, Georgia, Hawaii, Maine, Maryland, Massachusetts, Mississippi, New Hampshire, New Jersey, New York, North Carolina, Rhode Island, Vermont, and Virginia.

18. Constructed from U.S. Department of Energy, Energy Information Administration, *State Energy Overview,* DOE/EIA-0354 (83) (DOE, 1983).

19. Division of State Energy, State of Wisconsin Solar and Conservation Bank proposal to U.S. Department of Housing and Urban Affairs, November 1, 1982, p. 1.

blunt assessment was that "Iowa must become a more efficient manager of its energy resources in order to stem the tide of energy dollars leaving the State."[20]

Net oil- and gas-producing states (Texas, New Mexico, Louisiana, Oklahoma, Alaska, Montana, and Wyoming) did not develop strong conservation programs, but rather focused on production. As programs matured, some producing states used a portion of their fuel-related revenues to offset the rising impact of fuel prices by subsidizing retrofits. Of Alaska's $490 million in 1981–82 state financial subsidies, 2 percent was set aside to relieve rural electric rates, and another 5 percent was for conservation.[21] In the same period Nebraska used oil and gas severance taxes for public school energy conservation.

Assessment of State Performance

By and large states have received passing marks for their ability to organize and manage conservation programs. A 1979–80 General Accounting Office study of the state energy conservation program in New York, New Jersey, California, Indiana, Michigan, and Ohio found that federal funding "had been effective in terms of developing a State capability to manage energy programs."[22]

Deficiencies noted in program reviews were a lack of state-supplied resources for innovative programs, difficulty in coordinating programs that have incompatible federal governing regulations, lack of adequate data systems, and wide variations in technical quality.[23] Small states in particular had a hard time amassing the technical skills necessary to carry out programs, because they had so few staff positions funded. State legislatures were slow to grant funds to carry out the innovations that were successfully developed in other states, so the spread of effective state-initiated programs was slow.[24]

20. Policy statement of the Iowa Energy Policy Council, November 3, 1981, as cited in the State of Iowa's Solar Bank Proposal, app. A, November 15, 1982, p. 1.

21. State of Alaska Division of Energy and Power Development, *State of Alaska Long Term Energy Plan* (Anchorage, Alaska: The Division, 1981), p. IV-6.

22. General Accounting Office, *State Energy Conservation Program Needs Reassessing,* EMD-82-39 (GAO, 1982), p. ii.

23. DOE, *The Role of the States,* p. 12.

24. Nancy L. Ginn, *Ensuring Our Energy Future: State Initiatives for the 80s* (Washington, D.C.: National Governors' Association, 1980), pp. 2–3.

It is difficult to set goals and to measure what has been accomplished in a conservation program. Btus that weren't used are very hard to document, and it is even harder to prove that they weren't used because of the program's intervention. Evaluators tend to measure process goals and to get themselves entangled in elaborate debates about attribution of energy savings. A whole new discipline of conditional demand analysis has arisen to quantify the effects of energy prices, weather variations, and government interventions. Even so, evaluation after evaluation has reported the inability to measure the impact of indirect programs (anything that did not directly purchase a conservation measure) by means of recorded energy use. Too many variables change simultaneously to disentangle the individual contribution of small programs.

A comprehensive survey of state conservation programs that were in place as of December 1, 1979, found that the overall record was mixed. Seventeen states were ranked as "excellent" or "good" and almost half were rated as "unsatisfactory."[25] The rankings were based on fourteen tests: two efficiency standards, two types of state grants and loans, four utility price tests, planning and forecasting capabilities, and miscellaneous policies for bottle bills, gasohol, vehicle inspections, and new building design. For several of these tests energy conservation is a secondary goal. Vehicle inspection is an air pollution and safety issue; relatively little energy is saved. Mandatory bottle deposits are a garbage and resource issue; the energy benefits of recycling are used to justify the primary objective. A ranking of states' performance based strictly on energy conservation would not count programs for gasohol, vehicle inspection, and mandatory bottle deposits while neglecting to count appliance standards, commercial audits (two of the most energy-effective programs), tax credits, or industrial-agricultural incentives.

In assessing state performance, one must take into account which end uses a state program might reasonably be expected to influence. Energy consumption by end-use sector is roughly 20 percent residential, 15 percent commercial, 40 percent industrial, and 25 percent transportation. Well over half of all state efforts are directed at the residential sector, with most of the rest directed at local governments and small business. Transportation conservation is dominated by changes in auto design because of the federal fleet efficiency standards, and state programs have been limited to driver education, promotion of ridesharing-

25. Ted Stein, *The Path Not Taken: A Common Cause Study of State Energy Conservation Programs*, rev. ed. (Washington, D.C.: Common Cause, 1980), p. 21.

ing, and some fleet management. State officials rate transportation programs directed at the private car as their least successful activity.[26] By and large, industry has been leery of government conservation programs. A task force of business leaders called for letting the "free market point the way toward meeting energy needs" and to amend the "wishful thinking that relies on legislated solutions."[27]

A 1980 General Accounting Office study disparaged state energy savings achievements. It took the 5 percent energy-savings goal established in the SECP legislation as a serious target and assessed what energy savings had been reported. The auditors found that "the principal problems hampering program effectiveness in these areas were that the States"

> —undertook a large number of programs that account for minimal energy savings but a major share of State Energy Conservation Program funds,
>
> —undertook programs in the buildings areas using methods with serious limitations in encouraging energy savings,
>
> —set overly optimistic goals as to the population to be reached and the extent of compliance, or did not know the effect of programs on consumption because they failed to measure savings attributable only to the State Energy Conservation Program.[28]

The criticisms are valid. By law, states were required to plan to save 5 percent of an entire state's use by 1980. That was an ambitious undertaking when the states actually controlled less than 1 percent of the use. Savings of 3.1 quads, or 59 percent of the goal, were reported; the General Accounting Office thought even these savings were overstated or unsupported. There is a lesson here that goals selected without the participation of those who must carry them out and without an enforcement mechanism are rhetorical, not real. As one state agency observed, "We filled out the [federal reporting] forms, but we didn't take them seriously."

It is one of the anomalies of conservation that the original federal legislation called for achievement of measurable energy savings in the first year, but prohibited using funds to purchase hardware. The program designers desired quick, visible results but they wanted them without spending much money—a classic case of conflicting objectives. The prohibition on paying for measures led to all sorts of roundabout

26. Sawyer, "Improving Federal-State Energy Conservation Programs," p. 86.

27. California Roundtable Energy Task Force, "California Energy: A Program of Action" (San Francisco, June 1982), p. 2.

28. GAO, *State Energy Conservation Program Needs Reassessing*, p. i.

education and outreach efforts, whose effects have been less than memorable.

Outreach, Information and Education

Economics and engineering suggest that when the right technology is produced at the right price, the market will adjust. Innovation diffusion theory tells how this happens. Extensive research has shown that any innovation will be adopted by different socioeconomic groups in a fairly constant pattern.[29] The first adopters (2.5 percent) are of high social and economic status and are risk takers and innovators. Next to become involved (13.5 percent) are early adopters, who are also of high social and economic status and are opinion leaders. The innovation then spreads down through the majority, although the late majority (fully one-third of the market) does not adopt until the price is low enough and the pressures to adopt are strong. Last are the consumers with low social status and income. Lower-income individuals are slow to adopt new products, not because they wish to be, but because their cost of being wrong is proportionately much higher than for people who can afford to take risks.

In the early phase of government demonstration programs, the only realistic consumers are the innovators and the early adopters. But, because governments are expected to provide equal treatment for all citizens, such programs are often criticized for failure to reach the majority and lower socioeconomic groups. This leads to a constant pressure to get rapid societywide results. However, programs designed for innovators and early adopters will not serve the needs of those who are slow or last to adopt innovations. In particular, programs for lower-income individuals should be tailored with them in mind from the beginning and should not just replicate those that have succeeded with upper-income groups.

Conservation programs usually begin with outreach and education because of the planners' belief that if only consumers had better information, they would act rationally. Information campaigns are relatively nonthreatening, inexpensive, and—if they work—an easy

29. Avraham Shama, "Energy Conservation in U.S. Buildings: Solving the High Potential/Low Adoption Paradox from a Behavioral Perspective," *Energy Policy*, vol. 11 (June 1983), pp. 148–67. The article is an excellent synthesis of diffusion research and its application to conservation.

victory. A thousand examples abound—brochures, pamphlets, fliers, workbooks, posters, and energy fairs. Diffusion theory would suggest that an informative message, specialized media, and selective distribution are appropriate marketing strategies for innovators and early adopters. They are remarkably ineffective for the majority, who respond instead to persuasive messages, mass media and distribution, heavy personal selling, and publicity.

A review of one hundred conservation programs revealed remarkably little data on the effectiveness of information campaigns and showed that information programs are exceedingly difficult to document.[30] The few published examples of well-designed research do show, however, that information and outreach programs can be effective if they are targeted. In studies of programs as diverse as maintenance training for boiler operators, financing information for private apartment owners, and the basics of conservation for public housing authorities, workshop attendees have reported that they took follow-up actions as a result, at least in part, of the training that they received.[31] Studies have also found that the information-outreach respondents are innovators and early adopters. For example, a review of Minnesota's telephone information centers found that they were perceived as a useful service, callers were satisfied with the service and took more conservation steps than non-users, but they provided information to people who were already motivated to conserve energy.[32]

A review of information program evaluations found that program effectiveness is tied to the level of personal contact between the client and program staff.[33] Longer, more individual contact is obviously more

30. Colin K. Mick, Ulla Mick, and Daniel Callahan, *Human Factors, Information Campaigns and Energy Conservation* (Palo Alto, Calif.: Decision Information Services, 1982), pp. 25–35.

31. Katherine Tyrrell, "Evaluation of Return-on-Investment" (Sacramento: Office of Planning and Research, California Energy Extension Service, 1983); Eric Hirst, "Evaluating Energy Conservation Outreach Programs: A Case Study in Minnesota," *Energy,* vol. 5 (December 1980), pp. 1169–77; New York State Energy Office, Division of Conservation, *Evaluation of the Energy Conservation Training Program for Public Housing Authorities,* May 1982; and New York State Energy Office, Division of Conservation, *Evaluation of the Multi-Family Housing Energy Conservation Program* (Albany: Energy Office, 1981).

32. Eric Hirst and others, "Evaluation of Telephone Conservation Information Centers in Minnesota," *Journal of Environmental Systems,* vol. 10 (1980–81), pp. 229–48.

33. Gary Cullen, "Assessment of Residential Energy Conservation Programs," paper presented at the American Council for an Energy-Efficient Economy, *ACEEE 1982 Summer Study,* p. 10.

expensive, but adequate analysis has not been done on whether marginal investments in time result in sufficient energy savings to justify the additional cost.

The mass marketing techniques needed to reach the majority are not employed well by governments. Purchases of advertising space or media campaigns are regarded as a waste of money for government programs other than military recruiting. There are examples of successful government marketing, however. In 1981 New York State combined with 180 oil dealers in a joint advertising campaign to improve the efficiency of residential oil heaters. The dealers mailed 500,000 copies of the state-prepared information brochure and performed combustion efficiency tests free of charge while the program was advertised through radio and television public service announcements and weekly and daily newspapers. This well-instrumented campaign resulted in attributable program-induced savings of 100 to 320 gallons of oil annually per participating homeowner.[34]

If the lesson for the 1980s is for states to concentrate on proven programs with remaining potential, mass information-education campaigns are a poor future investment. A study found that the key factors in residential energy savings between 1973 and 1979 were changes in behavior, 43 percent; improvements in equipment efficiency, 44 percent; and improvements to the structure, 13 percent.[35] The easy actions—those most readily influenced by information campaigns—have been taken. Quality information campaigns require more personal contact. Because the trend in conservation funding has been downward, designing programs that require more staffing is counterproductive. If, as is likely, the early implementers have been reached, government doesn't have the diffusion tools to reach the majority and researchers couldn't document the results if they did. For the mid-1980s the question is whether other programs can induce changes in equipment and structural efficiency.

There are activities states can undertake to support marketing directed at the majority. Warranties for unusual products are one very good

34. New York State Energy Office, "Evaluation of the Oil Heat Efficiency Improvement Program" (Albany: Energy Office, January 1981).

35. *Factors in Residential Energy Savings since 1973* (Oak Ridge, Tenn.: Oak Ridge National Laboratory, 1980). This is supported by similar findings in Margaret F. Fels and Miriam L. Goldberg, "Post-embargo Conservation: A New Jersey Case Study," paper presented at the American Council for an Energy-Efficient Economy, *ACEEE 1982 Summer Study*.

example. A 1981 General Accounting Office report has pointed out that up until now states and local governments have not done much to reduce consumer fraud in conservation products.[36] Lack of technical expertise to evaluate claims and lack of resources to monitor claims or test products were the primary problems cited. Energy conservation products are a small part of the state and local consumer protection program, yet the home improvement market is infamous for consumer fraud.

Some states have adopted market cleanup programs. Florida has chosen to actively prosecute contractors with substandard work. The attorney general's office in Rhode Island joined with the Rhode Island Insulation Contractors' Association in 1982 to set insulation quality standards, a minimum one-year warranty, and a binding arbitration process. The federal residential conservation service does require contractors to agree to insulation standards on an individual basis, but states have never had the resources to investigate and prosecute fraudulent claims. A state-business partnership has a much higher likelihood of success.

Conservation through Financial Incentives

Reducing the cost of, or lowering the initial outlay for, conservation measures is a popular state approach. It sidesteps the complexities of designing information programs and produces easily measurable results. Conservation measures are cost effective without incentives; financial incentives are used to lower resistance caused by other market barriers. For example, the offer of a partial grant may convince a citizen that evaluating, finding, and installing home insulation is worthwhile. Loans and financing can be used to relieve capital access problems for the poor, small businesses, or public facilities.

PUBLIC FACILITIES. The blizzard of paperwork, the overlap of state and federal responsibilities, and the compressed grant cycle of the schools and hospitals program have all contributed to state-federal tensions. Arkansas attributed its success to the requirement of matching funds from the facilities, the encouragement of energy awareness through a required audit, and the use of professional and energy-savings criteria

36. General Accounting Office, "State and Local Agencies Have Problems Significantly or Rapidly Reducing Inaccurate and Misleading Energy-Saving Claims," in Brian J. Weberg, ed., *Energy Efficiency in Buildings: A State Policy Handbook* (Denver, Colo.: National Conference of State Legislatures, 1982), pp. 113–21.

in choosing projects.[37] Wisconsin also gave the program high marks, but pointed out that grantees sometimes invest in "what intuitively seems right" instead of picking the most cost-effective options from their audit reports.[38] A major finding of these evaluations is that the program stimulates new investment rather than paying for something that would have happened anyway. The program's effectiveness and high level of support is perhaps not surprising: energy costs are the most frequently cited cause of school financial problems, according to a 1982–83 poll of school superintendents.[39]

Public facility loans and grants, the oldest of the state financing programs, arose as companions to the federal grant program. Since most municipalities and school districts are restricted in their borrowing authority and in their capital budgets, public facility revolving loan funds have been successful and oversubscribed. Maryland, California, and Mississippi all have matching loan funds, while Nebraska and Florida provide matching grants. Maine and New Jersey have used state bonding authority to finance audits and energy improvements. Grants and loans for direct retrofit of schools and hospitals are successful state programs because their design is straightforward, the need is clear and otherwise unmet, and the benefits can be counted, appreciated, and publicized.

RESIDENTIAL GRANTS FOR WEATHERIZATION. For years, the low-income weatherization assistance program (administered by the Department of Energy) has been charged by both federal and state auditors with having problems of poor workmanship, insufficient data on energy savings, and inadequate financial management and program monitoring.[40] There have been numerous occasions of misuse of funds by the contract agencies and overstatement of both the number of homes weatherized and quality of work performed. Among twenty-seven low-income weatherization projects with valid evaluations, the median payback time was 9.2 years.

37. *The Institutional Conservation Program at Work in Arkansas* (Little Rock, Ark.: Energy Office, March 1982).

38. Martin Olle and others, *Energy Management in Wisconsin Public and Commercial Buildings: Results of the Institutional Conservation Program* (Madison, Wis.: Wisconsin Division of State Energy, 1984).

39. Shirley J. Hansen Associates, *School Finance and Energy through the Year 2000,* prepared for the U.S. Department of Energy, DOE/CE/64835-1 (1984). See also New York State Energy Office, Division of Conservation, *Controlling Energy Costs in Institutional Buildings: A Review of the Institutional Buildings Grants Program* (Albany: Energy Office, 1983).

40. General Accounting Office study of the Department of Energy's weatherization program as reported in *Energy Conservation Digest* (November 9, 1981), p. 4.

The program has been cost effective, but less so than for conservation investments by the population as a whole.[41] This is in part because the program is expected to both weatherize homes efficiently and provide employment for the disadvantaged. Any program with multiple objectives has built-in trouble.

Why has a troubled program hung on so successfully all these years? It is both an energy conservation program and a welfare program addressing the needs of the poor. Low-income energy assistance (administered by the Department of Health and Human Services) is pouring into the states at an annual rate of over $1 billion to pay daily utility bills, and that is not enough. By 1981 twice the actual level of funding would have been needed to lower the share of a poor family's annual income spent on energy just to the percentage spent by middle-income families.[42] Low-income energy assistance funds are often treated as general block grants for social support; in fiscal year 1983, 15 percent of these funds were either carried over or rolled out into other social service programs.[43]

Some states have experimented to strengthen the weatherization assistance program. Michigan tried having the local community action agencies identify eligible clients and perform preinspection of the homes and postinstallation inspections while the retrofit work was done by private contractors. The average cost per home weatherized was 22 percent less than the statewide average.[44] Starting in 1982, Colorado tested low-cost ($50) weatherization measures that are installed by the resident for some quick relief. It achieved measured utility bill savings of 11.6 percent in home heating bills and in the second year successfully directed half of its services to renters.[45]

A 1981 survey found twenty-six state-run weatherization programs in operation, up from the seventeen proposed or implemented in 1979. But there had been a trend away from direct, full payment for weatherization toward tax credits, rebates, and loans.[46] These are much less likely to get poor people's homes retrofitted.

41. Steven Ferrey, "Pulling a Rabbit Out of the Hat: Innovative Financing for Low-Income Conservation," in the American Council for an Energy-Efficient Economy, *Doing Better,* vol. H, p. 39.

42. David C. Sweet, "A Reduced Federal Role in Low-Income Energy Assistance: Implications for States," in Weberg, ed., *Energy Efficiency in Buildings,* p. 241.

43. Ferrey, "Pulling A Rabbit," p. 44.

44. "WAP: Innovative Programs," proceedings of All-States Energy Leaders Meeting (San Francisco: California Energy Extension, September 1982), p. 20.

45. State of Colorado, Office of Energy Conservation, *Low-Cost Weatherization Final Report: 1982–1983* (Denver: Office of Energy Conservation, 1984), p. 3.

46. Sweet, "A Reduced Federal Role," p. 238.

RESIDENTIAL LOANS. Theoretically, low-interest loans are a policy measure appropriate for the majority of consumers. Almost all states have some form of low-interest financing available from their regulated utilities. Four states (Connecticut, West Virginia, Alaska, and Pennsylvania) have chosen to sponsor their own loan programs in addition to or instead of utility funding. Experience has shown that all income classes will take loans, although lower-income groups may be frightened off if a lien is required for security or if utilities might be shut off for nonpayment.

Loan subsidies, principal reductions, and partial grants are now available in all states through the Department of Housing and Urban Development's Solar Energy and Energy Conservation Bank. Most states had great difficulty implementing this program, since it involved setting up new borrowing relationships with banks and other financial institutions. The Energy Bank is an interesting example of conflicting government objectives, since it uses private-sector lending institutions and yet requires all the detailed reporting and income verification common to federal aid programs. The banks have been unable to cope with the level of detail required, and most states have resorted to extensive state processing of the paperwork in order to make the bank work.[47]

Loan programs have received consistent positive evaluations in their ability to generate measurable conservation savings. A typical finding states that "the availability of loans seems to stimulate higher levels of retrofit investment and to produce more energy savings."[48]

TAX CREDITS. State tax credits are a curious phenomenon. They cost the state two to five times more than all other state conservation expenditures, yet seem to have an undramatic impact on purchases. Unlike the solar tax credits, which are necessary for the solar industry's survival, conservation credits seem to be a windfall for the purchaser of lower-cost items. Indications of lackluster performance come from three sources: no apparent surge in conservation measures sold the first year of a tax credit, econometric models that suggest other causality, and testimonials from industry associations. No marketing research has been done on the use of tax credits as an advertising feature nor on the credibility given products by the government's "seal of approval."

47. Findings reported at U.S. Housing and Urban Development All-States Meeting of Energy Bank Operators, Washington, D.C., June 26–28, 1984.

48. Linda Berry and Bruce Tonn, *Loan Impacts in Home Energy Audit Programs: A Minnesota Example,* ORNL/CON-145 (Oak Ridge, Tenn.: Oak Ridge National Laboratory, 1984), p. v.

Although they are not necessarily the most effective way to leverage state dollars, tax credits are generally accepted by members of both parties and by both business and consumer advocates. As a voluntary financial incentive, they have enormous surface appeal. Suggestions of marginal impact on additional purchases of conservation measures are taken as attacks on the conservation ethic, which reinforces the perception that tax credits' value is primarily emotional and political. Comparative research indicates that a rebate coming close to the time of purchase is more effective in generating new sales. That, plus an opportunity to cut revenue loss, may be what prompted Oregon in 1981 to repeal its $125 residential credit and to order utilities to design equivalent incentives.[49]

COMMERCIAL AND INDUSTRIAL LOANS. A newcomer to the field of state-funded initiatives and to tax-exempt financing is the state-sponsored loan pool for commercial and industrial conservation. Pioneered by North Carolina, these loan pools lessen financing costs by bundling conservation and alternative energy projects and passing through the proceeds of tax-exempt bonds. Six states—Maryland, California, Illinois, Minnesota, New York, and Oregon—have recently established commercial and industrial financing programs. Although most of these programs are not old enough to have a thorough evaluation, there is already some analytic question whether these are windfall gains to business. The argument followed is that businesses are much more motivated by energy prices than the residential sector and that they would have made the investment anyway. One study discounts over half the savings from these programs, asserting that they would have occurred anyway.[50]

THIRD-PARTY FINANCING. The greatest growth in state conservation programs has been in third-party financing and performance contracting. Close to half the states are experimenting with promoting third-party financing in state and municipal facilities. Over the years, states have

49. States giving conservation tax credits are Alaska (business), California (business and personal), Colorado, Hawaii, Montana, North Carolina, and South Carolina. North Dakota repealed its energy credit in 1983. California trimmed its credit from 40 percent to 35 percent, but extended its application. A deduction is allowed by Arkansas, Idaho, and Indiana; and Florida gives a sales tax exemption. *Energy Conservation Digest,* May 24, 1982, p. 9; and *All States Tax Handbook, 1982* (Prentice-Hall, 1981), p. 295.

50. Donald K. Schultz, "End Use Consumption Patterns and Energy Conservation Savings in Commercial Buildings," in the American Council for an Energy-Efficient Economy, *Doing Better,* vol. A, p. 120.

not been particularly successful in obtaining capital funds for retrofit. Third-party financing promises to plug that energy leak, since the user puts up no initial capital, owns the equipment after five to seven years, and pays for the installation through energy savings. The fact that energy savings provide a reliable source for paying off the lease is critical, because most public bodies are restricted by constitutions and bonding limits from making multiyear investments dependent on the "full faith and credit" of the government for repayment.

States are attracted to energy financing because it uses private capital to improve the public infrastructure and it has a high potential for being self-supporting without affecting tax revenues. State initiatives for increasing shared savings in state and municipal facilities undertaken since 1982 are:

—removing restrictions against multiyear liabilities through constitutional amendment, encouraging use of contracts that bar claims against general revenues, and creating loan guarantee funds (Arkansas, New Jersey, and Washington);

—developing procurement guidelines and model contracts (California, Delaware, Michigan, and New Jersey);

—conducting demonstrations (New York, New Jersey, California, Washington, Pennsylvania, New Mexico, Massachusetts, Minnesota, North Carolina, and Michigan).

By 1984, early enthusiasm had been dimmed by the realities of implementing a complicated concept. Why, one leading practitioner asked, should states have to share their energy savings potential with "high-powered lawyers, greedy financiers, and clever engineers"?[51] Hard lessons have been shared informally through contractor networks and scattered conferences, but too often a desire to accentuate the positive aspects of a demonstration has kept counterparts from learning the difficulties and disappointments of stretched-out negotiations, tax law intricacies, and endless briefings of disbelieving facility operators.

It is clear that in the 1980s states will be an eager and ready market for third-party financing. What is less clear is whether this will lead to a transition to efficient in-house energy management and whether third-

51. Robert A. Shinn and Anthony J. Rametta, "A Penny Saved Is Half a Penny Earned: Pennsylvania's Third Party (Shared Savings) Financing Program for Energy Conservation," in the American Council for an Energy-Efficient Economy, *Doing Better*, vol. L, pp. 102–12; and Mike Weedall, "The Emerging Role of the Public Sector in Third-Party Finance," in ibid., pp. 113–26.

party financing is an appropriate mechanism for states to promote for their citizens and businesses.

Conservation by Standard Setting

At the other end of the spectrum from outreach are minimum efficiency standards. The biggest energy savings of any state program have been obtained through building standards and appliance standards. For example, California's 1982 residential building standards lowered energy costs for new homes to one-fourth of those for homes built before any standards. Those standards will result in life-cycle energy savings of $20 billion.[52] Using cost effectiveness as the basis for policy choice, it is hard to argue against standards that are enforced. Standards that are not enforced, or that have no teeth because they were designed to be weak in order to get enacted, are disastrous. Mandatory retrofit of residences at time of sale is a prime example of the latter.

BUILDING STANDARDS. As early as December 1, 1979, forty-three states had established lighting standards for new state buildings, and thirty-eight had done so for new commercial buildings. Thermal standards had been established by forty-six states for new state buildings, by thirty-seven states for new residences, and by thirty-nine states for new commercial buildings.[53] Even though the federal government was supposed to develop performance standards for new buildings, New York, Florida, California, and Massachusetts went on to establish their own standards for new residential construction, Florida and California also established new nonresidential construction standards, and Minnesota and Wisconsin went even further by setting standards for existing residential units that are rented.

The 1975–79 standards, which were required by the SECP, focused on basic insulation measures. The strength of these standards was largely dependent on the quality of the building departments that enforced them. This, in turn, was affected by whether the state had a uniform building code, or whether local jurisdictions had leeway to adopt and pursue particular sections. Approximately one-third of the states performed only a training and advisory role in the implementation of their standards.

52. Ranny Eckstrom, *New Residential Building Standards* (Sacramento, Calif.: California Energy Commission, 1983).

53. Stein, *The Path Not Taken,* p. 126.

Another third added technical assistance to local agencies, and a final third carried out some enforcement functions. Two-thirds of the states delegated all enforcement responsibility to the local jurisdictions.[54]

Building standards do produce energy savings and life-cycle cost savings, even if they raise the initial cost of a new building. (Not all new standards raise costs; the new California office standards lower first costs because they allow for smaller sizing on the heating, ventilating, air conditioning, and lighting equipment.) The problems tend to be ones of implementation, such as inadequate product labeling and availability, conflicts with local codes on air exchanges, and technical complexity in the concepts, design manual, and documentation.[55] Effective standards require as much state resources to implement as to develop them in the first place. Builders, manufacturers, installers, and local officials must be trained. Extensive manuals to make compliance easy are needed. There must also be an exemption mechanism for unusual cases. Standards will not be accepted unless there is a long lead time before enforcement, so that inventories, whether of subdivisions or gas furnaces, can be cleared. The standards must be cost effective over the life of the product, and they must not increase first costs very much no matter how cost effective they are in the long run. Lastly, they must be enforced.

An example of the problems that can develop in implementation is Minnesota's program of mandatory minimum energy efficiency standards for rental housing, adopted in 1977. That program was ineffective, according to the state's evaluation, because the standards were weak and too simplistic for the variety of building types. Also, funding was never appropriated to inform owners of the requirements and to actively enforce compliance. Recognizing the standards' defects, Minnesota overhauled its program in 1983–84 to include "an effective set of standards that are widely publicized, with readily available energy audits, affordable financing, and a workable enforcement mechanism. Unless all of these components are available as a comprehensive package, significant improvements are highly unlikely."[56]

54. National Institute of Building Sciences, *States' Energy Conservation Standards for New Construction* (Washington, D.C.: NIBS, 1979), pp. 8–22.

55. National Institute of Building Sciences, *Energy Conservation for Buildings: A Case Study of California* (Washington, D.C.: NIBS, 1978), pp. 156–72.

56. Greg Hubinger, "Improving the Regulatory Approach to Increased Rental Housing Energy Efficiency: The Minnesota Case Study," in the American Council for an Energy-Efficient Economy, *Doing Better,* vol. C, p. 69.

Mandatory retrofit at time of sale has been considered as the equivalent of new residential building standards for the existing home market. Standards for existing housing start with one strike against them, for initial research indicates that while 60 percent of citizens accept regulations on new buildings, fewer than 20 percent support similar regulations on existing buildings.[57] Minnesota started with a mild version. Enacted in 1976, the home energy disclosure program went into effect in October 1980 and required that the results of an energy audit be made available to prospective homebuyers. The results of the first three months were dismal. Only one quarter of the houses sold had received their required evaluations.[58] Only 28 percent of buyers saw an audit while they were looking at homes (the majority received it at the time the purchase contract was signed or at close of escrow); 56 percent thought the report was inadequate. Research found that the audit did motivate the home purchasers to install measures in their new home, an interesting lesson for future program design.

Evaluation of California's local mandatory retrofit ordinances revealed similar problems to those found in Minnesota. Less than half the homes sold complied with the ordinances. There are repetitive problems with paying for the audits and the postinstallation inspections, creating a notification and record-keeping system, and a lack of enforcement. In 1983 one ordinance was repealed and one community decided to switch to a voluntary home rating and labeling system. The state is now testing a pilot voluntary home labeling and rating system as a substitute.

Wisconsin has pushed bravely on. In exasperation over the lack of success other approaches were having in getting the rental market weatherized, the legislature enacted mandatory standards for apartments. Starting in 1985, rental property was to be required to have an energy audit and to either have the energy standards met by the time the building is sold or have negotiations arranged with the purchaser for installation.[59]

APPLIANCE STANDARDS. The federal government was expected to set

57. Barbara J. Burt and Max Neiman, "Support for Local Government Regulation to Support Solar Energy," in the American Council for an Energy-Efficient Economy, *Doing Better,* vol. F, pp. 47, 50.

58. Frank Altman and others, "Minnesota Home Energy Disclosure Program," in Weberg, ed., *Energy Efficiency in Buildings,* pp. 201–16.

59. *Energy User News,* vol. 8 (January 3, 1983); and Brian Fay, "Voluntary Rental Living Unit Program," in the American Council for an Energy-Efficient Economy, *Doing Better,* vol. C, p. 28.

appliance standards. When it chose not to do so, Florida, New York, and California set multiple appliance standards, with Wisconsin, Minnesota, and Oregon joining the latter two in requiring intermittent ignition devices for gas appliances.

Appliance standards have a dramatic payoff. By 1984 California's appliance standards had reduced utility bills by almost $1 billion and peak load by 870 megawatts. By 1994 the existing standards will be saving more energy per year than is produced by all the hydroelectric power plants in the state (27 percent of electricity generation). Twice as many jobs are created by the existence of standards as would be by the purchase of fuel and construction of energy facilities if the standards were repealed.[60] After a lengthy attempt to overturn state appliance standards, even the U.S. Department of Energy has conceded that state appliance standards create sufficient energy savings to justify continuing the regulations.[61]

By far the most critical economic issue in the adoption of standards is how much savings would have been produced independently by market forces. In the case of appliances, evidence shows that energy efficiency has little influence on which appliance a consumer purchases compared with price, size, features, brand name, suitability, and color. The Institute of Heating and Air Conditioning Industries, Natural Resources Defense Council, Carrier Corporation, and General Accounting Office have all conducted studies indicating that appliance efficiencies, outside those governed by state standards, have not increased in response to price.[62] The observed discount rates for efficient appliance purchases fall into a range from less than 20 percent to more than 200 percent per year, too high to be the operation of a rational market.[63] Standards are especially effective for the new home and rental market, where the developer and landlord purchasers do not pay the operating cost and are chiefly concerned with the lowest first cost.

60. California Energy Commission, *California's Appliance Standards: An Historical Review, Analysis and Recommendations,* P400-83-020 (Sacramento: CEC, 1983), pp. vii, 69, 90.

61. "DOE Ruling Permits 5 States to Continue Appliance Rules Requiring Energy Efficiency," *Energy Conservation Bulletin,* vol. 3 (May–June 1984), p. 5.

62. California Energy Commission, *California's Appliance Standards,* pp. 77–80.

63. Henry Ruderman, Mark D. Levine, and James E. McMahon, "The Behavior of the Market for Energy Efficiency in the Purchase of Appliances and Home Heating and Cooling Equipment," LBL-15304 (Berkeley, Calif.: Lawrence Berkeley Laboratory, 1984).

Conclusions

Of the three levels of government, the states have been the most active in promoting energy conservation. Their programs have been diffuse and episodic, but seem to be cost effective to society. As programs have matured, they have taught the following lessons.

1. Program effectiveness is variable and is intertwined with the underlying perception of the public sector's role.

2. Information and education programs should be specific, personal, and aimed at conservation-oriented consumers.

3. Mass marketing should be rejected in favor of direct hardware purchase programs.

4. Matching grants, rebates, and loan subsidies are more effective than tax credits as incentives.

5. Programs should be sensitive to the high transaction costs of conservation purchases and to the high level of consumer awareness that is needed.

6. Low-income programs are not as cost effective as other conservation activities, and additional research is needed to ameliorate the growing gap between the share of income spent on energy by the poor and that spent by upper-income groups.

7. Off-budget options can be an acceptable method of financing retrofit of government facilities.

8. Standards for new buildings and appliances are an extremely cost-effective program option, but need to be buttressed by adequate training, compliance assistance, and enforcement.

9. Retrofit standards for existing buildings do not seem to be effective.

Comments by Eric Hirst

It is really surprising that one is unable to say much about the actual performance of the states in operating their programs and that there is so little data on the impact of the states' efforts. But there is good reason for it. The energy offices were born largely in response to the Arab oil embargo and 1975 federal legislation that optimistically and unrealistically mandated that the states should save 5 percent of their energy by 1980 and then gave them a tiny budget.

Half a dozen additional federal statutes were added during the late

1970s, and then the Reagan administration in 1981 simply cut off all that had gone before. Then in 1983 there was a resurgence of money because of the oil overcharge litigation. Overlaid on this chaotic federal role is the role of the state legislators themselves in providing funding in some cases for their energy offices and adding additional legislative mandates. As a consequence, the focus and purpose of state energy offices have tended to be ambiguous.

The preponderance of activities in states continues to focus on diffuse, mass-market kinds of information programs, which I consider inappropriate. I can't believe that more than ten years after the embargo people still need to be told to turn down their thermostats, drive at 55 miles per hour, and put insulation in their attics. But inertia is a powerful force, and a lot of the information programs set in place five or ten years ago continue to operate.

Another characteristic of state energy offices is their focus on the residential sector. It was the sector about which they knew the most, and it seemed the easiest one to start with. The expectation was that they would then move on to the commercial and industrial sectors. Unfortunately, that really hasn't happened.

Finally, state energy offices are conducting a large number of small, diffuse programs. From the point of view of management, that is terribly inappropriate. There is no way you can manage programs with annual budgets of $20,000, let alone even begin to evaluate them. These programs need to be consolidated.

It is also important to focus on the relationship between the state energy office and other institutions within the state, in particular the public utility commission and the utilities. State energy offices were created in the mid-1970s partly because the states and the Department of Energy felt that the commissions had become moribund. In the last few years, that has changed quite a bit. Both the commissions and the utilities have become much more active. There is a clear need now to eliminate or at least reduce the overlap of programs and responsibilities.

There is almost no analysis of actual program performance. This is primarily because the programs are so small that there is almost no hope of identifying their effects. Because there is so little analysis of energy savings, there is even less of program economics. Considerations of marginal and average cost values to society are almost never performed. Where they are done, they deal only with costs paid by the government and ignore the costs to other parties.

Despite these negative comments, my gut feeling is that the programs probably have had a modest, positive effect on the national energy situation. Much of the effect is probably indirect—that is, the states have served primarily to influence others who then in turn have taken action to save energy.

Comments by John Bryson

It is difficult to evaluate any of these conservation programs without considering the pricing of the energy form in question. The programs make sense primarily to the extent that the prices are inappropriate, as they likely are in two respects. First, with some limited exceptions, utility prices for natural gas or electricity are set on an embedded cost basis, rather than on the basis of marginal cost pricing. Second, even if energy, such as oil or gasoline at the pump, were priced at market levels unaffected by regulatory patterns, there are important externalities, such as the insecurity of world energy supplies.

State conservation programs need to be evaluated in the context of other programs, such as utility rate reform, which has potential in itself to improve price signals. Utility financing programs should be seen as related to the utility audit program that is mandated by the state energy office. There are also costs associated with the myriad levels of government involved (federal, several state agencies, local governments, and utilities) in developing conservation programs.

A related point is that study should be given to the most effective level of government involvement in energy conservation programs and to a better meshing of responsibilities among different agencies. There are substantial costs and waste that arise from the current fragmentation of responsibility. The residential conservation service program, for example, is a program in which federal officials invested an immense amount of time and energy in an effort to control the programs at the state level through extraordinary regulatory detail. After the federal and state energy offices finished writing regulations, the program moved to the utility commissions. The utility commissions needed to deal with the costs of the program, and the costs turned out to be extraordinary in relation to the apparent value of a pure information program. And there still is no serious evaluation data on that kind of auditing program.

Another example is the point-of-sale ordinances some municipalities in California adopted, which require the seller to do certain minimal weatherization measures at the time of sale. The rationale was that expenditures at the time of sale placed the least burden on the public because money was coming out of the transaction, and a small fraction of that money could be spent on retrofit. The problem is that the municipalities either didn't want to or weren't able to do the preaudit needed to tell the homeowner what he had to do in order to meet the standards or the postaudit to ensure the standards were met. The municipalities then started looking around for somebody else to do it. The idea arose that utilities could do it. But if a mandated audit by the utility is used to enforce a city ordinance, then a service or benefit is provided to that municipality at the cost of utility customers throughout the service area. In addition, utilities object to becoming the policeman for a municipality.

These are serious problems. Some further analysis needs to be given to determining the best delivery vehicle for energy conservation. What have been the costs or the benefits of the fragmented approach with federal money, heavy federal control, and the creation of state energy offices outside the traditional state line agencies?

JOHN H. GIBBONS, HOLLY L. GWIN,
and RICHARD B. POOL

Energy Conservation in the Federal Government

WE HOLD to the traditional meaning of conservation, "wise and thoughtful use." The federal government applies this notion of economic rationality to some resources, but some national leaders seem to equate energy conservation with varying degrees of misery. President Carter preached sacrifice rather than economic self-interest, and President Reagan likened energy conservation to being hot in the summer and cold in the winter rather than heating and cooling efficiently in well-built structures. To be sure, there have been and will be times when curtailment is a national necessity. But those exceptional times need to be distinguished carefully from the more fundamental purpose of conservation: using resources wisely.

Energy use and gross national product are not inextricably linked. Given time for adjustment, energy use is a very substitutable factor in the provision of goods and services, and economic growth can continue without a corresponding increase in energy consumption. Rising energy prices, like those experienced in the past decade, provide a powerful and effective incentive for consumers to become more energy efficient.

The federal government is the nation's largest energy consumer. In fiscal year 1982 the government used 2.5 percent of the national energy total at a cost of more than $13.6 billion.[1] The government's self-interest—using tax dollars with high efficiency—speaks for bringing that bill down if possible.

As the guardian of public health, safety, security, and natural resources, the federal government must contend with the nonmarket costs

1. U.S. Department of Energy, *Annual Report on Federal Government Energy Management, Fiscal Year 1982,* DOE/CE-0043/1 (DOE, 1984), p. 1.

Table 1. *Energy Use by Federal Agencies, Fiscal Years 1975–82*
Trillions of Btus unless otherwise indicated

Agency	*1975*	*1976*	*1977*	*1978*	*1979*	*1980*	*1981*	*1982*	*Percent change, 1975–82*
Department of Defense	1,504.9	1,386.8	1,401.2	1,365.7	1,384.2	1,394.8	1,455.5	1,484.3	−1.4
Department of Energy	86.5	91.7	88.3	86.3	86.3	83.3	85.7	89.6	+3.5
U.S. Postal Service	59.2	58.3	62.9	58.6	56.0	52.3	50.9	49.4	−16.6
General Services Administration	43.1	41.2	41.3	41.4	40.6	39.0	39.2	38.9	−9.7
Veterans Administration	39.2	36.5	37.9	39.4	38.5	37.7	37.5	38.0	−3.1
Department of Transportation	28.3	27.4	28.8	28.9	27.6	27.5	28.0	28.5	+0.8
National Aeronautics and Space Administration	26.8	25.3	24.0	22.5	22.5	21.3	21.2	21.8	−18.6
Department of the Interior	12.3	13.1	13.5	12.3	12.6	11.7	10.7	10.7	−12.9
Department of Agriculture	11.9	11.6	10.8	11.2	11.2	11.2	11.1	10.4	−13.0
Department of Health and Human Services	9.3	9.6	9.9	9.6	9.7	9.5	10.6	10.2	+10.7
Department of Justice	6.2	7.2	7.4	7.2	7.6	7.3	7.0	7.7	+25.3
Other[a]	9.3	10.5	11.2	11.5	11.5	11.4	11.8	12.4	+34.2
Total	1,836.9	1,719.2	1,737.2	1,694.7	1,708.2	1,706.9	1,769.1	1,802.0	−1.9

Source: U.S. Department of Energy, *Annual Report on Federal Government Energy Management, Fiscal Year 1982,* DOE/CE-0043/1 (DOE, 1984), p. A-1. Figures are rounded.

a. Includes Departments of Labor, Commerce, Housing and Urban Development, and State, and Panama Canal Commission, Tennessee Valley Authority, National Science Foundation, Office of Personnel Management, Interstate Commerce Commission, Small Business Administration, Federal Communications Commission, and Civil Aeronautics Board. Excludes Department of Treasury and Environmental Protection Agency.

of energy as well. Market prices do not reflect (1) the environmental costs of energy production and use; (2) the costs of defending Middle East oil production and shipping lanes; (3) the costs of purchasing and storing oil to meet emergencies; or (4) the costs to U.S. allies and the impoverished third world countries of U.S. competition for petroleum on the world market. The nonmarket cost of imported oil, even without supply interruptions, may be as high as $50 a barrel, compared with an average price of $31.87 a barrel in 1982.[2] The production of natural gas, coal, electricity, and other domestic sources of energy also entails major nonmarket costs. The government's unique ability to apprehend these costs speaks for a broad federal role in energy conservation efforts, particularly in research and development.

In this chapter, we examine the federal government's dual role in energy conservation—as a consumer of energy and as a promoter of the public welfare. The government's performance has not been impressive, particularly when compared with the private sector. We will show why this has been the case and where improvements could be made.

Energy Use in the Federal Government

Federal energy consumption declined fairly steadily from 1975, shortly after the first oil crisis, through 1980 (see table 1). Since 1980, however, federal energy use has increased. In fiscal year 1982 consumption was 1.9 percent greater than in fiscal 1981 and 5.6 percent greater than in fiscal 1980.

Not quite half the energy the federal government consumes is used to heat, cool, and operate its 500,000 buildings. It cost $4 billion in fiscal 1982 to provide their energy requirements of 0.8 quads. Building energy use has decreased since 1975, but progress has been minimal and inconsistent (see table 2). There are notable exceptions: the U.S. Postal Service achieved a 27.8 percent reduction and the National Aeronautics and Space Administration achieved a 22.7 percent reduction between fiscal years 1975 and 1982 in Btus consumed per gross square foot. The

2. Office of Technology Assessment, *Increased Automobile Fuel Efficiency and Synthetic Fuels: Alternatives for Reducing Oil Imports*, OTA-E-185 (Government Printing Office, 1982), p. 69.

Table 2. *Energy Use in Federal Buildings and Facilities, Fiscal Years 1975 and 1982*
Thousands of Btus per gross square foot unless otherwise indicated

Agency	*1975*	*1982*	*Percent change, 1975–82*
Department of Defense	271.0	235.4	−13.1
Department of Energy	1,028.8	866.6	−15.8
U.S. Postal Service	291.3	210.4	−27.8
General Services Administration	195.4	175.0	−10.4
Veterans Administration	360.9	318.0	−11.9
National Aeronautics and Space Administration	783.4	605.4	−22.7
Department of Transportation	552.1	495.3	−10.3
Department of Health and Human Services	456.3	465.4	+2.0
Department of Interior	179.8	153.0	−14.9
Department of Agriculture	325.5	284.4	−12.6
Department of Justice	313.8	352.7	+12.4
Other[a]	283.9	305.7	+7.7
Total Btus per gross square foot	292.8	254.2	−13.2

Source: DOE, *Annual Report on Federal Government Energy Management, Fiscal Year 1982,* p. A-6. Figures are rounded.
a. See note a, table 1.

total reduction throughout the federal agencies, however, was 13.2 percent; the goal was a 20 percent reduction by 1985.[3]

Energy use in general operations (transportation, tactical operations, research, and production and process operations within buildings) is shown in table 3. In fiscal year 1982 general operations accounted for 55 percent of total federal energy consumption at a cost of $9.6 billion. Vehicles and equipment consumed 95 percent of the energy used in general operations, and the Defense Department's use accounts for 96 percent of that amount. The Defense Department attributed its fiscal year 1982 increase of 2.3 percent over fiscal 1981 to increased readiness and mission support requirements. In 1982 the civilian agencies decreased energy use in general operations by 6.9 percent over 1975 and 3.1 percent over 1981.[4]

The Department of Defense is the federal government's largest energy

3. DOE, *Annual Report on Federal Government Energy Management, Fiscal Year 1982,* p. 1.
4. Ibid., p.1 and table 3A.

Table 3. *Energy Use in General Operations by Federal Agencies, Fiscal Years 1975 and 1982*
Trillions of Btus unless otherwise indicated

Agency and category	*1975*	*1982*	*Percent change, 1975–82*
Vehicles and equipment			
Department of Defense	858.9	899.3	+4.7
Department of Transportation	11.4	11.0	−3.1
U.S. Postal Service	11.2	10.5	−6.1
Department of Agriculture	5.2	4.5	−12.9
Department of Interior	3.4	2.8	−17.2
Department of Energy	1.9	2.5	+32.1
Department of Justice	1.9	1.9	+0.1
National Aeronautics and Space Administration	1.7	1.7	+2.6
Tennessee Valley Authority	1.1	1.1	+1.0
Department of Commerce	11.1	0.9	−16.0
Other[a]	3.5	2.4	−32.0
Total vehicles and equipment	901.3	938.8	+4.2
Facilities and production			
Department of Energy	24.5	30.5	+24.7
Department of Defense	15.9	19.7	+24.2
Total facilities and production	40.4	50.2	+24.5
Total general operations	941.6	989.0	+5.0

Source: DOE, *Annual Report on Federal Government Energy Management, Fiscal Year 1982*, p. A-4. Figures are rounded.

a. Includes Panama Canal Commission, National Science Foundation, Office of Personnel Management, Interstate Commerce Commission, Small Business Administration, Federal Communications Commission, Civil Aeronautics Board, General Services Administration, Veterans Administration, and Departments of Housing and Urban Development, State, Health and Human Services, and Labor.

user. It consumed almost 1.5 quads in fiscal year 1982, 82 percent of the federal total. Thus reduced use by Defense could contribute significantly to total federal energy conservation. For example, 38 percent of the Defense Department's energy consumption is used in buildings and facilities; conservation in that area would pose little risk of impairing military readiness. The civilian agencies also have much room for improvement in their energy use patterns.

History of Federal Conservation Efforts

The federal government first launched a coordinated program to conserve energy in 1973. President Nixon issued a directive requiring federal agencies to reduce energy consumption and established the federal energy management program to coordinate activities. Since then, both Congress and the executive branch have taken steps to influence federal energy use.

Congressional mandates include:

1. A requirement that the president develop and implement a ten-year plan to conserve energy in federal buildings (Energy Policy and Conservation Act of 1975).

2. A requirement that a Department of Energy (DOE) be organized. One of the purposes of the act is to promote maximum possible energy conservation measures throughout the federal sector (Department of Energy Organization Act of 1977).

3. A requirement that federal agencies audit their buildings with more than 1,000 square feet of floor space and implement energy conservation retrofit measures in buildings failing to meet certain standards (National Energy Conservation Policy Act of 1978).

4. A requirement that solar heating and cooling demonstrations take place in federal residential and commercial buildings and facilities (Solar Heating and Cooling Demonstration Act of 1974).

5. A requirement that an assistant secretary or assistant administrator from each major energy-using department and agency be designated as principal conservation officer (Department of Energy Organization Act of 1977).

6. A requirement that life-cycle costing methodology be developed for energy conservation investments (National Energy Conservation Policy Act of 1978).

These congressional acts are supplemented by several executive actions, including:

1. Executive Order 11912, which required the DOE to develop the ten-year plan required by the Energy Policy and Conservation Act.

2. Executive Order 12003, which set specific energy conservation goals for federal buildings. Federal agencies were directed to achieve a 20 percent improvement in the energy efficiency of existing buildings and a 45 percent improvement in new buildings between fiscal years 1975 and 1983. The executive order also required agencies to develop plans to conserve fuel in federally owned vehicles. These goals were to be accomplished through ten-year plans devised by each agency in addition to the overall ten-year plan.

3. Involvement of the Office of Management and Budget (OMB) in conservation efforts. The OMB has responsibility for promoting the

governmentwide implementation of sound energy management practices. Primarily, the OMB focuses on identifying funding for agency conservation projects and reviewing budget requests for carrying out energy conservation plans.

It should be noted that these mandates form the foundation of federal energy management and have little to do with other major federal energy legislation.

Federal Response

Some of the conservation mandates have been acted upon. Preliminary audits were made to identify the energy consumption characteristics of most federal buildings: size, type, rate of energy consumption, major energy-using systems, and regional climate. Life-cycle costing has been adopted as the primary criterion for carrying out conservation retrofits and for design of new buildings; the DOE is sponsoring workshops to educate federal officials in life-cycle costing techniques.

There also has been some success in meeting the goals for fuel economy in the federal government's civilian automobile fleet. The standard for cars purchased or leased for the federal civilian fleet for 1981 was 26 miles per gallon, 4 miles per gallon higher than the corporate average fuel economy standard for U.S. auto manufacturers. The actual average was 26.8 miles per gallon. In 1982 the federal fleet standard was lowered to 24 miles per gallon, the same as the corporate standard for that year. The actual average was 27.2 miles per gallon.[5]

The various presidential and congressional directives have generally been ignored, however. Energy conservation has not captured the interest of high officials: during a congressional investigation in early 1982, the head of conservation at the Interior Department stated that he did not participate in a single decision concerning energy conservation during 1981.[6] A 1984 General Accounting Office report indicated that "of the 11 designated principal conservation officers, only one has regularly attended the meetings [of the Interagency Federal Energy

5. General Services Administration, Office of Federal Supply and Services and Office of Transportation, *Federal Motor Vehicle Fleet Report, Fiscal Years 1981, 1982* (GSA, 1982, 1983), pp. 8, 7.

6. *Wasted Energy Dollars in the Federal Government,* Committee Print, Subcommittee on Oversight and Investigations of the House Committee on Energy and Commerce, 97 Cong. 2 sess. (GPO, 1982), pp. 294–97.

Policy Committee] since they resumed in 1982."[7] (The committee completely suspended operations from November 1980 through January 1982.)

The DOE estimates that by 1982 federal agencies had spent approximately \$1.5 billion on building retrofit actions, with associated cost savings of \$2.0 billion.[8] There are plans for more retrofit spending, but two important program elements are missing from many retrofit programs: technical audits to identify cost-effective energy conservation measures that would supplement the preliminary building audits and accountability to ensure that measures are implemented. For instance, a General Accounting Office study of the energy savings achieved by hospitals of the Navy, Veterans Administration, and Indian Health Service compared with that of five nonfederal hospitals having active energy management programs indicated that these federal agencies could save between \$16 million and \$56 million more each year if they adopted similar programs.[9]

Savings of 20 to 40 percent are normally attainable with retrofit programs that include careful data collection, good technical analysis, and on-site operator control. Many retrofit options are relatively inexpensive, considering their payoff. Improved insulation, reduced air leakage, and relatively simple modifications to heating, cooling, and lighting systems make dramatic differences in energy consumption and would yield far greater savings than have been realized in federal buildings over the past decade.

New buildings can be constructed at energy efficiencies much improved over today's structures, but replacement rates are not great enough to effect immediate significant reductions. And many new federal buildings fail to meet energy efficiency guidelines and criteria set by the General Services Administration. Since fiscal 1979 newly constructed federal buildings have used 20 to 200 percent more energy annually than they were designed to consume.[10]

7. Memorandum, J. Dexter Peach to Richard L. Ottinger, "Status of the Federal Energy Management Program," GAO/RCED-84-86, March 7, 1984, p. 6.

8. DOE, *Annual Report on Federal Government Energy Management, Fiscal Year 1982*, p. 5.

9. General Accounting Office, *Millions Can Be Saved through Better Energy Management in Federal Hospitals*, GAO/HRD-82-77 (GAO, 1982), p. 13.

10. GAO, *GSA Could Do More to Improve Energy Conservation in New Federal Buildings*, prepared for the U.S. Department of Energy, GAO/PLRD-82-90 (GAO, 1983), p. 12.

On the whole, increased services cannot explain the government's poor performance in energy conservation. An example from the private sector provides a good comparison with the government's poor performance. The Bell System used 12 percent less energy during the first two-thirds of 1982 than it did in the same period of 1973, even though its volume of business had grown 97 percent in the interim. Like the government, Bell has operations in every climate zone and operates vehicles, buildings, manufacturing operations, and office systems.[11]

Improvements have been made in federal conservation efforts, but there are serious deficiencies. The DOE took over seven years to write an overall ten-year plan for buildings that is still seriously flawed. It contains sparse documentation to justify the use of industry lighting efficiency standards rather than the more stringent federally developed standards; it does not give the Interagency Federal Energy Policy Committee a significant role in promoting federal energy efficiency; and it uses out-of-date fuel cost projections in life-cycle cost analyses.[12] Overall federal building energy use is down only 13.2 percent after seven years, badly trailing the record of the private sector (see table 2).

The performance of the federal energy management program, which is still vested with responsibility for overall coordination of federal energy conservation, is perhaps the most distressing aspect of federal energy conservation efforts. It was established to provide individual agencies with the guidance necessary to implement presidential and congressional initiatives, to monitor and evaluate conservation performance, to analyze federal energy cost trends, and to provide technical assistance. A victim of budget cuts, personnel shifts, and lessened status, the program never achieved its potential. In mid-1981 four of the program's twelve positions were eliminated as a result of a major reorganization of the DOE's conservation program. At the same time, the DOE's top officials reduced the status of the program from an office to a branch, the department's lowest organizational unit. Finally, the administration announced its intent to terminate it in fiscal year 1983,[13] although Congress rejected this proposal in its continuing resolution.

A renewed federal energy management program is essential to effec-

11. Energy Research Advisory Board, Conservation Panel, *Energy Conservation and the Federal Government: Research, Development, and Management,* prepared for the U.S. Department of Energy, DOE/S-0017 (ERAB, 1983) p. 36.

12. Memorandum, Peach to Ottinger, "Status of Federal Energy," p. 5.

13. Ibid., pp. 7–8.

tive energy management in the federal government. It should be established as a high-level office reporting directly to the under secretary of the Energy Department, who by law has primary responsibility for energy conservation.[14] The program needs to be well staffed with professionals and to have very strong support from the administration. An adequate control system should be installed to develop plans, establish goals, establish cost accountability, and measure progress. This system must begin at the lowest level where energy can be measured and be assigned to a responsible manager. The president should be advised of the progress of all the federal departments on a semiannual or annual basis.

Steps to Success

We have noted repeated instances of government laxity in pursuing conservation efforts. Those federal agencies most successful in their energy conservation efforts attribute their success to three main factors: commitment by top management, a dedicated staff, and the clear-cut importance of cost reduction to the agencies. These factors are commonly found in private-sector energy conservation efforts and are essential to any federal success.

Commitment from those with responsibility and authority for conservation is essential to an organization's energy conservation program. In a private corporation, commitment and accountability begin with the chief executive officer and move down to division vice-presidents, subdivision managers, plant managers, and finally to first-line supervisors. Each management level within a federal agency should make an analogous commitment.

The effort required to achieve high energy efficiency goes well beyond the time available to top management in both the public and private sectors. Therefore an effective staff must be set up to manage the program for the chief executive. In the private sector, staff from the corporate, division, and plant levels is typically required. A parallel contingent is needed in each federal agency. The duties of these groups will change at each level; however, each of them has a number of responsibilities, including implementing the policies; establishing a

14. GAO, *The Federal Government Needs a Comprehensive Program to Curb Its Energy Use,* EMD-80-11 (GAO, 1979).

system for controlling and monitoring energy conservation progress; interpreting energy conservation results and advising management of corrective actions necessary; and timely reporting of progress and establishing goals for future performance.

Federal agencies should maintain some in-house engineering personnel with energy system expertise to analyze and install energy-saving projects and should supplement that staff with consultants. Agency heads should recognize the accomplishments of both the engineers and the managers with appropriate ceremonies and awards.

Promoting Energy Conservation throughout the Economy

Normally, when the relative price of something falls, consumers use more of it. Yet the energy required to produce a unit of GNP in the United States has been falling for about sixty years despite a long decline (until the 1970s) in the real price of energy—an indication of just how attractive conservation investments can be. If a conservation investment makes sense when the price of energy is falling, it makes even more sense when the price starts to rise. Rising prices are the most powerful and effective incentive for consumers to become more energy efficient.

Research done at the Oak Ridge National Laboratory estimates that without the conservation measures taken since 1970, U.S. energy demand would now be greater by sixteen quads.[15] Probably the most influential factors in lowering consumption have been high energy prices and the threat of future shortages. The Oak Ridge report attributes 70 percent of the energy savings to price response, but says that five quads of the savings in 1981 result from nonmarket forces, including government conservation programs. These programs include automobile fuel economy standards, industrial information programs, and the residential conservation service. Thus the savings to the U.S. economy because of these programs may have amounted to as much as $3 billion to $12 billion

15. Eric Hirst and others, *Energy Use from 1973 to 1980: The Role of Improved Energy Efficiency*, ORNL/CON-79 (Oak Ridge, Tenn.: Oak Ridge National Laboratory, 1981); David L. Greene and others, *Estimating the Total Impact on Energy Consumption of Department of Energy Conservation Programs*, ORNL-5925 (Oak Ridge, Tenn.: Oak Ridge National Laboratory, 1982); and Eric Hirst and others, "Recent Changes in U.S. Energy Consumption: What Happened and Why," *Annual Review of Energy*, vol. 8 (1983), pp. 193–245.

in 1980, or up to twelve times as much as the government spent on them in that year. The accompanying but less quantifiable values of improved air quality and decreased dependence on imported oil are also important. The federal role in translating interest in energy efficiency into productive action has begun to make its mark in private-sector programs, but not in the federal agencies themselves.

Spreading the Word

Federal efforts over the past decade have provided much helpful information on energy costs, the nature of demand, and the opportunities for conservation. Such information and education help build a long-term awareness about resources as well as a factual basis for making productive energy decisions in the near term. Without such activities from a central resource, the national awareness of energy issues would inevitably fall, leaving only the inherently incomplete signals provided by market prices. A network for disseminating technical information among federal agencies, other levels of government, and the private sector is prerequisite to an effective energy policy and is heavily dependent upon federal leadership.

FEDERAL INFORMATION PROGRAMS. There are many different types of information programs in the federal government. The residential conservation service oversees the performance of energy audits and provides advice on efficiency improvements. The *Gas Mileage Guide* aids consumers in their choice of new cars. The Office of Industrial Programs participated in cost-sharing demonstration projects with industry and provided information to help small businesses. These programs and others have recently been threatened by the rationale that because of energy price deregulation there is now sufficient market incentive to support such activities within the private sector.

The residential conservation service assures that utilities provide audits to customers to inform them of potential savings. It is, in effect, a service for both the utilities, whose construction costs are escalating beyond reason, and consumers, who must pay the price for excessive capacity buildup. Attempts have been made to repeal the law establishing this service as well as the energy extension service, the prototypical program that provides energy conservation advice to building owners and other energy users. Funding has also been cut for energy analysis and diagnostic centers, which provided technical assistance to small industries that wanted to adopt energy conservation. This move has halted the expansion of a program that obtained implementation of its recommendations in one out of every two visits and yielded savings ten times greater than the federal investment in the program.[16]

In 1982 the Reagan administration reduced by almost 90 percent the number of copies it published of the *Gas Mileage Guide*, a brochure comparing new-car fuel economy for car buyers, and eliminated a semiannual update of the brochure. Thus information necessary for consumers to purchase fuel-efficient automobiles has been made less available. In addition, the administration canceled plans to publish a guide to tires' impact on fuel efficiency, identified by manufacturer and model. It would have provided information that could have helped save 400,000 barrels of oil per day.[17]

Despite praise for the DOE's Office of Industrial Programs, its programs have been substantially reduced. A National Academy of Sciences study concluded, "On balance, the Office of Industrial Programs has done a commendable job in implementing the federal role in industrial energy conservation . . . and it has spent the monies appropriated to it in a prudent manner, as evidenced by the the results of its efforts to date and those projects that appear to have future potential. . . . Federal support of the present and planned DOE industrial conservation program is an important effort to achieve additional energy conservation."[18] This recommendation has apparently been ignored.[19]

ENERGY CONSUMPTION IN HOUSING. The federal government could provide information on conservation to a major energy-consuming sector while saving itself some money.[20] The housing sector uses 25 percent of the nation's energy. The Department of Housing and Urban Develop-

16. Office of Technology Assessment, *Conservation and Solar Energy Programs of the Department of Energy: A Critique*, OTA-E-120 (GPO, 1980), p. 77.

17. William U. Chandler, "The Fuel Efficiency of Tires by Manufacturer and Model" (Washington, D.C.: Environmental Policy Institute, 1981).

18. National Academy of Sciences, National Materials Advisory Board, *An Assessment of the Industrial Energy Conservation Program*, vol. 1: *Summary*, NMAB 395-1 (Washington, D.C.: National Academy Press, 1981), p. 9.

19. *Department of Energy Oversight*, Hearings before the Subcommittee on Energy Conservation and Power and the Subcommittee on Fossil and Synthetic Fuels of the House Committee on Energy and Commerce, 97 Cong. 2 sess. (GPO, 1982).

20. This section draws heavily from *Review of Federal Policies and Building Standards Affecting Energy Conservation in Housing*, Hearings before the Subcommittee on Housing and Community Development of the House Committee on Banking, Finance, and Urban Affairs, 98 Cong. 2 sess. (GPO, 1984), pp. 3–21.

ment (HUD) is paying at least part of the energy bill in 3.6 million households—those involved in public housing, section 8 or section 202 housing, and various other federal programs. Measured in terms of number of dwellings, HUD is operating the fifth largest state in the country. And because many private dwellings are constructed so as to make them eligible for federal financing, HUD and the other government mortgage associations exert enormous influence over conservation standards throughout the housing construction industry.

The energy bill for public housing was about $1 billion in 1982. (Data on the amount of energy used are very scant.) It is clearly in HUD's (and the nation's) long-term financial interest to invest in cost-effective weatherization and other retrofit measures. HUD recently began an extensive conversion program from master metering to individual apartment metering in order to induce energy savings. However, heavy reliance on this method of providing clearer price signals to the consumer could impede HUD's progress in encouraging structural improvements for energy efficiency.

Such measures as replacing poorly fitting windows, plugging air leaks, adding ceiling and floor insulation, and retrofitting furnaces would make more significant reductions in energy use. It has been estimated that an average investment of $1,300 per dwelling unit ($1.5 billion total) would yield average annual savings of $325 per unit over a payback period of four years, while creating a source of gainful employment for thousands of people.[21] HUD could make this investment itself or encourage utilization of a new concept in energy conservation by contracting with energy conservation companies (ECCOs).

ECCOs are private firms that will contract with a building owner or public housing authority to reduce energy consumption. ECCOs put up the capital for efficiency improvements and are paid for their efforts from the savings generated. For instance, a company may guarantee to reduce consumption by 10 percent. If consumption is reduced by only 10 percent, the building operator will owe a smaller energy bill, but the ECCO will not realize any profit. If, however, consumption is reduced by a greater amount, the building operator will pay the company the amount of excess savings out of the fund that otherwise would have been paid to the utility. An alternate method of contracting is an agreement to share any savings that result. Usually the ECCO takes the greater

21. Will Perkins and the Ehrenkrantz Group, *An Evaluation of the Physical Condition of Public Housing Stock*, vol. 1: *Final Report*, HUD Report H2850, prepared for the Department of Housing and Urban Development (HUD, 1980).

portion for the first few years in order to recoup its capital investment, and the split evens out as the years go by.

If the government worked with ECCOs, it would save energy, avoid large initial outlays of capital, demonstrate the effectiveness of energy conservation technology and new management techniques, and provide itself with an example of beneficial reliance on private-sector ingenuity. Yet HUD is discouraging such contracting efforts by public housing authorities by demanding that it receive 50 percent of any savings realized, thus preventing an adequate rate of return for the ECCOs in early years and decreasing the incentive for public housing authorities to explore this new area.[22]

In purchasing appliances for its 3.5 million units, HUD can influence private markets and manufacturers. If HUD insists that refrigerators or water heaters installed in units where it pays the energy bills meet certain efficiency standards, then manufacturers will begin to make them available and builders will begin to install them in order to keep the government as a customer.

The private housing market is influenced by the federal government's standards for FHA and VA loans, its standards for mobile home construction, and its policies governing the use of secondary mortgage financing. Up to 80 to 90 percent of new dwellings meet federally established minimum property standards because builders want buyers to be able to qualify for federal financing. Unfortunately, minimum property standards fall far short of reasonable technical and economic goals. Mobile homes account for one-fifth of all new dwelling units each year, and energy efficiency standards for their construction could make a major impact on national energy consumption. If the Federal National Mortgage Association and Federal Home Loan Mortgage Corporation began to consider energy payments in the same way they consider principal, interest, taxes, and insurance when they review a purchaser's ability to qualify for a loan, it would greatly encourage energy efficiency improvements in existing housing.

Energy Conservation Research and Development

In a competitive market economy, business, constantly seeking profits, responds to perceived consumer needs.[23] This system works

22. Norris McDonald, "Energy Efficiency Strategies for Multifamily Rental Housing" (Washington, D.C.: Environmental Policy Institute, 1981).

23. This section draws heavily on John Sawhill, ed., *Energy Conservation and Public Policy* (Prentice-Hall, 1979).

best when market signals are clear, that is, when the full cost of a good or service is visible in its price. This is not the case in the energy market, where prices are obviously influenced not only by technology and resource availability, but also by regulatory practices and international cartels. In the face of large nonmarket costs and great and uncontrollable uncertainties about future energy prices, it is difficult for the private sector to justify extensive investment in research and development (R&D) for greatly improved energy efficiency. Thus federal investment in the energy sector is made to ensure reliability and minimum cost of the necessities and amenities that energy helps provide. As energy market prices rise, government research is justified to help develop alternative price-competitive supplies and ways to provide goods and services using less energy, again in order to minimize cost.

The national self-interest in energy productivity is enormous, especially when related national security costs are taken into account. Public benefits of generic R&D in energy productivity include the following:

1. Energy savings can lighten the heavy burden of balance of payments, and new world markets will open to eventual private-sector producers of new energy-efficient technologies.

2. Existing supplies of energy resources will last longer, providing more time for developing alternatives and increasing resilience to short-term interruptions.

3. The health and environmental impacts of energy conservation can be understood and dealt with before widespread implementation.

4. Less developed nations will have a better chance for economic growth if energy efficiency in the major energy-consuming countries can hold down the rate of energy price increases.

Both government and industry R&D investments in the energy sector have risen sharply since 1975. Before 1975 R&D in energy conservation was essentially nonexistent in government and nearly so in industry, because energy prices had been declining for decades. Despite its promise as a cost-effective way to ease energy problems, federally sponsored research in energy productivity is still not significant compared with corresponding commitments to energy supply.

The DOE's Energy Research Advisory Board reviewed the proposed fiscal year 1982 budget for energy conservation R&D and concluded, "The overall level of Federal R&D funding for conservation and improved utilization programs is too low in view of their potential for energy improvements and the inability of many important energy-consuming sectors to conduct R&D. Moreover, Department-wide, the balance between supply oriented R&D and conservation R&D is too heavily weighted toward the supply side."[24] The story for 1983 was even worse: the conservation request represented only 0.5 percent of total budget authority and was a 97 percent reduction from the 1981 appropriation of $821 million.

Admittedly there have been problems with federal R&D in energy conservation, particularly the emphasis on near-term payoffs. In its efforts to accelerate a near-term national shift to higher efficiency, DOE placed primary emphasis on research and programs that emphasized technology with a high chance for payoff and near-term savings. In this regard, DOE acted somewhat like an industrial entrepreneur and chose actions with the lowest risk and highest rate of return. While such a federal strategy may be defended for the short run, it seems inappropriate for the long run because a competitive market system should be able to attract private venture capital when potential returns are sufficiently high (or risks sufficiently low). Energy supply research has traditionally emphasized development of very long-term options such as fusion, breeders, and advanced solar electric concepts. For the longer term and in the national interest, conservation R&D should give priority to those situations in which the risks (and potential rewards) are so great, the time for commercialization so long, or the potential returns (based on present energy price) so low that private investment alone cannot rationally be expected to suffice.

Even a cursory examination of energy use in contemporary society reveals major opportunities for improvement in efficiency, especially over the long term (corresponding to replacement of capital stock). For the most part, we have not begun to approach the limits to conservation posed by physical laws. Studies of the trade-off between efficiency of use and the price of energy indicate that large improvements in efficiency of energy-using devices are economically attractive in response to modest increases in production cost. One role of conservation R&D is to expand the boundaries of efficiency that economically match a given energy price. This is ultimately reflected in the amount of energy required to sustain a given level of goods and services.

Long-term research also provides improved insight into the nature and trends of our energy-consuming society—the choices we make, how

24. Energy Research Advisory Board, *Federal Energy R&D Priorities*, prepared for the U.S. Department of Energy, DOE/S-0031 (ERAB, 1981), p. 45.

and why we adopt or reject technology. Similarly, research yields improved understanding of the social and economic effects of energy conservation on employment, social equity, freedom of choice, resilience in the face of emergencies, international security, environment and health, and urgent demands for new supply development.

Many major long-term conservation opportunities cannot attract private capital. Thus the national need for work on various conservation measures is substantial and continuing. A federal R&D program in conservation should: (1) examine substitution of technological innovation for consumption of purchased energy, especially oil, with emphasis on providing technical options that will not result from private-sector R&D; (2) develop new institutional mechanisms to facilitate the development and adaptation of resource-conserving technologies; and (3) focus on new technologies or management techniques that are environmentally benign or no more damaging than many new energy supply technologies.

To achieve these goals, a federal energy conservation R&D program could perform the following specific tasks:

1. Support basic research on fundamental understanding of physical, chemical, and biological properties, such as high electrical and thermal resistivity and conductivity; high and low heat capacity; high chemical and thermal energy density; high strength-to-weight materials; low friction; and high-strength materials at elevated temperatures.

2. Organize R&D support that encourages new ways of doing things. The greatest strides in energy productivity will likely emerge from investments in fundamental process development.

3. Develop increased opportunities for energy conversion at point of use. There are three possible areas of inquiry: production of gases and liquids from primary energy resources and deemphasis of large central station generation of electricity; decentralized production of electricity (such as smaller fossil-fueled plants, direct solar conversion, or fuel cells); and siting of moderate to large power plants close enough to industrialized and urbanized areas so that "waste" energy can be economically utilized by various consumers.

4. Support long-term technical, microeconomic, and social research to improve understanding of the role and future of energy and its substitutes in the economy.

5. Improve the knowledge base about the processes of transfer, adoption, modification, and rejection of technological innovation by ultimate users.

6. Research ways to assess the full costs of energy and to devise equitable ways to introduce such cost signals into the marketplace.

7. Systematically delineate the implication of existing public policies—price controls, real estate taxation, freight rules, direct and indirect transportation subsidies, and corporate tax policy with regard to R&D as well as capital investment—for energy and other resources, and devise productive changes.

Performance by Other Governments

Most nations had adopted explicit energy policies by 1980, with varying degrees of active involvement by their governments. The common theme for petroleum-importing nations has been that of increased self-reliance through the strategies of diversified sources of imports, domestic energy resource development, and increased efficiency of use. The latter two strategies are the only possible near-term strategies for some countries, such as Japan. Western European nations are deeply involved in diversifying their imported sources of energy (for example, natural gas from Russia), and supplementing those efforts with supply development and fuel switching (for example, from petroleum to nuclear electric in France).

France has embarked on a national plan to provide substantial economic growth (5 percent per year) between 1980 and 1990, a plan that relies in part on conservation to "supply" the energy equivalent of a 20 percent expansion of supplies. Such a program will require substantial investment capital (about 40 billion francs per year), but will create 300,000 jobs during the decade.[25]

One of the most impressive national programs is Japan's, where efforts are proceeding on three fronts: development of domestic supply sources; fuel switching (petroleum to natural gas and coal); and conservation. Imported oil accounted for 72 percent of Japan's energy in 1979, with 70 percent of that oil coming from the Middle East. Japan reduced its ratio of energy to GNP by 25 percent (34 percent in the industrial sector) between 1973 and 1980. This remarkable change was, in part, due to the shifts in the composition of Japan's GNP. Nonetheless, this improvement appears to be unexcelled by any nation. By comparison,

25. Gaston Rimareix, paper presented at the Third International Energy Symposium, 1982 World's Fair, Knoxville, Tennessee, May 1982.

the same ratio for the United States fell by about 13.2 percent during that same period. The difference in the two countries' ratios is partly due to the difference in leadership and policies provided by the different governments. Japan plans to achieve an additional 15 percent decline between 1980 and 1990.[26]

The International Energy Agency is composed of representatives from industrialized, oil-importing nations and acts as a coordinator and clearinghouse on information and activities including energy demand and conservation. Information about activities in less industrialized countries is less helpful in making comparisons with the United States, but does indicate that there is intense interest in the issue of energy efficiency and a commitment to act. One difficulty frequently encountered, especially in developing nations, is a lack of good data on energy consumption patterns.

The lessons to be learned by the United States in comparisons with other countries include: (1) energy efficiency is making impressive inroads into national energy demand growth, albeit obscured by the impact of recession; (2) other nations, under strong government leadership, are doing much better than the United States in conserving energy and have put in place policies designed to make further improvements; (3) technologies associated with high energy efficiency are likely to be sources of products and services in international commerce; and (4) a major difference between current attention to energy demand in the United States and in other countries is that the U.S. government virtually ignores the demand side while other governments pay considerable attention to policies to foster efficient use.

Conclusions

The federal government should strive to be a model for responsiveness to the national need for energy efficiency. To be most effective, leadership in this kind of economic husbandry should begin with the White House. The managers of federal agencies should be even more attentive to energy efficiency than their most active private-sector counterparts. The opportunities for direct energy savings in governmental operations

26. Toyoaki Ikuta, "Japan's Energy Strategy," paper presented at the Third International Energy Symposium, 1982 World's Fair, Knoxville, Tennessee, May 1982.

are enormous: a 1 percent change in federal agency energy consumption presently amounts to $125 million per year. These savings are multiplied by the additional actions outside government that are influenced by government activities.

Markets cannot function properly without complete and accurate information. The federal government is the only entity organized to provide the kind of information needed to make improvements in energy efficiency nationwide. Thus far the federal government has not done a very good job of collecting the information needed to make good decisions in savings in its own operations. In addition, it has recently been seeking to undo other information programs. Reversing that trend is of the utmost importance.

It is indeed unfortunate that most operations of the federal government, with incentives that should transcend those that exist in the private sector, now seriously lag behind the private sector. One way to cut federal expenditures is to eliminate functions of government; another is to increase the efficiency of governance.

Comments by Grant P. Thompson

It is convenient to think of the issues that this paper raises under three subcategories: First, there is the research and development that the federal government funds as a traditional exercise of government power. Second, there are those functions that only government can undertake such as taxing, regulation, subsidy, and providing and collecting data and information. Finally, there is government as the proprietor and manager of a very large-scale enterprise that uses energy in manufacturing, housing, and transportation.

First, let us look at government as a provider of research and development. The authors are quite correct in pointing out that there are enormous benefits to be gained by research and development, provided that two conditions are met: the results of the R&D must be accepted by the market, and the R&D would not have been conducted in a timely fashion without government funding.

The authors are right in viewing with the proper sense of alarm the deep and unthinking cuts that the Reagan administration has made in the R&D budget year after year. Indeed, every independent assessment that has been made over the last three years of the Department of Energy's conservation budget has concluded that it is badly out of balance when compared with the opportunities that exist for meaningful government-sponsored R&D.

On the other hand, defenders of existing programs ought to feel an obligation to differentiate between those projects that are worthy of support and those that should be left to the private sector to fund (if they are funded at all). Like it or not, we are in an era of restraint. The era of free and easy money for dealing with energy problems is past. As a political reality we need to give some guidance.

Three general observations are worth making about government-funded R&D. First, people often have opportunities to make investments in conservation that have quite favorable economic returns, yet they do not make the investments. This suggests that there are noneconomic factors that are influencing their decisions. Understanding those additional factors would provide useful information, yet provide no benefit that any single company could capture. Government ought to support R&D on behavioral and other nontechnical issues; historically it has been loath to do so.

Second, as the paper points out, if the nation is going to concentrate public R&D money any place, it should be on the buildings sector, where the potential for cost-effective payback is very high. The private sector is ill equipped and ill organized to provide that research.

Finally, the government ought to avoid being ideological in determining what R&D it will support. For example, this administration has consistently said that industrial research belongs entirely in the private sector. Yet if one looks at "industry" not as a single monolith but as a collection of quite diverse companies, one can see that some segments are very well equipped to conduct research while others are poorly equipped. Simple repetition of the mantra that only long-term, high-risk, high-payoff, generic R&D should be supported by the federal government has a mind-numbing effect that prevents more careful analysis. It will be critical to identify both suitable individual R&D projects to be performed at the federal level and to develop a methodology to decide what the government should do and what it should leave to others.

I turn now to those actions that government takes that affect private decisionmaking—information programs, penalties, subsidies, taxation, and regulation. Here again, there has been an enormous turnaround in government activism. The paper hints at a distinction that I think is important: on the one hand, some government programs classified as "energy" programs (that is, weatherization or fuel assistance payments) really are a specialized way of delivering welfare; on the other hand, other energy programs (such as labels on appliances or automobile standards) truly affect all consumers. Budget cuts, the loss of experienced managers, a continual barrage of deferments of spending, and attempts to repeal underlying legislation have sapped these latter programs' continuity and vitality over the last three years. It is very hard to measure the effectiveness of programs that have been in a defense mode, rather than trying to get their job done.

Nonetheless, it is not helpful merely to lament the loss of programs without saying what we should do about it. The answer of more money is simply not going to be accepted. We ought to concentrate on evaluating individual programs rather than the conservation program in its entirety. Such evaluations should compare the programs with other alternatives, including simply letting the market work. I am convinced that fair-minded assessments would conclude that many of the programs are worth continued funding, while a few deserve to be replaced, improved, or extinguished.

I think the authors would do well to confront more directly than they do the issue of the proper role of government in energy conservation programs. The purest viewpoint, which says that the market is the only proper instrument of policy, is clearly foolish, yet a more reasoned defense of the alternative is required.

An articulate statement of why certain sectors of the economy need government programs in order to encourage cost-effective conservation should include the following points. First, conservation is diffuse. No business entity exists that can organize its delivery in many sectors. Second, information for individual actions is hard to get and hard to believe when it comes from vendors of products. Third, for some products (for example, automobiles that are fuel efficient but have high first costs), the net present value of various possible purchasing decisions is identical for consumers, although it has very different results for the nation as a whole. Finally, conservation has a good number of positive externalities that no one seller or buyer can capture. Taken together, I think these points make a convincing case for a less doctrinaire approach toward standards, regulations, taxes, and subsidies than is the current fashion in Washington.

Finally, let me turn to the government as the owner and manager of buildings, fleets of vehicles, and industrial enterprises. The authors rightly place an emphasis on this, not only because the government is the largest single user of energy but because it is a frustrating and difficult problem to organize the bureaucracy to save energy that is purchased with taxpayers' funds.

I think the authors somewhat mistakenly spend a good deal of space discussing why government departments ought to save energy as if it were a moral imperative. Indeed, the reason they use so much energy is simple—no member of the civil service directly bears expense or responsibility for energy use, and no department suffers if costs rise. Energy is simply treated as an outside event, beyond the control of budget managers.

The traditional incentives to improving efficiency—that is, cost pressures placed on those in a position to make decisions and reap the rewards of those decisions—are missing in the government service. It is unlikely that civil service reforms will coalesce around the energy conservation issue, yet there are at least a few improvements possible.

First, the authors are clearly correct that top management has to be visibly interested in the issue. Unless the boss takes conservation seriously, no one else will. Second, there need to be clear measures of productivity. Data must be collected and results of the data collection must be regularly and usefully communicated to those who control energy usage. Third, investments that save energy need to be facilitated by financing decisions that don't punish investments with higher first costs. In this connection, I think it might be fruitful to explore some shared-saving energy schemes.

The authority should exist to hire private entrepreneurs to save energy for the government. But I would also give the departments the option of trying to do better themselves, allowing the savings accrued to be placed in discretionary funds for the department to carry out projects dear to the hearts of those in charge. To be particularly daring, the government might provide cash awards to be shared by offices or services that achieved verifiable savings.

It is in looking for actual programs and policies and orders that the solutions to the government's energy consumption problems must be found, not in general prescriptions or moral imperatives.

Comments by Arthur H. Rosenfeld

There are several developments in Western Europe that support the point of view of this paper. The attitudes there about efficient use of energy are really quite different from here. The United States sees fairly constant electricity and oil prices right now. But the price of oil internationally is pegged to the dollar. In France in 1983 every two weeks when I went to fill up my gas tank the price of gasoline had just gone up another percentage point. So the signals are different. As Bill Hogan tells us, it is the signals that count.

When the French government looks at energy use in the public sector of a city, they don't distinguish particularly between a national building, a military building, a school, or a hospital. It is all money that the French taxpayer is paying for energy services, and they want to do something about that.

The scheme that they have worked out is something we ought to import. They are installing computerized energy management systems in all schools, hospitals, and other public buildings. They have developed a standard chip that goes into the energy management computer control systems (EMCS). This extra chip allows phone communication with the system by officials in city hall. The city energy manager can now obtain by telephone the up-to-date energy use of every school in the city, for example. He can then arrange meetings among all the school custodians to exchange information and experience. And on Monday morning there can be comparisons of school energy use on the desks of the principals of all the schools. In addition, the schools are given energy budgets. If a school saves money, that can go into the principal's discretionary fund. These EMCS systems are cheap, about $7,000, and the extra chip that allows all of them to communicate is about $100.

The French also have building standards for new homes, new commercial buildings, and so on, which they ratchet down about every five years as the price of energy goes up. Space heating for a typical French dwelling consumed approximately two and one-half tons of oil per dwelling before the 1973 oil embargo. Then the French developed 1975 standards requiring new homes to reduce consumption down to two tons. The standards were revised in 1979 down to one and one-half tons, and then in 1982 revised again down to one ton. Now the question is, what do they do in 1985?

The cream has pretty much been skimmed. It is a tough decision as to what to do next. It depends a bit on the offerings by the manufacturers of furnaces and how well triple glazing works and that sort of thing. What the French decided to do is to introduce the idea of building-use labels. They have one star, two stars, three stars, and four stars. One star says that a building's use is 15 percent better than the standard, two stars is 25 percent, and three stars is 35 percent. The government defrays a substantial amount of the increased first cost by offering low-interest loans.

The French expect to give out about 1,000,000 labels a year. But they are interested in the three and four stars because that is where they save the most energy. In return for the label, building owners agree to let the government look at their energy-use bills every month for the next two years. The buildings that are interesting and potentially successful will get data loggers to measure everything from those buildings for the next two years. Two years from now there will be 20,000 buildings all over France with everything about them measured, and therefore inspiring the confidence of the building industry.

That is different from the way we have been bumbling through things in the United States. It does not do any good to say that owners of a building should do this or that. There are two things that you have to do to get the attention of the owner of a building or the principal of a high school. First, they need to know daily what their energy use was and how much it costs. Second, they have to retain the profits. Somehow or other we have got to get the federal system doing that.

Just to drive that point home, let me give three examples of how misinformed a high school principal can be about the cost of wasted energy use in his high school. The principal at one high school told a student that the high school's energy bill was $14,000 a year. The student bet the principal that the $14,000 was a monthly figure, not an annual one. The student won the bet. The high school used $150,000 worth of energy a year, and that was about two-thirds wasted. I pointed out to another principal that every security light in the stairwell that is on all the time cost him $80 a year. He thought I meant the whole stairwell—but it is every 100-watt bulb. His understanding was that much off. Finally, at another high school, we found a hot water faucet dripping at a half a gallon a minute. That was costing the school $580 a year. That kind of loss would show up on a sophisticated feedback system.

Until the lobby of every public building—schools, hospitals, or whatever—has some sort of monthly accounting of energy use that everybody can look at while waiting for the elevator, we are not going to make any progress. That is my message.

Conference Participants

with their affiliations at the time of the conference

John H. Alschuler, Jr. *Santa Monica City Government*
Francis Bator *Harvard University*
Edward H. Blum *Merrill Lynch, Pierce, Fenner and Smith*
John Bryson *Morrison and Foerster*
I. C. Bupp *Harvard University*
Charles Cicchetti *University of Wisconsin*
Linda Cohen *Brookings Institution*
Richard Cotton *Dewey, Ballantine, Bushby, Palmer and Wood*
Robert W. Crandall *Brookings Institution*
Angus Duncan *Windfarms NorthWest*
Alan R. Erwin *Public Utility Commission of Texas*
S. David Freeman *Tennessee Valley Authority*
Dermot Gately *New York University*
John H. Gibbons *Office of Technology Assessment*
Karen Griffin *California Energy Commission*
Robert E. Hall *Honeywell*
David Harrison, Jr. *Harvard University*
Robert F. Hemphill, Jr. *Applied Energy Services*
Eric Hirst *Oak Ridge National Laboratory*
William W. Hogan *Harvard University*
Henry Lee *Harvard University*
Roger Naill *Applied Energy Services*
Merton J. Peck *Yale University*
Richard B. Pool *Kaiser Aluminum and Chemical Corporation*
Perry D. Quick *Roosevelt Center for American Policy Studies*
Alice M. Rivlin *Brookings Institution*
Arthur H. Rosenfeld *Lawrence Berkeley Laboratories*
Samir Salama *Energy and Environmental Analysis*

Arnold W. Sametz *New York University*

Anthony Saunders *New York University*

Maxine Savitz *Lighting Research Institute*

John C. Sawhill *McKinsey and Company*

Stephen Sawyer *University of Maryland*

Sam H. Schurr *Electric Power Research Institute*

Patrick J. Scullion *Michigan Consolidated Gas Company*

Granville J. Smith, III *Energenics Systems*

Robert B. Stobaugh *Harvard University*

Grant P. Thompson *The Conservation Foundation*

Jon Veigel *North Carolina Alternative Energy Corporation*

Index